The Biblical Accommodation
Debate in Germany

Hoon J. Lee

The Biblical Accommodation Debate in Germany

Interpretation and the Enlightenment

Hoon J. Lee
Trinity Christian College
Chicago, IL, USA

ISBN 978-3-319-87092-2   ISBN 978-3-319-61497-7 (eBook)
DOI 10.1007/978-3-319-61497-7

© The Editor(s) (if applicable) and The Author(s) 2017
Softcover reprint of the hardcover 1st edition 2017
This work is subject to copyright. All rights are solely and exclusively licensed by the Publisher, whether the whole or part of the material is concerned, specifically the rights of translation, reprinting, reuse of illustrations, recitation, broadcasting, reproduction on microfilms or in any other physical way, and transmission or information storage and retrieval, electronic adaptation, computer software, or by similar or dissimilar methodology now known or hereafter developed.
The use of general descriptive names, registered names, trademarks, service marks, etc. in this publication does not imply, even in the absence of a specific statement, that such names are exempt from the relevant protective laws and regulations and therefore free for general use.
The publisher, the authors and the editors are safe to assume that the advice and information in this book are believed to be true and accurate at the date of publication. Neither the publisher nor the authors or the editors give a warranty, express or implied, with respect to the material contained herein or for any errors or omissions that may have been made. The publisher remains neutral with regard to jurisdictional claims in published maps and institutional affiliations.

Cover illustration: INTERFOTO/Alamy Stock Photo

Printed on acid-free paper

This Palgrave Macmillan imprint is published by Springer Nature
The registered company is Springer International Publishing AG
The registered company address is: Gewerbestrasse 11, 6330 Cham, Switzerland

To Susie, Wyatt, and Ford

Acknowledgements

I would like to thank John Woodbridge for his guidance during the writing of this book. Not only did he introduce me to the issue of accommodation, he has provided invaluable insight through numerous conversations and readings of drafts. In addition, I have benefited from the Douglas Sweeney's careful reading of the book. His comments helped me focus the work.

Several libraries facilitated tracking down sources, including the Herzog August Bibliothek and their support through the Günther Findel-Stiftung Fellowship, the Staatsbibliothek in Berlin, and the Thüringer Universitäts-und Landesbibliothek at the University of Jena.

I am indebted to my family, who has supported me throughout the entire process. My deepest gratitude is for my wife, to whom this book is dedicated. Without her encouragement, patience, and sacrifice, this project would not have been completed.

Contents

1 Introduction   1

2 Accommodation in the Seventeenth-Century Dutch Republic   23

3 Accommodation in Early Eighteenth-Century Germany   61

4 The Beginning of the Accommodation Debate, 1761–1789   99

5 The Middle Years of the Accommodation Debate, 1790–1799   141

6 The End of the Accommodation Debate, 1800–1835   177

7 Conclusion   211

Bibliography   223

Index   245

Abbreviations

BJHP   British Journal for the History of Philosophy
BJRL   Bulletin of the John Rylands Library Manchester
CTJ   Calvin Theological Journal
CTQ   Concordia Theological Quarterly
CQ   The Covenant Quarterly
HTS   Harvard Theological Studies
Int   Interpretation
JETS   Journal of the Evangelical Theological Society
ZTK   Zeitschrift für Theologie und Kirche

CHAPTER 1

Introduction

Throughout the history of Christianity interpreters of the Bible have strived to faithfully understand Scripture and accurately interpret its meaning. The significance of properly grasping God's revelation has not been lost on exegetes, whether the occasion was a great ecumenical council or a small private affair. Through tireless determination, the study of the Bible continues to grow and offer profound insight into God and his work throughout creation. Ultimately, interpreters have sought to understand the Bible in a manner worthy of God's communication to man.

However, the depth of Scripture, for better or worse, has often led to a wide variation of interpretations. As differing readings of the Bible show no sign of waning, the history of biblical interpretation has helped readers discern between various interpretive methods and streams. As an essential tool for modern exegesis, the study of how the Bible was interpreted in the past has aided our present pursuit of a faithful reading of Scripture, serving as an arbiter over present issues by bolstering the strengths and exposing the weaknesses of modern interpretative methodologies.

One of the most contentious topics in the history of biblical interpretation and in current scholarship is historical criticism.[1] Since the

---

[1] V.P. Furnish defines historical criticism as having five characteristics: (1) "a concern to understand the relation between biblical teachings and the data derived from experience"; (2) "an assumption that the Bible is a proper object for rational investigation";

seventeenth and eighteenth centuries, historical criticism has developed and tested the boundaries of faithful exegesis. With the introduction of unconventional methodologies, it has provided a wealth of new information, but accompanying these inroads is an ongoing debate over the validity of some aspects of the historical-critical method and its conclusions. For example, scholars often debate whether the premise of historical criticism desacralizes Scripture. Is reading and interpreting the Bible in the same manner as other ancient Near Eastern texts appropriate for God's revelation?

As interpreters go on contesting the legitimacy of historical criticism, they have neglected a vital element of its history. In the modern discussion of hermeneutical methods, contemporary scholarship has yet to fully address the doctrine of accommodation, especially its development in the eighteenth century. Thus Graham A. Cole, speaking to the history of biblical interpretation, writes, "one of the most fertile ideas generated in such discussion is the idea of divine accommodation."[2] Urging for a renewal of the doctrine of accommodation, D. A. Carson argues that a "restatement of that doctrine would be salutary today."[3] Despite the significance of accommodation, the doctrine remains an elusive principle and is sorely misunderstood in current biblical scholarship. This volume aims to redress this confusion.

Footnote 1 (continued)

(3) "a conviction that this investigation must proceed with attention to the individuality of the writers"; (4) "a commitment to the distinction between the words of the New Testament and the Word of God"; and (5) "an acceptance of a thoroughgoing historical view of the canon itself." "The Historical Criticism of the New Testament: A Survey of Origins," *BJRL* 56, no. 2 (1974): 336–370. Also see Ernst Troeltsch, "Historical and Dogmatic Method in Theology," in *Religion in History*, trans. James Luther Adams and Walter F. Bense, with an introduction by James Luther Adams (Minneapolis: Fortress, 1991), 11–32.

[2] Graham A. Cole, "The Peril of a 'Historyless' Systematic Theology," in *Do Historical Matters Matter to Faith?: A Critical Appraisal of Modern and Postmodern Approaches to Scripture*, ed. James K. Hoffmeier and Dennis R. Magary (Wheaton, IL: Crossway, 2012), 63.

[3] D. A. Carson, *The Gagging of God: Christianity Confronts Pluralism* (Grand Rapids, MI: Zondervan, 1996), 130.

Defining Accommodation

Historically, theologians used accommodation to harmonize creaturely and supernatural realities in the Bible. While they affirmed the divine inspiration of the Bible, they also recognized that it had human authors, and thus the text reflected human characteristics. The question that accommodation sought to answer was, how does the reader account for both divine and human authorship in the Bible? The doctrine dictates that by utilizing human authors, ideas, and language, God accommodated his revelation to humankind's level of comprehension.

Richard Muller defines accommodation as follows:

> accommodation occurs specifically in the use of human words and concepts for the communication of the law and the gospel, but it in no way implies the loss of truth or the lessening of scriptural authority. The accommodation or condescension refers to the manner or mode of revelation, the gift of the wisdom of infinite God in finite form, not to the quality of the revelation or to the matter revealed.[4]

Due to man's limited capacity, God must accommodate himself in order to be understood. According to Muller's definition, accommodation affects the manner, mode, and form of God's revelation and not the actual matter. Elsewhere, Muller states, "God does not accommodate his truth to human sin—rather he accommodates his truth to human ways of knowing."[5] In other words, accommodation, as it was traditionally understood, does not compromise the truth or authority of divine revelation.

John Calvin's (1509–1564) use of accommodation is commonly cited to illustrate the Augustinian understanding of accommodation.[6] The reformer appropriated Augustine's (354–430) definition of the doctrine

---

[4] Richard A. Muller, *Dictionary of Latin and Greek Theological Terms: Drawn Principally from Protestant Scholastic Theology* (Grand Rapids, MI: Baker, 1985), 19.

[5] Richard A. Muller, *Post-Reformation Reformed Dogmatics: The Rise and Development of Reformed Orthodoxy, ca. 1520 to ca. 1725*, vol. 1, *Prolegomena to Theology*, 2nd ed. (Grand Rapids, MI: Baker, 2003), 262.

[6] Since Calvin's accommodation is dependent upon an earlier historical definition, his use of accommodation was not unique to Reformed theology. As we will see, the reformers' understanding of the doctrine was shared by other Protestants, such as Lutherans and Catholics alike. In addition to Reformed, Lutheran, and Catholic theology, John Wesley too held the same understanding of accommodation. John Woodbridge, "Foreword," in Hoffmeier and Magary, *Do Historical Matters Matter to Faith?* 17.

and proposed the principle as a tool for reconciling the creaturely and supernatural realities in the Bible. For Calvin, accommodation was the key to understanding why the Bible often included matters that seemed to contradict truth. However, these contradictions only *appeared* to be so due to the accommodated nature of the biblical text. Not only did accommodation aid as an exegetical principle in interpreting certain passages, it also served to uphold the inspiration, authority, and inerrancy of the Bible.[7] For example, Genesis describes both the sun and the moon as the "two great lights." Yet Calvin understood that the moon's surface consisted of a reflective element and thus did not emit light itself. However, Calvin maintained that Moses did not err in his description of the moon. Rather, Moses wrote in accommodated fashion.[8] Despite having a fuller understanding, Moses adapted scientific truth to the visual perception of man and the use of phenomenological language, which meant the Bible remained fully inerrant in all matters.

Despite a well-established tradition of accommodation going back to Augustine and the patristic fathers, Faustus Socinus (1539–1604) developed a contrary definition of accommodation. Socinus altered the historical understanding of accommodation by including the "wrong opinions of the people of the day."[9] In *De Auctoritate Sacrae Scripturae* (1588), Socinus proposed that God used the erroneous beliefs of the biblical authors as an accommodation to their ideology.[10] Rather than merely adopting the manner, mode, and form of divine revelation to man, God chose to adapt the *matter* of revelation by incorporating the misunderstandings of man. Christ instructed his apostles according to the "level of the people" when it came to such matters as bodily resurrection, and both the apostles and Christ "accommodated themselves in the opinions of men which at the time largely prevailed" in their teaching

---

[7] For a definition of inerrancy, see B. B. Warfield, *The Inspiration and the Authority of the Bible* (Philadelphia: Presbyterian and Reformed, 1948); A. A. Hodge and B. B. Warfield, "Inspiration," *Presbyterian Review* 2 (1881), 225–260.

[8] John Calvin, *Commentaries on the First Book of Moses, Called Genesis*, trans. John King (Edinburgh: Calvin Translation Society, 1847), 1:86.

[9] Martin Klauber and Glenn Sunshine, "Jean-Alphonse Turrettini on Biblical Accommodation: Calvinist or Socinian?" *CTJ* 25, no. 1 (1990): 14.

[10] Faustus Socinus, *De Auctoritate Sacrae Scripturae* (Amsterdam: n. p., 1588), 13. The work was originally published under the pseudonym Dominicus Lopez by the false publisher Lazarum Ferrerium in Seville. The 1611 edition carried the title *De Sacrae Scripturae Auctoritate*.

of hell.[11] Whereas accommodation of manner—the Augustinian-Calvinist form—does not impact Scripture's authority, accommodation of matter—the Socinian form—resulted in an errant Bible. Socinus's definition of accommodation reversed Calvin's accommodation, thus compromising the inspiration, authority, and inerrancy of Scripture. While sharing the same name, the two definitions of accommodation had contrary approaches to the Bible, resulting in greatly differing conclusions.

During the rise of historical criticism in the second half of the eighteenth century, scholars in Germany heatedly debated the nature of accommodation. Gottfried Hornig estimates that between 1763 and 1817 no less than 31 works on accommodation were published in Germany.[12] In his 1804 translation of Georg Friedrich Seiler's (1733–1807) *Biblische Hermeneutik oder Grundsätze und Regeln zur Erklärung der Heil. Schrift des Alten und Neuen Testaments* (1800), Jodocus Heringa (1765–1840) identified more than 15 scholars involved in the debate over accommodation.

The debate dealt with the relationship of accommodation to biblical authority and inerrancy, especially in conjunction with the recent critical methods of interpreting the Bible. At stake was not just the factual accuracy of the Bible but also biblical inspiration, biblical authority, and the doctrinal core of Christianity itself. Proponents of a Socinian accommodation contended for an errant Bible: just as the biblical authors were wrong about the moon's light, so too were they wrong about matters of creation, the spirit world, Jesus's earthly ministry, the atonement, and the resurrection. What theologians had previously understood as Christian truth may just have been an accommodation to an errant notion common during the time of the Bible's writing.

As historical criticism made its way to America, the debate over accommodation followed. Charles Hodge (1797–1878) was quite aware of the pivotal role accommodation played in the formation of historical criticism. In the inaugural volume of *The Biblical Repertory* (1825),

---

[11] Faustus Socinus et al., "Epitome of a Colloquium Held in Rakow in the Year 1601," in *The Polish Brethren: Documentation of the History and Thought of Unitarianism in the Polish-Lithuanian Commonwealth and in the Diaspora, 1601–1685*, ed. George Huntston Williams, HTS 30 (Missoula, MT: Scholars Press, 1980), 1:121, 105.

[12] Gottfried Hornig, *Die Anfänge der historisch-kritischen Theologie* (Göttingen: Vandenhoeck & Ruprecht, 1961), 211.

Hodge attributed the pervading historical-critical methodologies to Socinus's and Johann Salomo Semler's (1725–1791) use of accommodation.[13] Hodge worried that with a Socinian understanding of accommodation, an exegete would be free to interpret the Bible in any fashion he desired:

> It must be perceived that if the principle contended for be admitted, every one will be at liberty to assert, that any doctrine he may see fit to object to, is a mere accommodation to Jewish opinion… Every individual's opinions, or what he calls his reason, is made the supreme judge on matters of religion.[14]

Hodge concluded that due to the various definitions of accommodation, one must be diligent in deciphering between competing uses of the doctrine and in discarding illegitimate implementations of accommodation.

Hodge was not the only one aware of the importance of untangling the numerous definitions and uses of accommodation. Patrick Fairbairn in his *Hermeneutical Manual* (1858) traced the origin of "false" accommodation to Johann Jakob Wettstein (1693–1754). According to Fairbairn, Wettstein's position on accommodation attributed "ambiguous, sometimes erroneous, opinions of the multitude" to the Bible.[15] Fairbairn contended that Semler derived his understanding of accommodation from Wettstein, witnessed in Semler's 1764 edition of Wettstein's *Prolegomena ad Novum Testamentum*. As the major progenitor of this type of accommodation, Semler argued that due to the historical nature of Scripture, large portions of the Bible applied only to the time in which they were written. Fairbairn observed that Semler's use of false accommodation negated the doctrines of the Trinity, the divine Sonship of the messiah, the atonement, the personality of the Holy Spirit, bodily resurrection, and the eschatological judgment.[16]

As opposed to false accommodation, Fairbairn stipulated that "true" accommodation was an accommodation of form. God adapted the form

---

[13] Charles Hodge, "Introduction to Charles Christian Tittmann on Historical Interpretation," *Biblical Repertory* 1 (1825): 125–127.

[14] Hodge, "Introduction to Tittmann," 126.

[15] Patrick Fairbairn, *Hermeneutical Manual: Or, Introduction to the Exegetical Study of the Scriptures of the New Testament* (Edinburgh: T & T Clark, 1858), 91.

[16] Fairbairn, *Hermeneutical Manual*, 92.

and manner of communication, not its content or matter. Within true accommodation, Fairbairn distinguished between a "general" and a "specific" accommodation. General accommodation referred to the universal limitation of man and God's general response; that is, humanity was inherently limited regardless of anyone's specific time in history. Specific accommodation spoke of the particular time in history when Scripture was written; for example, the nation of Israel differed contextually from the present day. Hence, God's specific (rather than general) accommodation reflected the constraints of their particular historical context.

Toward the end of the century, Milton Terry argued very similarly to Fairbairn. While not applying his terminology of "false" and "true" accommodation, Terry held many of the same views. Not unlike Hodge, Terry identified Semler's use of accommodation as unsound and as being the progenitor of Socinian accommodation.[17] Also, as with Fairbairn, Terry affirmed a legitimate use of accommodation that aided in the explanation of creaturely realities.

The association between Semler and Socinian accommodation was also identified in *The Catholic Encyclopedia* (1907–1912). A. J. Maas wrote that Theodore of Mopsuestia and the Socinians sought to "destroy the value of the Messianic prophecies" through their use of accommodation.[18] Maas went on to state, "The first to adhere to the principle of Biblical rationalism was Semler (d. 1791), who denied the Divine character of the Old Testament, and explained away the New by his 'system of accommodation,' according to which Christ and the Apostles only conformed to the views of the Jews."[19] Adhering to the Augustinian position on accommodation, Catholic theology contended for the use of accommodation in keeping with biblical authority and inerrancy.[20]

---

[17] Milton S. Terry, *Biblical Hermeneutics: A Treatise on the Interpretation of the Old and New Testaments* (New York: Phillips & Hunt, 1883), 166. Also see 511–513.

[18] A.J. Maas, "Exegesis," *The Catholic Encyclopedia*, ed. Charles G. Herbermann, Edward A. Pace, Condé B. Pallen, Thomas J. Shahan, and John J. Wynne (New York: Encyclopedia Press, 1907–1912), 5:695.

[19] Maas, "Exegesis," 705.

[20] The *New Catholic Encyclopedia* (1967) does not uphold the same position as *The Catholic Encyclopedia*. This may be partially due to the format change between the two encyclopedias and perhaps to a theological shift as well.

As one can see, the doctrine of accommodation can have a significant impact on how Scripture is interpreted. Hodge warned his readers of the dangers of a Socinian understanding of accommodation. This is not to say that all use of accommodation is contrary to biblical authority and inerrancy. As Fairbairn indicated, there is a difference between *false* accommodation and *true* accommodation; the latter followed the definition used throughout the history of the church.

HISTORIOGRAPHY

Scholars have not always been careful to distinguish between these two kinds of accommodation, but that has not stopped them from using their understanding of accommodation to argue for a particular view of the history of biblical authority. It behooves us to trace some of these developments in the literature before proceeding.

An important work for providing a historical perspective on accommodation throughout Christian and Jewish history is Stephen D. Benin's *The Footprints of God* (1993). As a student of Amos Funkenstein, Benin's study extends what Funkenstein began in *Theology and the Scientific Imagination* (1986). I will not attempt a full assessment of the work and its subject matter here but will merely mention the author's helpful distinction between positive and negative accommodation.

Accommodation was most prolific during the patristic period, though not exclusive to the era. Benin identifies two forms: positive accommodation accounts for God's revelation communicated according to human capacity, while negative accommodation is the polemic tool against Judaism and their continual belief in rituals such as sacrifices. Benin writes, "In patristic texts, accommodation is viewed negatively when it is applied to the Jews and Jewish ritual practice... [T]he Lord permitted certain ceremonies, such as sacrifices, to keep his people from becoming idolaters. Negative accommodation then is both punitive and prophylactic."[21] The church fathers, Benin claims, argued that God never desired rituals such as sacrifices but merely allowed them due to the Israelites' immaturity. This allowance was for a specific period of time, which has

---

[21] Stephen D. Benin, *The Footprints of God: Divine Accommodation in Jewish and Christian Thought* SUNY Series in Judaica (Albany: State University of New York Press, 1993), 1.

since passed. It is important to note that neither Benin nor the primary material he quotes alludes to any understanding that God was wrong to accommodate to the limitations of the nation of Israel or that Scripture was errant. The fathers' use of negative accommodation was intended to criticize Judaism, not God or the authority of Scripture.

Unfortunately, Benin's treatment of the eighteenth century, limited to nine pages, is rather brief and incomplete. Benin identifies Gotthold Lessing (1729–1781), Johann Georg Hamann (1730–1788), and Johann Herder (1744–1803) as proponents of the doctrine, contending that Lessing's use of accommodation reflected the pedagogical attitude of the Enlightenment toward the Bible. As reflected in the publication of Hermann Samuel Reimarus's (1694–1768) *Wolfenbüttel Fragments* (1774–1778), the "primer," in this case, Scripture was for that day and that day only.[22] Despite calling Herder a critic of the Enlightenment, Benin presents him as being in line with Lessing's definition of accommodation. As for Hamann, Benin makes little mention of the "Magus of the North."

If Benin had developed his discussion of Hamann, he would have presented a fuller understanding of the Enlightenment and moved beyond a paradigmatic view that unfairly depicts the Enlightenment simply as a rationalistic movement. Also, with a fuller examination of Hamann's use of accommodation, we would have not only learned about his Trinitarian expression of the doctrine but also gained a greater grasp of how contradictory definitions of *accommodation* existed during the Aufklärung (the German term often translated "Enlightenment"). However, even more significant than these omissions is that Benin seems unaware of not only Semler's theory of accommodation but the entire accommodation debate. At the very least, with Semler the most noted user of accommodation in the eighteenth century, Benin would need to include a discussion of the Halle theologian. Without a treatment of the debate, Benin fails to acknowledge the various definitions of *accommodation* and its impact on the interpretation of the Bible.

On the other hand, Gottfried Hornig, in *Die Anfänge der historisch-kritischen Theologie* (1961), does discuss Semler's use of the doctrine. Without drawing a connection to Socinus, Hornig not only attributes to Semler a similar understanding but also deems him the most prominent

---

[22] Benin, *Footprints of God*, 203–204.

adherent. However, Hornig does not identify Semler as the originator. Instead, he rightly draws attention to the fact that Semler never claimed this title for himself.[23] According to Hornig, Semler was aware of the different uses of accommodation in the seventeenth century, but only after he developed the doctrine in the eighteenth century did accommodation become so prevalent.[24]

Hornig is also aware of various understandings of accommodation in the eighteenth century. He writes,

> The dispute revolved around the question whether and to what extent it could be maintained that Jesus and the apostles in their preaching especially employed the manner of speech that would have adapted religious presentations and the general world picture of their listeners. Closely connected was the other question how such time-limited elements of the New Testament are judged from the standpoint of modern scientific insight. The way in which these questions were answered, had not only considerable consequences for systematic theology, but rather also for direct practical preaching.[25]

According to Hornig, Semler rejected the orthodox definition of accommodation in favor of a more progressive understanding.[26]

Though not speaking specifically to the use of accommodation in eighteenth-century Germany, Jack Rogers and Donald McKim's work should be mentioned because of the central role accommodation plays in their overall objective. In *The Authority and Interpretation of the Bible* (1979), the authors challenge the doctrine of scriptural inerrancy through a historical study of the church, paying particular attention to the doctrine of accommodation. They contend that Francis Turretin's (1623–1687) "innovative" theology was adapted by the Princetonians of the nineteenth century as a tool against historical criticism. As a result, the Princetonians mistakenly attributed scriptural inerrancy to Calvin. Rogers and McKim write, "They thought of themselves as followers of

---

[23] Hornig very briefly mentions that others claim Baruch Spinoza (1632–1677) as the progenitor of this particular strand of accommodation. Hornig, *Die Anfänge*, 213.

[24] Hornig, *Die Anfänge*, 211.

[25] Hornig, *Die Anfänge*, 211.

[26] Hornig reasons that the orthodox position on accommodation was a tool to support verbal inspiration. Accommodation can be used to harmonize the errors that verbal inspiration cannot otherwise account for. Hornig, *Die Anfänge*, 214.

Calvin. But in actuality, they believed and taught a theological method regarding the authority and interpretation of the Bible that was rooted in a post-Reformation scholasticism, an approach almost the exact opposite of Calvin's own."[27]

At the heart of the authors' thesis is their belief that because the historical church advocated a doctrine of accommodation, they could not have held to inerrancy. Thus they argue that, with the early church fathers, Calvin affirmed that Scripture was written in accommodated fashion according to the historical culture of that day, which included errors. They contend,

> Scripture was not used as a sourcebook for science. Early theologians accepted God's accommodated style of communication. God, like a good father or mother, adopted the thought and speech of children in order to relate to them. Theology was meant to be a practical discipline, enabling people to understand God's relationship to them.[28]

On the other hand, Turretin and other Protestant scholastics based the authority of Scripture on inerrancy with "no trace of the central Christian tradition of accommodation."[29] The historical and cultural importance of Scripture gave way to propositional truths. This "innovation" became solidified with the import of Common Sense Realism and the fight against biblical criticism.[30] The authors write,

---

[27] Jack B. Rogers and Donald K. McKim, *The Authority and Interpretation of the Bible: An Historical Approach* (San Francisco: Harper & Row, 1979), xvii.

[28] Rogers and McKim, *Authority and Interpretation*, 458.

[29] Rogers and McKim, *Authority and Interpretation*, xvii.

[30] A. T. B. McGowan argues that the doctrine of inerrancy was not a direct result of Common Sense Realism. Other scholars held to Common Sense Realism, including some of the Princetonians' opponents, yet promoted an errant Bible. A. T. B. McGowan, *The Divine Authenticity of Scripture* (Downers Grove, IL: IVP Academic, 2007), 101–102. Also see J. Ligon Duncan III, "Common Sense and American Presbyterianism: An Evaluation of the Impact of Scottish Realism on Princeton and the South" (master's thesis, Covenant Theological Seminary, 1987). Similarly, Paul Helseth contends that the Princetonians were in line with Reformed thinking concerning the use of reason. Though they used Common Sense Realism, the root of their understanding of reason lay in Christian faith and not pure reason. Paul Kjoss Helseth, *"Right Reason" and the Princeton Mind: An Unorthodox Proposal* (Phillipsburg, NJ: P&R, 2010).

Scholasticism assumed that reason had at least equal standing with faith in religious matters, with the consequence that revelation was often relegated to a secondary position. The Reformation concept of accommodation was dropped and Western logic was assumed to reflect the working of the mind of God.... Theology was no longer viewed as a practical, moral discipline exclusively directed toward the salvation of people and their guidance in the life of faith. Theology now became an abstract, speculative, technical science that attempted to lay foundations for philosophical mastery of all areas of thought and life. Further, and equally far-reaching in its consequences, the concept of accommodation was discarded.[31]

Because the nature of their work deals with biblical authority and historical criticism, and because the authors uphold the importance of accommodation, one would expect a treatment of the German accommodation debate. However, Rogers and McKim conduct no study of the eighteenth-century debate and its relation to the rise of historical criticism. Had they discussed the accommodation debate, Rogers and McKim would have come to a better understanding of the doctrine. Their confusion over Socinian accommodation would have been clarified, leading them to the conclusion either that they had misconstrued the position of scholars such as Calvin or that Socinian accommodation was the historical position but was opposed by orthodox supernaturalists in the seventeenth and eighteenth centuries.

John Woodbridge, in *Biblical Authority: A Critique of the Rogers/McKim Proposal* (1982), offers a careful examination of Rogers and McKim. Woodbridge begins by identifying ten methodological errors that Rogers and McKim commit. Many relate to the polemical and selective use of data that depends heavily on secondary literature. Woodbridge states that Rogers and McKim's presuppositions are in many ways a reflection of Karl Barth (1886–1968) and G. C. Berkouwer (1903–1996). He writes,

> By this we mean that the later Berkouwer's "historical disjunctions" probably became Rogers and McKim's working premises. Since Berkouwer does not believe in complete biblical infallibility and argues that the Bible's chief function is to reveal salvation truths (pp. 428–29), then those figures of the past who declared that the Bible reveals salvation truths also

---

[31] Rogers and McKim, *Authority and Interpretation*, 186–187.

did not believe in complete biblical infallibility. Since Berkouwer thinks that God's accommodation to us in human language necessitates an errant Bible (pp. 431–33), then those individuals who spoke of accommodation denied complete biblical infallibility. Since, Berkouwer argues that according to the Bible 'error' relates solely to 'sin and deception' (p. 431), then Augustine, Calvin, and Luther only describe error in that way. Since Berkouwer does not believe that the Bible's incidental comments about history and science are always reliable, then Augustine, Wycliffe, Calvin, Luther, and others did not believe this either. Evidently, Rogers and McKim took the later Berkouwer's premises and crushed them down on whatever data they encountered.[32]

Woodbridge's study accurately defines accommodation and exposes the difference between Rogers and McKim's definition, as it is read back into past Christian scholars, and the actual understanding of the doctrine held by those whom Rogers and McKim study. His careful review of Rogers and McKim's citations reveals that the authors often misquote or misrepresent past users of accommodation to align them with the Socinian position. He shows that Rogers and McKim's definition of accommodation is not in line with the church's historical definition; rather, the authors' doctrine follows that of Socinus.

RECENT USES OF ACCOMMODATION

More recently, the issue of accommodation has come to the forefront through works such as Peter Enns's *Inspiration and Incarnation* (2005), in which he uses accommodation alongside historical criticism to aid in modern biblical interpretation. He writes, "the problems many of us feel regarding the Bible may have less to do with the Bible itself and more to do with our own preconceptions."[33] Keeping this in mind, Enns proceeds to pose three questions: Why does the Bible appear to share many commonalities with other ancient Near Eastern literature? Why are there contradictory statements within the Bible? Why do some of the New Testament authors interpret the Old Testament in such particular

---

[32] John D. Woodbridge, *Biblical Authority: A Critique of the Rogers/McKim Proposal* (Grand Rapids, MI: Zondervan, 1982), 147–148.

[33] Peter Enns, *Inspiration and Incarnation: Evangelicals and the Problems of the Old Testament* (Grand Rapids, MI: Baker, 2005), 15.

fashions?[34] The remainder of the work seeks to address these three issues by juxtaposing the divine and human nature of the Bible to each topic through the use of accommodation.

According to Enns, the reason why the creation account in Genesis shares similarities to texts such as the *Enuma Elish* is that the two works were derived from the same myth. The Genesis account is not unique or original. God's accommodation took the common myths of that day and utilized them for the recounting of God's creation of the universe. This borrowing of myth does not negate divine inspiration or authority but rather serves as the channel through which God communicates his revelation.

Accommodation is also responsible for the "diversity" in Scripture. The reason why the Bible contains diverse, contradictory, and erroneous statements and beliefs is because "to be understood, [God] condescends to the conventions and conditions of those to whom he is revealing himself."[35] Similar to Rogers and McKim, Enns contends that regardless of whether these "conventions" are correct, God chooses to accommodate his revelation to these standards. The diversity of Scripture is not to be rejected or explained away but instead accepted as part of the way the Bible has been written as accommodated revelation.

Lastly, due to the Second Temple context of the New Testament authors, one should expect the New Testament authors to read the Old Testament in accommodated fashion. Modern readers should not force modern standards of exegesis onto the New Testament context. New Testament accommodation situates the exegetical approach of the authors in a Second Temple hermeneutical model. Enns does make a distinction between accommodation to the authors' understanding and the authors' accommodation to their readers. In Enns's opinion, New Testament accommodation is the former and not the latter. The authors worked within their Second Temple context because that was their understanding and not because they "knew better" and were merely accommodating to their readers.

Enns demonstrates the important connection between accommodation and modern historical criticism. While one may not agree with his conclusions or his Socinian definition of accommodation, we can benefit

---

[34] Enns, *Inspiration and Incarnation*, 15–16.

[35] Enns, *Inspiration and Incarnation*, 109.

from Enns's efforts to resurrect the doctrine for biblical interpretation. However, Enns never indicates any awareness that the concept of accommodation is quite varied among its users. Nor does he ever allude to the differences between Augustinian and Socinian accommodation or to the doctrine's impact on historical criticism.

Kenton Sparks also advocates the important relationship between historical criticism and accommodation. In *God's Word in Human Words* (2008), Sparks contends for an evangelical appropriation of historical criticism based on a Socinian definition of accommodation, though he does not identify it as Socinian.[36] In a more epistemologically focused work than Enns's, Sparks begins with three central concepts. First, a Cartesian totalistic hold on knowledge and truth is unwarranted. Second, all interpreters are firmly situated within their context and thus adhere to the exegetical practices of their day. This contextualization does not exclude the authors of the Old or New Testament. Third, arguing from what he calls a "postmodern practical realist perspective," Sparks claims that we should expect the adequacy of communication in everyday life to be present in the Bible. For Sparks, God's accommodation to man includes the use of man's adequate communication, which is characterized by imperfection. He writes, "Might it be the very height of divine wisdom, of inerrant wisdom, for God to speak to us from an *adequate* human horizon rather than from his divine, inerrant viewpoint?"[37]

Arguing similarly to Enns, Sparks contends that accommodation was integral to the way the church throughout history has addressed the diversity in the Bible.[38] Sparks defines accommodation as "God's adoption in inscripturation of the human audience's finite and fallen perspective. Its underlying conceptual assumption is that in many cases God does not correct our mistaken human viewpoints but merely assumes them in order to communicate with us."[39] He argues that accommodation is "theologically necessary only if we believe that errors

---

[36] Kenton L. Sparks, *God's Word in Human Words: An Evangelical Appropriation of Critical Biblical Scholarship* (Grand Rapids, MI: Baker, 2008).

[37] Sparks, *God's Word in Human Words*, 55. Sparks also identifies practical realism as the catalyst for his rejection of the traditional evangelical understanding of inerrancy, which he deems Cartesian.

[38] Sparks, *God's Word in Human Words*, 230.

[39] Sparks, *God's Word in Human Words*, 230–231.

appear in Scripture."⁴⁰ He states the necessity of accommodation without consideration of the natural chasm between God and man, due to the limited capacity of man, which requires condescension regardless of sin. For Sparks, an admission of accommodation is always an admittance of error within divine revelation. Based on his Socinian understanding of accommodation, it is no wonder Sparks finds evangelicals wary of accommodation.

Not unlike Enns, Sparks reads his definition of accommodation into the history of the church without accounting for various definitions of accommodation. For example, Sparks states that Chrysostom's definition contains the "true nature" of accommodation. However, when we compare Sparks's definition against Chrysostom's, we see a subtle yet significant difference. Sparks quotes Chrysostom as saying, "What is condescension? It is when God appears and makes himself known, *not as he is*, but in the way one incapable of beholding him is able to look upon him. In this way God reveals himself proportionally to the weakness of those who behold him."⁴¹ In Sparks's definition, the "underlying conceptual assumption" is that God allows error to remain within divine revelation. However, Chrysostom's definition contains no inkling of such a sentiment. Sparks inserts his definition into Chrysostom's statement.

In his effort to remind evangelicals of the importance of general revelation, Sparks contends that recognizing the accommodated nature of Scripture will relieve some of the tensions between special and general revelation. He writes, "In the case of Copernicus, it seems that God's word in creation properly trumped his word in Scripture because the latter had been accommodated to an ancient and partially mistaken view of the cosmos."⁴² Sparks extends this reasoning to theological themes. For example, by comparing how ancient Egyptians understood deity to the theology found in Genesis 1–3, Sparks contends that God accommodated the Bible to the general revelation that existed at that time; in short, Genesis 1–3 was an accommodation to the general revelation shared by all ancient Near Eastern cultures—Egyptian, Israelite, or otherwise. Sparks concludes, "So we will not go far wrong if we say that Scripture functions not so much by giving us new theology as by

---

⁴⁰ Sparks, *God's Word in Human Words*, 247, 256.
⁴¹ John Chrysostom, quoted in Sparks, *God's Word in Human Words*, 239.
⁴² Sparks, *God's Word in Human Words*, 275.

ordering, correcting, and extending the natural theology that we already possess."[43]

In the end, Sparks's understanding of accommodation leads him in the direction of trajectory theology or theology "beyond the Bible."[44] Since the Bible is accommodated to the limited and erroneous understanding of the people at the time it was written, modern exegesis and theology must improve upon what is found in the written text. He observes, "as I have suggested, the Bible sometimes accommodates the errant views of its human authors and audiences, and that our search for the truth on some issues will therefore require that we move beyond the Bible for better insights."[45] Sparks rejects a division of science and theology in the Bible. Hence, moving beyond the Bible is not merely a matter of science but of theology as well. Sparks contends that the very nature of accommodated revelation requires modern readers to "trump the Bible" with God's continual communication to the church and not be content with the accommodated revelation of Scripture.[46]

METHODOLOGY AND SIGNIFICANCE OF THIS STUDY

While modern biblical scholars have renewed efforts to utilize accommodation once again, they appear to be confused over what the doctrine entails. A historical treatment of accommodation, especially in the period when it was discussed most extensively, would thus benefit modern scholarship. Given the use of historical criticism in modern biblical scholarship, a thorough examination of the accommodation debate, which occurred in conjunction with the formative years of historical criticism, is most warranted.

In hopes of gaining a better understanding of accommodation and its relationship to biblical inerrancy, authority, and historical criticism, this project seeks to answer the question, what understandings of accommodation did German scholars involved in the accommodation debate from 1761 to 1835 propose? This study identifies and locates the relevant

---

[43] Sparks, *God's Word in Human Words*, 276.

[44] For a treatment of the relationship between accommodation and "beyond the Bible" theology, see I. Howard Marshall, *Beyond the Bible: Moving from Scripture to Theology* (Grand Rapids, MI: Baker Academic, 2004).

[45] Sparks, *God's Word in Human Words*, 288.

[46] Sparks, *God's Word in Human Words*, 295.

works within the second half of the eighteenth century. In the pages that follow, I conduct a thorough examination of the pertinent works, again with a particular emphasis on the relationship between accommodation, inerrancy, biblical authority, and historical criticism. While eighteenth-century accommodationists may not have operated out of these same specific categories, they will help in assessing which particular understanding of accommodation they were promoting. In doing so, I will be looking at issues such as cosmology, demonology, and the extent to which Jesus accommodated his teaching to his hearers.

In answering this driving question, I seek to address three matters. First, despite Hodge and Fairbairn's admonition, scholars such as Jack Rogers, Donald McKim, Peter Enns, and Kenton Sparks continue to confuse and misappropriate the doctrine of accommodation. While demonstrating the value of accommodation for modern interpretive methodology, their failure to distinguish between Augustinian accommodation and heterodox accommodation only confuses the use of accommodation. New discussion must be initiated to develop the appropriate use of accommodation.

Second, there is a need to continue researching the eighteenth century and the nature of the era we commonly call the Enlightenment. Without a systematic treatment of the accommodation debate, our understanding of the period is limited to select scholars such as Semler and fails to recognize the important role of accommodation in eighteenth-century exegesis. A study of the debate will provide perspective on well-known historical figures, such as Immanuel Kant, but will focus on their role as accommodationists, which often goes unaddressed. It will also offer an opportunity to reflect on understudied eighteenth- and nineteenth-century scholars who played significant roles in the discussion. The examination of the variety of scholars represented in the debate thus contributes to a better comprehension of the Enlightenment. Countering the paradigmatic perception of an exclusively rationalistic Enlightenment, the accommodation debate reveals a fuller picture of the theological and hermeneutical diversity within the Enlightenment.

Third, a greater understanding of accommodation will add an accurate representation of the rise of historical criticism in the eighteenth century. I argue that Socinian accommodation and historical criticism formed a partnership that resulted in the modern use of the former. Beyond just the scholarship of Semler, many early promoters of historical criticism utilized this partnership. With a greater understanding of accommodation in eighteenth-century Germany, we gain further insight into the presuppositions of historical criticism and its subsequent development.

STRUCTURE OF THE STUDY

To proceed with this study, we first need to establish the backdrop of the debate. Thus, the second chapter addresses accommodation in the seventeenth-century Dutch Republic. By studying the use of accommodation by the Voetians and Cartesio-Cocceians, we will gain an understanding of historical accommodation and the development of Socinian accommodation, which had a significant bearing on the later accommodation debate in Germany. Beginning with Christopher Wittichius (1625–1687) and culminating with Balthasar Bekker (1634–1698), Cartesio-Cocceians combined Cartesian principles with Socinian hermeneutics. Though forgoing the strict Cartesian dualism, Baruch Spinoza (1632–1677) popularized Socinian accommodation.

In Chap. 3, I turn to the first half of the eighteenth century in Germany. Orthodox scholars such as Valentin Ernst Löscher (1673–1749) and their Pietist counterparts Joachim Lange (1670–1744) and Johann Jacob Rambach (1693–1735) combatted a Wolffian form of Socinian accommodation found in Siegmund Jakob Baumgarten (1706–1757). In addition to the Wolffian influence, we will see a decline in Cartesio-Cocceian accommodation but a progression of Spinozist accommodation. The chapter ends with a treatment of Johann Georg Hamann (1730–1788), who was perhaps the most prolific user of accommodation in this period.

The next three chapters address the accommodation debate from 1761 to 1835. Whereas the previous chapters deal with scholars who used or addressed the issue of accommodation within writings of a larger scope, the authors of the accommodation debate often wrote works exclusively on the doctrine. Rather than approaching the debate thematically, the chapters are divided into chronological sections, 1761–1789, 1790–1799, and 1800–1835, to preserve a sense of the historical development over these decades.

In the conclusion, I advocate for two definitions of the doctrine of accommodation. By summarizing our findings I will demonstrate the differences between Socinian and Augustinian accommodation. And I will suggest ways that the study of the accommodation debate contributes to our understanding of historical criticism in modern interpretation.

Bibliography

Benin, Stephen D. *The Footprints of God: Divine Accommodation in Jewish and Christian Thought.* SUNY Series in Judaica. Albany: State University of New York Press, 1993.

Calvin, John, *Commentaries on the First Book of Moses, Called Genesis.* Translated by John King. 2 vols. Edinburgh: Calvin Translation Society, 1847.

Carson, D. A. *The Gagging of God: Christianity Confronts Pluralism.* Grand Rapids, MI: Zondervan, 1996.

Cole, Graham A. "The Peril of a 'Historyless' Systematic Theology." In *Do Historical Matters Matter to Faith?: A Critical Appraisal of Modern and Postmodern Approaches to Scripture*, edited by James K. Hoffmeier and Dennis R. Magary, 55–69. Wheaton, IL: Crossway, 2012.

Enns, Peter. *Inspiration and Incarnation: Evangelicals and the Problems of the Old Testament.* Grand Rapids, MI: Baker, 2005.

Fairbairn, Patrick. *Hermeneutical Manual: Or, Introduction to the Exegetical Study of the Scriptures of the New Testament.* Edinburgh: T&T Clark, 1858.

Furnish, V. P. "The Historical Criticism of the New Testament: A Survey of Origins." *Bulletin of the John Rylands Library Manchester* 56 no. 2 (1974): 336–70.

Helseth, Paul Kjoss. *"Right Reason" and the Princeton Mind: An Unorthodox Proposal.* Phillipsburg, NJ: P&R, 2010.

Hodge, A. A. and B. B. Warfield, "Inspiration," Presbyterian Review 2 (1881), 225–60.

Hodge, Charles. "Introduction to Charles Christian Tittmann on Historical Interpretation," *Biblical Repertory* 1 (1825): 125–27.

Hornig, Gottfried. *Die Anfänge der historisch-kritischen Theologie.* Göttingen: Vandenhoeck & Ruprecht, 1961.

Klauber, Martin, and Glenn Sunshine. "Jean-Alphonse Turrettini on Biblical Accommodation: Calvinist or Socinian?" *Calvin Theological Journal* 25, no. 1 (1990): 7–27.

Maas, A. J. "Exegesis," *The Catholic Encyclopedia*, ed. Charles G. Herbermann, Edward A. Pace, Condé B. Pallen, Thomas J. Shahan, and John J. Wynne. New York: Encyclopedia Press, 1907–1912, 5:695.

Marshall, I. Howard. *Beyond the Bible: Moving from Scripture to Theology.* Grand Rapids, MI: Baker Academic, 2004.

McGowan, A. T. B. *The Divine Spiration of Scripture: Challenging Evangelical Perspectives.* Nottingham: Apollos, 2007.

Muller, Richard A. *Dictionary of Latin and Greek Theological Terms: Drawn Principally from Protestant Scholastic Theology.* Grand Rapids, MI: Baker, 1985.

———. *Post-Reformation Reformed Dogmatics: The Rise and Development of Reformed Orthodoxy, ca. 1520 to ca. 1725.* 4 vols. 2nd ed. Grand Rapids, MI: Baker, 2003.

Rogers, Jack B., and Donald K. McKim. *The Authority and Interpretation of the Bible: An Historical Approach.* San Francisco: Harper & Row, 1979.
Socinus, Faustus. *De auctoritate Sacrae Scripturae.* Amsterdam: n.p., 1588.
Socinus, Faustus, et al. "Epitome of a Colloquium Held in Rakow in the Year 1601." In *The Polish Brethren: Documentation of the History and Thought of Unitarianism in the Polish-Lithuanian Commonwealth and in the Diaspora, 1601–1685,* edited by George Huntston Williams. Harvard Theological Studies 30. Missoula, MT: Scholars Press, 1980.
Sparks, Kenton L. *God's Word in Human Words: An Evangelical Appropriation of Critical Biblical Scholarship.* Grand Rapids, MI: Baker, 2008.
Terry, Milton S. *Biblical Hermeneutics: A Treatise on the Interpretation of the Old and New Testaments.* New York: Phillips & Hunt, 1883.
Troeltsch, Ernst. "Historical and Dogmatic Method in Theology." In *Religion in History.* Translated by James Luther Adams and Walter F. Bense, with an introduction by James Luther Adams. Minneapolis: Fortress, 1991.
Warfield, B. B. *The Inspiration and the Authority of the Bible.* Philadelphia: Presbyterian and Reformed, 1948.
Woodbridge, John D. *Biblical Authority: A Critique of the Rogers/McKim Proposal.* Grand Rapids, MI: Zondervan, 1982.
———. "Foreword." In *Do Historical Matters Matter to Faith?: A Critical Appraisal of Modern and Postmodern Approaches to Scripture,* edited by James K. Hoffmeier and Dennis R. Magary, 13–18. Wheaton, IL: Crossway, 2012.

CHAPTER 2

Accommodation in the Seventeenth-Century Dutch Republic

The appropriateness of beginning a discussion of the eighteenth-century German accommodation debate with an examination of seventeenth-century Dutch biblical exegesis is at first questionable—on account of both chronology and geography. However, we have good reason to begin with the Dutch Republic rather than proceeding straight to the debate. Though the accommodation debate occurred in Germany roughly during the period from the last third of the eighteenth century to the first third of the nineteenth century, the country's seventeenth-century neighbors foreshadowed the debate.

The doctrine of accommodation has a long history, extending back to the patristic age, particularly through the work of Augustine. Calvin popularized Augustinian accommodation, but Luther also used it, and post-Reformation scholars of both Lutheran and Calvinist confessions developed it further. Through Socinus, a heterodox understanding gained a hearing in the sixteenth century. Yet while introduced in the sixteenth century, it was not until seventeenth-century Dutch Reformed scholars combined Socinian accommodation with Cartesian philosophy that this heterodox understanding became widely accepted. The popularity of this newly formed Socinian doctrine sparked contention among orthodox Calvinists, resulting in a major dispute.

Socinian accommodation did not become a fully defined concept for German scholars until the eighteenth century. Rather than emerging from a Lutheran origin, Socinian accommodation came to the Germans via seventeenth-century Dutch Reformed Cartesio-Cocceians. To admit an acceptance of Socinianism, as with Spinozism, was tantamount to admitting atheism. Hence, it was advantageous for these Germans to be able to show a theological lineage from the Cartesio-Cocceians rather than from Socinus. In addition to appropriating Socinian accommodation from the Cartesio-Cocceians, eighteenth-century adherents of this heterodoxy inherited Cartesio-Cocceians' practices, applying the doctrine to similar issues and biblical passages as they did. The early stages of the accommodation debate in Germany thus continued the cosmological discussion central to the earlier Dutch dispute and further developed the beginnings of doctrinal accommodation found in late seventeenth-century Dutch accommodation.

On the other hand, in defense of Augustinian accommodation, eighteenth-century orthodox Lutherans and Pietists turned to their seventeenth-century Lutheran heritage. We will discuss their argument further in Chap. 4, but it is important to note here that while the orthodox Lutherans and Pietists were acquainted with Voetian accommodation, they did not need to make the geographical and confessional jump that Germans embracing the Socinian definition did because they could trace a progression directly from Luther to post-Reformation Lutheran theology. Also, as Augustinian accommodationists combatted eighteenth-century heterodox accommodation, they distanced their opponents from the Cartesio-Cocceians and associated heterodox accommodation directly with Socinus. Hence, while the accommodation dispute in seventeenth-century Reformed circles differed from the accommodation debate, a clear historical and theological development links the two. It would be a disservice to study the latter without discussing the former.

THE VOETIANS AND THE CARTESIO-COCCEIANS

Acquainted with the Dutch Republic through his military service to the country, a family tradition, René Descartes (1596–1650) established himself in the United Provinces of the Netherlands after his military service and several years of travel. Despite being born near Tours in France, Descartes preferred life in the Dutch Republic, especially given the greater level of privacy there. Thus, before its dissemination throughout Europe, Cartesian philosophy found its home in the Dutch Republic. The controversial work *Meditations on First Philosophy* (1641) created an immediate response of both admiration and dismay in Dutch academia.

Among Descartes's critics was a professor of theology named Gijsbert Voetius (1589–1676). After completing his education in Leiden and briefly serving as a minister, Voetius was appointed professor of theology at Utrecht in 1634. Throughout the 1630s, Voetius served as the leader for orthodox Calvinists in the Dutch Republic, but it was not until the 1640s that this network of Dutch Calvinists gained the title "Voetians." Associated with this title was a reputation for combatting heterodoxy and upholding Reformed theology in the orthodox tradition.[1]

As part of their endeavor to uphold orthodoxy, Voetians refuted Cartesian philosophy.[2] In their estimation, the mechanistic worldview of Descartes rid the world of God, or at the very least distorted God's role in the universe. Also, Cartesian doubt undermined the foundation of Christianity, to the extent of questioning the very existence of God.[3] Lastly, the Cartesian system replaced revelation with reason, elevating philosophy to the stature of the Bible. The Voetians argued that scriptural truth was limited by Cartesian dualism to matters of morality, while philosophy became the sole interpreter of natural science.[4] As a result, they reduced the Bible to a collection of moral principles, void

---

[1] For further information concerning their Aristotelian nature, see Paul Dibon, "Die Republik der Vereinigten Niederlande," in *Die Philosophie des 17. Jahrhunderts*, vol. 2, *Frankreich und Nierderlande*, ed. Jean-Pierre Schobinger, Grundriss der Geschichte der Philosophie (Basel: Schwabe, 1993), 42–86; Richard A. Muller, "Reformation, Orthodoxy, 'Christian Aristotelianism,' and the Eclecticism of Early Modern Philosophy," in *Nederlands Archief voor Kergeschiedenis*, n.s. 81, no. 3 (2001): 306–325.

[2] Paul Dibon, "Der Cartesianismus in den Niederlanden," in Schobinger, *Die Philosophie des 17. Jahrhunderts*, vol. 2, *Frankreich und Nierderlande*, 349–374; Dibon, "Scepticisme et orthodoxie reformée dans la Hollande du Siècle d'Or," in *Scepticism from the Renaissance to the Enlightenment*, ed. Richard H. Popkin and Charles B. Schmitt, Wolfenbüttler Forschungen 35 (Wiesbaden: In Kommission bei O. Harrassowitz, 1987), 55–81.

[3] Jacobus Revius, *Methodi Cartesianae consideratio theologica* (Leiden: Hieronymum de Vogel, 1648), 60–71. Also see Revius, *Kartesiomanias pars altera, qua ad secundam partem rabiosae Assertionis Tobiae Andreae respondetur* (Leiden: Hieronymum de Vogel, 1655), 318–319, 385–386; Revius, *Analectorum theologicorum disputatio XXI* (Leiden: Johannis Nicolai van Dorp, 1647).

[4] Ernst Bizer, "Die reformierte Orthodoxie und der Cartesianismus," *Zeitschrift für Theologie und Kirche* 55, no. 3 (1958): 347. Also see Gijsbertus Voetius, *Thersites heautontimorumenos. Hoc est, Remonstrantium hyperaspistes: catechesis, et liturgiae Germanicae, Gallicae, et Belgicae denuo insultans* (Utrecht: Abrahami ab Herwiick et Hermanni Ribbius, 1635), 266–267.

of universal truth or salvific force.⁵ On the other hand, they endowed philosophy with revelatory status as infallible and divine truth.⁶

Despite the concerted efforts of the Voetians, by the late 1640s Cartesian thought permeated much of Dutch academia. By the 1650s, the Voetian camp was countered by a group of scholars led by the Leiden theology professor Johannes Cocceius (1603–1669). Born in Bremen, Cocceius studied in Germany and the Netherlands. After returning to Bremen as a professor in 1630 and back to Franeker in 1636, Cocceius eventually earned the theology chair at Leiden, which he maintained until his death.

Open to Cartesian thought, Cocceius appropriated some of the new developments in biblical exegesis associated with Cartesian scholars. Jonathan Israel describes Cocceius's hermeneutical principle as follows: "parts of Scripture were intended only to be figurative and allegorical, tailored to the ignorance and superstition of the ancient Israelites," while "the real meaning and relevance can only be distilled by means of sophisticated exegetical methods."⁷ With the realization of the accommodated nature of the text, proper interpretation of the Bible required new exegetical methods. For instance, passages that recounted supernatural occurrences could be interpreted figuratively or allegorically, rather than literally, which often meant using accommodation to harmonize scientific accuracy with the biblical authors' inaccurate perception.

Israel rightly argues that this understanding of the Bible solidified the connection between the Cartesians and the Cocceians.⁸ However, the Cocceians used Cartesian philosophy to varying degrees. Cocceius himself refrained from appropriating Cartesian doubt, a principle employed by Cocceians such as Abraham Heidanus (1597–1678), Francis Burmann (1628–1679), Johannes Braunius (1628–1708), Christophorus Wittichius (1625–1687), and Balthasar Bekker (1634–1698).⁹ Willem van Asselt argues that while Cocceius showed limited

---

⁵ Bizer, "Die reformierte Orthodoxie," 283.

⁶ Jonathan Israel, *Radical Enlightenment: Philosophy and the Making of Modernity 1650–1750* (New York: Oxford University Press, 2001), 25–26.

⁷ Jonathan Israel, *The Dutch Republic: Its Rise, Greatness, and Fall, 1477–1806* (Oxford: Clarendon, 1995), 666.

⁸ Israel, *The Dutch Republic*, 892.

⁹ Willem J. van Asselt, "Scholasticism in the Time of High Orthodoxy (ca. 1620–1700)," in *Introduction to Reformed Scholasticism*, ed. Willem J. van Asselt, trans. Albert Gootjies,

interest in Cartesian philosophy, the Leiden professor never envisioned developing this line of thinking within his own theology. Despite Cocceius's original intentions, many Cocceians established their whole theology on the basis of a partnership with Cartesian philosophy.[10] Hence, a certain amount of discontinuity existed between Cocceius and Cocceians who appropriated Cartesian philosophy in their theology.

Wiep van Bunge attempts to identify the link between the Cartesians and Cocceians as Calvin's doctrine of accommodation.[11] Descartes, in his second *Replies*, alluded to the Bible's accommodation to "ordinary understanding."[12] Thus, van Bunge argues, accommodation served as a tool for the reconciliation of the Bible with this new science by bridging Reformed theology with Cartesianism. He claims that the Voetians, not the Cocceians, were the ones who departed from the Calvinistic tradition. They limited their theology by adhering to a literalistic reading of Scripture, thus "categorically refusing the hermeneutical principle of accommodation."[13]

Upon closer examination of van Bunge's argument, we can see three areas in which his assessment of Cartesio-Cocceian accommodation fails. First, while van Bunge rightly identifies the use of accommodation by Cartesio-Cocceians, he is wrong to dissociate Voetians from the doctrine. As we will see shortly, Voetians did not reject Calvin's understanding of accommodation; rather, they objected to the way in which the Cocceians apprehended the doctrine.

Second, van Bunge employs an antiquated and false understanding of Calvin's accommodation. Following Ford Lewis Battles, van Bunge argues that Calvin based his concept of accommodation on his rhetorical

---

Footnote 9 (continued)

Reformed Historical-Theological Studies (Grand Rapids, MI: Reformation Heritage, 2011), 149.

[10] Willem J. van Asselt, *The Federal Theology of Johannes Cocceius (1603–1669)*, Studies in the History of Christian Thought 100 (Leiden: Brill, 2001), 81.

[11] Wiep van Bunge, *From Stevin to Spinoza: An Essay on Philosophy in the Seventeenth-Century Dutch Republic*, Brill's Studies in Intellectual History 103 (Leiden, Brill, 2001), 50–51.

[12] René Descartes, *Philosophical Writings*, trans. John Cottingham, Robert Stoothoff, and Dugald Murdoch (Cambridge: Cambridge University Press, 1984–1991), 2:102. Cf. in van Bung, *From Stevin to Spinoza*, 50.

[13] Van Bunge, *From Stevin to Spinoza*, 51.

training.[14] While perhaps not Battles's intention, this perception of Calvin separates the reformer's use of accommodation from his theological convictions. van Bunge's position allows him to connect Calvin to the Cartesio-Cocceians through the tradition of rhetoric while bypassing the need to prove theological cohesion.

Jon Balserak contends that a rhetorical matrix neglects the theological context in which Calvin was using the doctrine.[15] For Calvin accommodation was not merely a rhetorical tool but a theological principle that upheld the authority of the Bible. Balserak states that Calvin's use of accommodation "rarely, if ever, suggests a conception of the Bible which understands its truth as being historically–relative, as seems to have been the case with these later proponents of accommodation such as Christoph Wittich," a prime example of Cartesio-Cocceian accommodation.[16]

Third, in contrast to Calvin, Cartesio-Cocceian accommodation rested on the foundation of a Cartesian dualism separating moral truth from natural philosophy. Cartesianism thus voided the Bible's claims of possessing natural truth. And so, unlike Calvin, Cartesio-Cocceians distinguished between the moral truth of Scripture and matters of nature. Viewing the world mechanistically, Cartesio-Cocceians implied that when biblical authors recounted supernatural occurrences in the Bible, they simply betrayed their own misunderstanding of how nature really functions. Whereas Calvin used accommodation to harmonize Scripture with science, Cartesio-Cocceians used accommodation to detach the Bible from science. Thus Bekker stated, "it is certain that philosophy contemplates all that is accessible to reason; it is theology that teaches what transcends the power of the human mind, as the Apostle testifies."[17] Bekker went on to state that the "principle" of philosophy is

---

[14] Ford Lewis Battles, "God Was Accommodating Himself to Human Capacity," *Int* 31, no. 1 (1977): 20. E. David Willis presents a similar view in "Rhetoric and Responsibility in Calvin's Theology," in *The Context of Contemporary Theology: Essays in Honor of Paul Lehmann*, ed. Alexander J. McKelway and E. David Willis (Atlanta: John Knox, 1974), 43–64.

[15] Jon Balserak, *Divinity Compromised: A Study of Divine Accommodation in the Thought of John Calvin*, Studies in Early Modern Religious Reforms 5 (Dordrecht: Springer, 2006), 8–9.

[16] Balserak, *Divinity Compromised*, 166.

[17] Balthasar Bekker, *De Philosophia Cartesiana Admonitio Candida & Sincera* (Wesel: Hoogenhuysen, 1668), 10.

reason, while for theology it is revelation. These two concepts of truth consist of two different ontological principles. Though they can never contradict each other, for both are from God, they also never intersect with each other. In short, van Bunge fails to account for the dualism found in Cartesio-Cocceian accommodation, which would be anathema to Calvin.

CHRISTOPHER WITTICHIUS AND CARTESIO-COCCEIAN ACCOMMODATION

As a leading Cartesio-Cocceian, Christopher Wittichius's (1625–1687) 1652 disputation *Dissertationes Duae, Quarum prior De S. Scripturae in rebus Philosophicis abusu examinat* is a prime example of Cartesio-Cocceian accommodation. Born in Brzeg, Wittichius studied theology under Tobias Andreae (1604–1676) at Groningen, in addition to his studies at Bremen and Leiden. After short teaching stints at Herborn and Duisburg, Wittichius spent a more extended period at Nijmegen and eventually settled down in Leiden. He worked to reconcile Cartesian philosophy and Reformed theology throughout his career, but his influence was felt most during his last two positions.

Wittichius characterized Scripture as "accommodat mediatè." For Wittichius, accommodation meant that Scripture "often speaks in the opinion of the common people."[18] As a pedagogical tool, the erroneous thinking of the biblical audience was incorporated into the text. The common man did not benefit from the scientific knowledge of the learned. Thus, rather than relating certain matters such as natural science as it actually exists in reality, the Bible was written so that the common man would understand. For the greater purpose of communicating spiritual truth, the authors accommodated the erroneous perceptions of the biblical figures to their readers.

This definitional difference did not stop the Cartesio-Cocceians from turning to their Reformed history for the purposes of establishing credibility. Wittichius cited Calvin's comments on Genesis 1:16 to support his

---

[18] Christopher Wittichius, *Dissertationes Duae, Quarum prior De S. Scripturae in rebus Philosophicis abusu examinat* (Amsterdam: Ludovicum Elzevirium, 1653), 3. I refer to the 1653 published edition, which contains minor changes from the original 1652 disputation.

use of accommodation.[19] While the Bible described the moon as a lesser light, the modern man knew that the moon is merely a reflection of the sun and does not emit light itself. Rather than confusing ancient Israel with an irrelevant discussion of the moon, the biblical author chose to include this misconception in order to teach the greater truth that God is Creator of all. As a father adapts difficult subjects in a way that is appropriate to his child's capacity, so too the Bible "condescends to the understanding of the common people" by using their "erroneous opinions."[20]

Accommodation, for Wittichius, was to be held in conjunction with the senses. The Bible relates natural matters by "accommodation to the appearance of the senses."[21] For instance, the first chapter of Ecclesiastes addressed the rise of rivers, yet the passage was relating not scientific truth but rather the appearance of the river according to the senses.[22] What distinguished Wittichius from Augustinian accommodation was his literalistic fashion of interpreting the text without taking account of phenomenological language. For Wittichius, when the Bible spoke of the ends of the earth, as in Isaiah 13:5 or Deuteronomy 30:4, the authors were mistaken about the nature of earth. Because of the "fallacy of sight," the biblical authors truly believed that the earth came to an end.[23]

For many Cartesio-Cocceians, their definition of accommodation treated the senses of ancient Israel and scientific truth as mutually exclusive. Throughout his work, Wittichius's doctrine of accommodation juxtaposed the concepts "according to the appearances of the senses and the common people" and "not according to truth."[24] With regard to "things of nature," the Bible "does not speak accurately but according to the erroneous opinion of the common people."[25] Being forced to accommodate to the understanding of "the weak," passages that contain matters such as natural science are not to be trusted. Hence, the modern reader "cannot draw knowledge of natural philosophy" from Scripture.[26]

---

[19] Wittichius, *Dissertationes Duae*, 6–7. Wittichius also connected Augustine's use of accommodation with Descartes. Wittichius, *Dissertationes Duae*, 249.

[20] Wittichius, *Dissertationes Duae*, 91.

[21] Wittichius, *Dissertationes Duae*, 56.

[22] Wittichius, *Dissertationes Duae*, 5.

[23] Wittichius, *Dissertationes Duae*, 51.

[24] Wittichius, *Dissertationes Duae*, 64. Also see, Wittichius, *Dissertationes Duae*, 30–31.

[25] Wittichius, *Dissertationes Duae*, 92.

[26] Wittichius, *Dissertationes Duae*, 3.

In the same year, Martin Schoock (1614–1669), who held the chair in philosophy at Groningen, published his incomplete *De Scepticismo* (1652). He had originally defended this disputation in the early 1640s as a student of Voetius, who encouraged him to develop it into a fuller treatment. Though the project never came to fruition, Schoock did manage to publish the first part ten years later. The delayed timing of the publication explains why Schoock made no mention of Wittichius's accommodation.

Rather than taking on Wittichius, Schoock targeted Philip van Lansbergen (1561–1632) and Paulo Foscarini (1600–1647). He rejected their idea that the Bible incorporated "erroneous common opinion."[27] Such an understanding of accommodation implied that the Holy Spirit could not communicate truth without the inclusion of error.[28] He agreed with the Cocceians that the primary focus of Scripture was for the teaching of salvation. However, with Voetius, he argued that Scripture's objective did not negate other matters included in the Bible, such as natural science. Accommodation aided in the purpose of Scripture "but not so that it lies with the liars and errs with the erring."[29] Schoock's doctrine recognized the Holy Spirit's need to condescend in the Bible but simultaneously affirmed the Spirit's ability to communicate spiritual matters alongside scientific truth. Contrary to Wittichius, Schoock presented an Augustinian accommodation, fully in agreement with Calvin, which upheld the Bible's authority and inerrancy.

Strengthening Socinian Accommodation Within the Cartesio-Cocceian Camp

In opposition to Schoock stood Cocceians such as Lambert van Velthuysen (1622–1685). Van Velthuysen earned his degree in philosophy at Utrecht in 1644. Although he never held an academic chair, van Velthuysen served as a leading member of the Cartesio-Cocceians and the "College der Scavanten," a circle of academic, pastoral, and lay Cartesio-Cocceians in Utrecht. He began his career in Utrecht as a

---

[27] Martin Schoock, *De Scepticismo* (Groningen: Henrici Lussinck, 1652), 401.
[28] Schoock addressed this issue repeatedly in *De Scepticismo*, 399–426.
[29] Schoock, *De Scepticismo*, 406.

medical doctor and later became a trustee of the West Indian Company. In 1667, he changed careers once again, becoming Utrecht's magistrate. Some of his early scholarships included a work on the difference between mathematical infinity and God's infinite nature. He also published a study of Hobbesian ethics drawn from Cartesian arguments for the existence of God. His methodology was rooted in a dualistic approach to science and theology.

Between 1654 and 1656 van Velthuysen entered into a dispute with Jacobus du Bois (?–1661) over the interpretation of Joshua 10. The passage recounts Joshua's conquests and God's provision to have the sun stand still so that Joshua's forces could continue in victory. In the anonymously published *Bewys, Dat het gevoelen van die genen, die leeren der Sonne Stilstandt* (1655), van Velthuysen claimed that the Voetians disregarded the Copernican theory due to their opposition to Cartesianism. Since the Bible's account contradicted the scientifically verified heliocentric universe, Voetians continued to adhere to a geocentric universe because biblical passages described the sun as moving around the earth. By incorporating cosmology into their theological framework—rather than theology into a scientifically verified cosmological framework—the Voetians rejected a heliocentric world on the basis of what van Velthuysen saw was a false foundation.[30]

As with Wittichius, van Velthuysen believed that the Bible did not contain consistent natural truth, or at least that natural truth was never the Bible's intention. Since the Bible's primary purpose was to teach about moral and spiritual truth, the modern reader could discard treatments of nature and science in Scripture. Contrary to the Voetians, van Velthuysen argued that not everything contained in the Bible was inspired by the Holy Spirit. Some matters could be understood as truth or dogma, while other matters were to be cast aside as remnants of the historical context of the Bible.[31]

Van Velthuysen attempted to maintain within his hermeneutics both Reformed and Cartesian principles. In accordance with the Reformed tradition, he sought the *verus sensus* of Scripture through an understanding of the circumstances surrounding the writing of the Bible. At the

---

[30] Lambert van Velthuysen, *Bewys, Dat het gevoelen van die genen, die leeren der Sonne Stilstandt, En des Aertycks Beweging niet strydich is met Godts-Woort* (Utrecht: Jaer onses Herren, 1655), 4.

[31] Van Bunge, *From Stevin to Spinoza*, 76.

same time, he propped up Cartesian reason as the sole judge when distinguishing between truly inspired passages and parts of Scripture that were a by-product of the writing process.[32]

Though van Velthuysen's main targets were du Bois and the Voetians who rejected the heliocentric theory, he also criticized Wittichius's understanding of accommodation. Van Velthuysen admonished his fellow Cartesio-Cocceian's claim that the Bible spoke *ad captum vulgi*. Instead, he argued, we should understand certain texts that lacked the inspiration of the Holy Spirit as the result of the historical circumstances of the Bible. These passages were not accommodations of God but merely the views of the authors. For van Velthuysen, admitting that the Bible spoke *ad captum vulgi* would be claiming that the Bible "lies."[33]

Though he rejected Wittichius's doctrine of accommodation, only a year later van Velthuysen reversed his position on accommodation. In response to du Bois's criticism of *Bewys, Dat het gevoelen van die genen, die leeren der Sonne Stilstandt,* van Velthuysen reiterated his earlier arguments in his similarly titled *Bewys, Dat noch de Leere van der Sonne Stilstant* (1656).[34] There is little difference between the two works except for van Velthuysen's endorsement of Wittichius's *De Stylo Scripturae* (1656) and his use of accommodation.[35] What van Velthuysen denounced in his first work, he advocated in his second.

Van Bunge suggests that van Velthuysen's about-face resulted from Wittichius's concerted effort to coax him toward his view.[36] Despite the lack of an academic chair, van Velthuysen held considerable sway

---

[32] Wiep van Bunge, "Balthasar Bekker's Cartesian Hermeneutics and the Challenges of Spinozism," *BJHP* 1, no. 1 (1993): 67.

[33] Van Velthuysen, *Bewys, Dat het gevoelen van die genen*, die leeren der Sonne Stilstandt, 9–14.

[34] See Jacobus du Bois, *Naecktheyt van de Cartesiaensche Philosophie: Ontbloot in een antwoort Op een Cartesiaensch Libel Genaemt Bewys, dat het gevoelen van die gene die leeren der Sonne-Stilstandt* (Utrecht: Johannes van Waesberge, 1655), for his critique of van Velthuysen's earlier work. Also see du Bois's *Dialogus theologico-astronomicus* (Leiden: Petrus Leffen, 1653).

[35] Lambert van Velthuysen, *Bewys, Dat noch de Leere der Sonne Stilstant, En des Aertryx Bewegingh, Noch de gronden vande Philosophie van Renatus Des Cartes strijdig sijn met Godts Woort. Gestelt tegen een Tractaet van J. du Bois* (Utrecht, Dirck van Ackersdijck and Gijsbert van Zijll, 1656), 7.

[36] Van Bunge, *From Stevin to Spinoza*, 84.

in the propagation of Cartesian thought. In an effort to solidify the Cartesio-Cocceian camp, Wittichius wrote to van Velthuysen, requesting that he reconsider opposition to his understanding accommodation. In addition, Wittichius petitioned Johannes de Raey (1622–1702) to personally present a copy of Wittichius's newly published *De Stylo Scripturae* to van Velthuysen. Regardless of whether van Velthuysen's reversal was as much a political move as a theological change, he nonetheless became a staunch defender of Cartesio-Cocceian accommodation.

The propagation of Socinian accommodation can be attributed not only to the numerous writings of Wittichius but also to van Velthuysen's leadership within the Cartesio-Cocceian party. While Wittichius provided much of the theological advancement of Socinian accommodation, van Velthuysen's shift on accommodation symbolized the unification of the Cartesio-Cocceians. Perhaps the most important element we can glean from this episode was that the doctrine possessed great enough significance for Wittichius to actively seek reconciliation with van Velthuysen. Socinian accommodation became one of the critical principles behind which the Cocceians rallied, who deemed it essential to their theology. Van Velthuysen's seal of approval not only solidified the Cartesio-Cocceian position but also validated Socinian accommodation as a central component to Cocceian hermeneutics.

These now familiar themes were reiterated by Wittichius in his *Consensus veritatis in Scriptura divina et infallibili revelatae cum veritate philosophica a Renato Des Cartes detecta* (1659). In it, he maintained a Cartesian dualism that separated natural and spiritual matters, a bifurcation that characterized the Bible's address of natural matters as "accommodating to the opinion of the common people."[37] Whereas Augustinian accommodation upheld biblical authority in all matters, Wittichius's understanding of the doctrine included error within God's condescension. Once again he juxtaposed the two concepts: "Scripture often speaks according to the opinion of common people, not according to the accurate truth."[38] For Wittichius, the two were mutually exclusive categories.

---

[37] Christopher Wittichius, *Consensus veritatis in Scriptura divina et infallibili revelatae cum veritate philosophica a Renato Des Cartes detecta* (Leiden: Cornelii Boutesteyn & Cornelii Lever, 1682), 297. I am using the second edition.

[38] Wittichius, *Consensus veritatis*, 6.

Turning to exegetical matters, Wittichius discussed passages such as Genesis 1 where the moon is said to be a lesser light. Since the Bible never intended to teach natural science, it used the accommodated language of common and ordinary phrases.[39] The use of accommodation extended to the apostles as well. They "condescended" to the capacity of their audience in their oral and written teaching.[40] When it came to supernatural accounts in the Bible, modern readers, Wittichius argued, must understand the accommodated nature of the Bible in order to appropriately interpret miracles. For example, when we read about Moses's parting of the Red Sea, we must keep in mind that the dividing of water was only a description through the limited understanding of ancient Israelites and not according to truth.[41] Hence, according to Wittichius, "it is not possible to know matters regarding natural philosophy claimed in Scripture."[42] Israel deems Wittichius's "Cartesianism infused with liberal Calvinist theology" as the first "genuinely 'critical,' scientifically orientated, Protestant Biblical hermeneutics," and he goes on to state, "it was not long before this stance [Wittichius's accommodation] was pre-empted, and his very maxim captured and radicalized, by Spinoza and his followers."[43]

THE *PHILOSOPHIA S. SCRIPTURAE INTERPRES* CONTROVERSY

The publication of Lodewijk Meyer's (1629–1681) *Philosophia S. Scripturae Interpres* (1666) added a new dimension to the ongoing dispute between the Voetians and Cocceians. Born in Amsterdam, Meyer returned as a physician after completing doctorates in both medicine and philosophy at Leiden. He worked closely with the theater, while also writing lexical works and serving as a Latinist. He and Spinoza became close friends, and they fostered a mutual respect and often sought each other's opinions. Their philosophical commonality was evident in Meyer's 1663 edition of and Preface to Spinoza's *Renati des Cartes Principia philosophiae*.

---

[39] Wittichius, *Consensus veritatis*, 238.
[40] Wittichius, *Consensus veritatis*, 36.
[41] Wittichius, *Consensus veritatis*, 351.
[42] Wittichius, *Consensus veritatis*, 28. Also see Wittichius, *Consensus veritatis*, 29.
[43] Israel, *Radical Enlightenment*, 450.

Though Meyer exerted much time and energy in promoting Spinoza's philosophy, he was also an accomplished thinker in his own right. His *Philosophia S. Scripturae Interpres* was published anonymously, predating Spinoza's *Tractatus Theologico-Politicus* (1670) by four years, and quickly became a success in the clandestine book market. The following year Meyer published his Dutch translation of the work. The second Latin edition was released in 1674, often together with the *Tractatus Theologico-Politicus*. For the third edition published in 1776, Semler added a new introduction and critical notes. Not until Meyer's death in 1681 was the authorship revealed.

The controversial book was premised on the idea that philosophy was the sole interpreter of the Bible. Meyer contended that the "true and certain knowledge of things" was the only decipher of the Bible's difficult texts.[44] With new scientific knowledge, he could not accept a literal interpretation of Scripture, as the Voetians promoted. Meyer's solution was to extend the scope of Cartesian philosophy to areas of theology and biblical exegesis. What Wittichius and van Velthuysen merely implied in their works, Meyer stated explicitly in the *Philosophia S. Scripturae Interpres*. For our purposes, Meyer's work is significant due to the responses that followed its publication by both Cocceians and Voetians. Though Meyer only briefly mentioned accommodation in sections such as his prologue and epilogue, he forced his fellow Cartesians to defend their philosophical hermeneutic and use of Socinian accommodation.

In a frantic attempt to separate themselves from Meyer's Cartesian interpretation of Scripture, the leading Cartesio-Cocceians denounced the *Philosophia S. Scripturae Interpres*. They were unsettled by the extent to which Meyer had utilized Cartesian philosophy in biblical exegesis. While Meyer may have based his premise on Cartesian thought, he took the philosophical system beyond the boundaries established by the Cartesio-Cocceians. Van Velthuysen's response, *Dissertatio de usu rationis in rebus theologicis* (1668), led the Cartesio-Cocceian disconcertion with *Philosophia S. Scripturae Interpres*. However, van Velthuysen could not convincingly condemn Meyer's system due to the obvious similarity between the *Philosophia S. Scripturae Interpres* and his own work. Both elevated the role of reason and specifically Cartesian philosophy in biblical interpretation. Both contended that the Bible was filled with

---

[44] Lodewijk Meyer, *Philosophy as the Interpreter of Holy Scripture*, trans. Samuel Shirley (Milwaukee: Marquette University Press, 2005), 37, 52–53, 126.

obscurity that required a philosophical perspective in their interpretive methodology. And both expressed the same understanding of accommodation. Due to these similarities, van Velthuysen was often accused of writing Meyer's work himself. *Philosophia S. Scripturae Interpres* was perceived as the natural progression from van Velthuysen's earlier works.

It was Cartesio-Cocceian Lodewijk Wolzogen's (1633–1690) response in *De Scripturarum Interprete adversus Exercitationem Paradoxum* (1668) that created the most uproar. Wolzogen served as a pastor in Utrecht and would later become a professor of theology. He was part of the "College der Scavanten" and a close associate of van Velthuysen. As with van Velthuysen, whom Wolzogen defended against charges that he wrote the *Philosophia S. Scripturae Interpres*, Wolzogen denounced the work and attempted to distance Cartesio-Cocceian thought from what was perceived as the natural outcome of Cartesian philosophy. However, in attempting to separate himself from Meyer's system, Wolzogen assimilated his thought to a Socinian approach to Scripture.[45] As a result, Wolzogen was not only unsuccessful in distancing himself from Meyer but was now charged with Socinianism.

Agreeing with Meyer, Wolzogen contended that natural science could not contradict the Bible. However, he objected to Meyer's use of philosophy as the exclusive interpreter of Scripture. The accommodated nature of Scripture requires methods besides philosophy. Since the Bible was written "according to the use of common language," the language of the Bible is the best interpreter of Scripture.[46] Thus, the exegete must know the circumstances in which Scripture was penned, since it was written according to the common opinion of the ancient Near East. In fact, the biblical writers were ignorant of the actual cause of various phenomena, and they wrongly attributed natural events to supernatural forces, which inevitably led to the inclusion of errors.[47] This was done so that the Bible would be "understood by the ignorant" and not just by the educated.[48] Meyer and Wolzogen were in agreement on this last point, but they differed on how best to interpret these accommodations.

---

[45] Lodewijk Wolzogen, *De Scripturarum Interprete adversus Exercitatorem Paradoxum* (Utrecht: Linde, 1668), 221, 225–226. Also see Israel, *Radical Enlightenment*, 206.

[46] Wolzogen, *De Scripturarum Interprete*, 72.

[47] Wolzogen, *De Scripturarum Interprete*, 43.

[48] Wolzogen, *De Scripturarum Interprete*, 70.

Not only did the *Philosophia S. Scripturae Interpres* affect the argumentation of the Cartesio-Cocceian camp, it also forced a response from a wide range of scholars. The Groningen professor Samuel Maresius (1599–1673) had previously held a middle ground between the Voetians and Cocceians. However, after the publication of the *Philosophia S. Scripturae Interpres*, Maresius, who was no friend of Voetius, sided with the Voetians because he perceived the work to be the natural outcome of Cartesian philosophy.

Maresius was the son of a former naval officer turned judge with a Reformed heritage that extended far back on both sides of the family. Upon completing his studies at Paris and Geneva, he entered into ministry at Laon and Crépy. After some time, Maresius took a hiatus in order to complete his doctorate at Leiden. The following years were filled with various ministry positions that moved him from Sedan to Maastricht and then to Hertogenbosch. In his final position, he succeeded Franciscus Gomarus (1563–1641) as a theology professor at Groningen. Maresius had planned to accept a position in Leiden but died before he was able to make the transition.

The year after the *Philosophia S. Scripturae Interpres* was published, Maresius held a series of lectures dedicated to the work and to what he perceived was an attack on orthodox theology. That same year Maresius expressed his discontent in *Disputationes Theologicae prior refutatoria libelli de philosophia Interprete Scripturae* (1667). According to Maresius, Meyer misunderstood the significance of the Bible as a historical text. Since the Bible spoke in the "human style" according to its day, Maresius argued, we must understand what exactly that meant in ancient Near Eastern times.[49] Philosophy could not provide the insight that a historical and philological study could.

Maresius condemned not only Meyer's use of accommodation but also Wolzogen's understanding of the doctrine. For Maresius, accommodation did not mean adapting to the erroneous understanding of the common man. To have the Bible written according to the "public and ordinary meaning" stipulated not erroneous thinking but merely plain speaking.[50] Whereas Cartesio-Cocceian accommodation construed

---

[49] Samuel Maresius, *Disputationes Theologicae prior refutatoria libelli de philosophia Interprete Scripturae* (Groningen: Johannis Collenus, 1667), 3:9.

[50] Maresius, *Disputationes Theologicae*, 3:11.

certain passages as full of errors or misunderstandings, Maresius's accommodation employed "common sense" and interpreted passages as phenomenological language.[51] Maresius continued his criticism of Socinian accommodation in his systematic polemic against Cartesianism, *De Abusu Philosophiae Cartesianae* (1670). As a culmination of his thoughts on Cartesianism and also as a response to Wittichius's lecture annotations to his students, this work became a significant resource for refuting Cartesian philosophy.

BENEDICT DE SPINOZA AND THE *TRACTATUS THEOLOGICO-POLITICUS*

In the midst of the *Philosophia S. Scripturae Interpres* controversy, Spinoza published his *Tractatus Theologico-Politicus* (1670), introducing a new dimension to biblical hermeneutics and the use of accommodation. Not only did Spinoza incorporate Socinian accommodation within his argument for theological and political freedom, but he also implemented the doctrine at a level previously unseen. Central to the work was Spinoza's belief that the Bible "does not teach philosophical matters but only piety, and everything in Scripture is adapted to the understanding and preconceptions of the common people."[52]

The prophets' superiority was contingent upon a high level of imagination, not knowledge. They were not privileged in matters of natural or spiritual truth.[53] What allowed the prophets to write the biblical books was nothing more than a vivid imagination, and it was to these "understandings and preconceptions" that revelation was adapted. However, accommodation was not only necessary but also necessarily errant. Spinoza wrote,

> It is not in the least surprising, therefore, that God adapted Himself to the imaginations and preconceived opinions of the prophets and that the faithful have held conflicting views about God.... Nor is it at all surprising that the sacred books express themselves so inappropriately about God

---

[51] Maresius, *Disputationes Theologicae*, 3:16.

[52] Benedict de Spinoza, *Theological-Political Treatise*, trans. Michael Silverthorne and Jonathan Israel (Cambridge: Cambridge University Press, 2007), 186.

[53] Spinoza, *Theological-Political Treatise*, 27.

throughout.... They are here manifestly speaking according to the [utterly deficient] understanding of the common people, whom Scripture strives to render not learned but obedient.[54]

The Bible was a result of accommodation to the historical context of the ancient Near East. It inevitably included the contradictory and erroneous preconceptions of that day in an effort to advance the piety of its readers.

Before examining the *Tractatus Theologico-Politicus*, we must note a couple of points. First, as Jay M. Harris contends, Spinoza's understanding of accommodation took a turn just before the *Tractatus Theologico-Politicus*.[55] Prior to 1670, Spinoza extended the use of accommodation to the prophets of the Bible. In this view, the prophets knowingly adapted their writing to their audience to better communicate their message. However, in the *Tractatus Theologico-Politicus*, Spinoza no longer held this position. The prophets were not superior in knowledge; rather, they held the same views as the rest of the nation of Israel. Accommodation applied universally to both prophet and audience. Second, Spinoza secularized the doctrine of accommodation to further the objectives of the *Tractatus Theologico-Politicus*. Gregory W. Dawes writes, "Spinoza's use of the traditional language of 'accommodation' seems to be little more than a transposition into traditional theological terms of Spinoza's conviction that prophetic knowledge was primarily a matter of the imagination."[56]

In support of these two points, J. Samuel Preus traces in Spinoza's writings a form of accommodation similar to Maimonides up to 1665. However, in *Tractatus Theologico-Politicus* Spinoza "puts an end to the traditional doctrine of accommodation."[57] Preus argues that Spinoza's accommodation radically departed from the "mainline Christian tradition" because he utilized the language of accommodation to "destroy supernaturalism" and to advance his hermeneutic of history.[58] Amos

---

[54] Spinoza, *Theological-Political Treatise*, 177.

[55] Jay Michael Harris, *How Do We Know This?: Midrash and the Fragmentation of Modern Judaism* (Albany: State University of New York Press, 1995), 125–126.

[56] Gregory W. Dawes, *The Historical Jesus Question: The Challenge of History to Religious Authority* (Louisville: Westminster John Knox, 2001), 50.

[57] J. Samuel Preus, *Spinoza and the Irrelevance of Biblical Authority* (Cambridge: Cambridge University Press, 2001), 173.

[58] J. Samuel Preus, "Prophecy, Knowledge and Study of Religion," *Religion* 28 (1998): 129.

Funkenstein states that while being influenced by Abraham Ibn Ezra's (1093–1167) understanding of accommodation, Spinoza "put [accommodation] on its head—or, if you wish, on its feet."[59] To the detriment of Ibn Ezra and the Augustinian definition of accommodation, Spinoza's doctrine undermined the "authentication of the Bible as a superhuman document."[60] By redefining accommodation, Spinoza used the principle to void the Bible of its theological content. Funkenstein describes Spinoza's primary purpose of accommodation as emptying "theological language" of its content before abandoning it altogether or having it "turned on its head."[61]

Spinoza began *Tractatus Theologico-Politicus* by integrating his understanding of accommodation into his discussion of prophecy and the role of the prophet. According to Spinoza, prophets were those who interpret God's revelation. However, the prophets "were not endowed with more perfect minds than others but only a more vivid power of imagination."[62] Also, despite the prophets' role as interpreters of revelation, they still had limitations. Prophets "cannot themselves achieve certain knowledge of them and can therefore only grasp by simple faith what has been revealed."[63] Thus, the prophet was limited to his existing preconceptions of God, which were often mistaken and even contradicted other prophets. For example, due to Joshua's misconceptions concerning the stationary position of the sun, Scripture recorded that the sun stood still. However, Joshua's account was not a phenomenological depiction of the motion of the sun from an earthly perspective. Rather, Joshua was ignorant of the orbit of the earth around a fixed sun. On that particular

---

[59] Amos Funkenstein, *Theology and the Scientific Imagination: from the Middle ages to the Seventeenth Century* (Princeton: Princeton University Press, 1986), 220.

[60] Funkenstein, *Theology and the Scientific Imagination*, 220.

[61] Funkenstein, *Theology and the Scientific Imagination*, 221. Spinoza's accommodation differed from someone like Galileo Galilei (1564–1642), who on the one hand maintained that God accommodated to the biblical authors without them accommodating their writings while on the other contended for an error-free Bible. See Hoon J. Lee, "'Men of Galilee, Why Stand Gazing Up into Heaven?': Revisiting Galileo, Astronomy, and the Authority of the Bible," *JETS* 53, no. 1 (2010): 103–116.

[62] Spinoza, *Theological-Political Treatise*, 27.

[63] Spinoza, *Theological-Political Treatise*, 13.

night, Joshua was unaware of the sun's reflection on atmospheric ice, which caused an unusually bright night.[64]

The errors of the biblical authors were not limited to scientific matters but extended to their understanding of God. The Bible's anthropomorphic language was an outcome of the common notions of that time. When Scripture used the phrase "spirit of God," the prophet was describing God according to what he knew of man. Thus, "spirit of God" was the prophet's way of saying God was like a man and had a "mind, i.e., heart, passion, force and the breath of the mouth of God."[65] Not only did the prophets attribute human qualities to God, but they also limited God to human characteristics. For example, Adam was unaware of God's omnipresence and omniscience and thus presented God as lacking knowledge of Cain's deeds and location.[66] Moses too failed to understand these attributes of God. In questioning God's command to speak to the enslaved Israelites, Moses revealed his failure to grasp God's omniscience.[67]

As God accommodated to individuals, so too did he accommodate to the entire nation of Israel. God's election of the nation was an accommodation to "childish" thinking. Spinoza explained,

> When therefore Scripture states that God chose the Hebrews for himself above other nations (see Deuteronomy 10:15) so as to encourage them to obey the law, and is near to them and not to others (Deuteronomy 4:4–7), and has laid down good laws solely for them and not for others (Deuteronomy 4:2), and has made himself known to them alone, in preference to others (see Deuteronomy 4:32), and so on, Scripture is merely speaking according to their understanding.... Moses desired to teach the Hebrews in such a manner and inculcate into them such principles as would attach them more closely to the worship of God on the basis of their childish understanding.[68]

---

[64] Spinoza, *Theological-Political Treatise*, 34.
[65] Spinoza, *Theological-Political Treatise*, 23.
[66] Spinoza, *Theological-Political Treatise*, 35.
[67] Spinoza, *Theological-Political Treatise*, 36.
[68] Spinoza, *Theological-Political Treatise*, 43, 44. This is how Spinoza interprets 1 Cor. 9:19–23. Paul was not establishing a special status for Israel; he was merely appeasing the need for such recognition. Spinoza, *Theological-Political Treatise*, 53.

God did not intend to privilege Israel in any fashion. The special relationship between God and Israel was due to the Israelites' need for status. To promote piety, God allowed the Israelites to believe that they were unique.

In addition to a childish mindset, Spinoza perceived an inherent slavery mentality within the Israelites. Due to centuries of Egyptian rule, the Israelites were unable to make a mental exodus from the concept of *law*. In order to work within this slavery mentality, God created the Mosaic Law. The Law provided simplistic teaching geared toward a life of servitude and gratitude for God's rescue from slavery. Thus Spinoza argued that the Israelites understood God as a "legislator obliging them to live well by command of the law" or as a "ruler, legislator, king, merciful, just, etc., despite the fact that the latter are merely attributes of human nature and far removed from the divine nature."[69] The universal nature of God deemed such laws irrelevant; however, God established a system of laws for the temporary benefit of the Israelites. In truth, "God acts and governs all things from the necessity of his own nature and perfection alone, and his decrees and volitions are eternal truths and always involve necessity."[70]

Spinoza distinguished between accommodation to the prophets and to Christ. He argued that God did not need to adapt his revelation because Christ had perfect knowledge. God revealed himself to Christ directly and not through "words or visions." Christ was not a mere prophet but a "mouth-piece" of God. Thus, "it would be equally irrational to think that God adapted his revelations to Christ's beliefs as that he had previously adapted his revelations to the beliefs of angels (i.e., to the beliefs of a created voice and of visions) in order to communicate his

---

[69] Spinoza, *Theological-Political Treatise*, 39, 63.

[70] Spinoza, *Theological-Political Treatise*, 65. As human law is directly tied to the nature of man and the limited understanding of the human mind, so too are the ceremonies described in the Old Testament. Spinoza contended that Isaiah "promises as the reward for liberating [the oppressed] and practicing charity, a healthy mind in a healthy body and the glory of God after death, but the reward for ceremonies is merely the security of the state, prosperity, and worldly success." Spinoza, *Theological-Political Treatise*, 70. He wrote, "As for ceremonies, or those at least which are narrated in the Old Testament, these were instituted for the Hebrews alone and were so closely accommodated to their state that in the main they could be practiced not by individuals but only by the community as a whole." Spinoza, *Theological-Political Treatise*, 68.

revelations to the prophets."[71] Christ understood God's revelation as it truly was and not through the medium of accommodation.

In addition, Christ was sent not only on behalf of the Jews but for all humanity. When Christ spoke in laws, he was not speaking through his weakness of mind, as the prophets did, but as an adaptation of universal truth to the mindset of his hearers. The capacity of his audience determined how Christ spoke to them. To those who were weaker, Jesus taught through parables and obscurity, but to those with a greater capacity, he spoke eternal truth.[72] Christ alone had the ability to receive unmediated revelation and freely adapt it to his audience as he deemed appropriate.[73]

As stated previously, Spinoza's accommodation implied that the Bible included contradictory and erroneous views. This notion impacted not only the authority of the Bible but also the way in which we interpret it. In Spinoza's view, Scripture spoke in a "wholly inexact manner" for the purpose of spurring devotion and imagination.[74] Because prophecy did not add to wisdom but was merely accommodated to preconceived beliefs, one is under no obligation to follow its instruction in "philosophical" or "natural and spiritual matters."[75] For instance, Jesus stated in Matthew 12:26 that demons who pledged loyalty to Satan cannot stand divided, but this statement did not attest to the existence of demons or Satan. Jesus was merely accommodating to the Pharisees' erroneous belief in demons without commenting on their existence.[76]

Spinoza also applied this line of reasoning to the interpretation of miracles. In his view, nothing was contrary to the laws of nature. Miracles were not events that occurred outside of natural law but rather were a way to accommodate an explanation through the imagination of the common person. Thus, the interpreter must often spiritualize the text to discover the true meaning of the passage. Rather than a literal

---

[71] Spinoza, *Theological-Political Treatise*, 63–64.

[72] Spinoza, *Theological-Political Treatise*, 64.

[73] Though Christ was unique in his ability to receive and adapt divine revelation, a small, select group of biblical authors occasionally accommodated their writings. Spinoza argued that Rom. 3:5 and 6:19 evinced Paul's tendency to speak in "human terms" when ascribing characteristics such as "pity, grace, anger, etc." to God.

[74] Spinoza, *Theological-Political Treatise*, 91.

[75] Spinoza, *Theological-Political Treatise*, 40.

[76] Spinoza, *Theological-Political Treatise*, 41.

interpretation, one must recognize the accommodated nature of the text. For instance, Spinoza denied the resurrection and spiritualized it as a message of piety. He wrote,

> I therefore conclude that Christ's resurrection from the dead was in fact of a spiritual kind and was revealed only to the faithful according to their understanding, indicating that Christ was endowed with eternity and rose from the dead (I here understand "the dead" in the sense in which Christ said "Let the dead bury their dead"), and also by his life and death he provided an example of surpassing holiness, and that he raises his disciples from the dead in so far as they follow the example of his own life and death.[77]

At times, the Bible was referring not to a spiritual message but to a natural occurrence that the biblical authors could *not* explain. Though a natural explanation could have been provided, the limited capacity of the audience prohibited them from articulating such a complicated process. Instead, the author gave the natural phenomenon a supernatural explanation in order to simplify the matter. Attributing the event to supernatural factors satisfied the common person and thus provided the sole "criterion" for defining a miracle.[78] Such would not do for Spinoza and other interpreters in the early modern era, who were more advanced in their understanding of science. Rather than limiting themselves to the way Scripture accommodated complicated explanations of natural phenomena, they were free to disregard miracles and discover the true explanation through science.

Due to the accommodated nature of Scripture, the modern reader also had to become acquainted with the culture and beliefs of that day. Since revelation was contextualized to the times of the Old and

---

[77] Benedictus de Spinoza, Letter 75, in *The Letters*, trans. Samuel Shirley, with an introduction and notes by Steven Barbone, Lee Rice, and Jacob Adler (Indianapolis, IN: Hacket, 1995), 338. Johannes Bredenburg (1643–1691) argues that a straightforward literal reading of 1 Cor. 15:13–15 makes the historical occurrence of the resurrection explicit. According to Bredenburg, Spinoza's claim is simply weak and cannot ignore the biblical claim for dogmatic truth. Wiep van Bunge, "Van Velthuysen, Batelier and Bredenburg on Spinoza's interpretation of the Scriptures," in *L'hérésie spinoziste: La discussion sur le Tractatus theologico-politicus, 1670–1677, et la réception immédiate du spinozisme*, ed. Paolo Cristofolini (Amsterdam: APA-Holland University Press, 1995), 63.

[78] Spinoza, *Theological-Political Treatise*, 84.

New Testaments, it was critical to understand these accommodations as cultural depictions of "apparitions and imaginary things" that were "adapted to the beliefs of those who passed them on to us as they appeared to them, namely as actual events."[79] Spinoza proposed that exegetes should interpret Scripture in the same manner as scientists study nature. As with nature, a history of Scripture must be established, from which one can draw definitions and principles. He wrote,

> Provided we admit no other criteria or data for interpreting Scripture and discussing its contents than what is drawn from Scripture itself and its history, we will always proceed without any danger of going astray, and we shall have the same assuredness in discussing things that surpass our understanding as in discussing things that we learn by the natural light of reason.[80]

Thus, knowledge derived from the Bible had to be interpreted in light of the Bible's historical context.

This principle was not only ideal but also necessary for interpreting Scripture properly. Due to the Bible's instruction of piety, the "teachings of true piety are expressed in the most everyday language, since they are very common and extremely simple and easy to understand."[81] The Bible simply cannot be interpreted purely through reason or philosophy because it accommodated the common notions of humanity. Interpretation of such accommodations was based not on philosophical truths but rather on the history of the Bible. Spinoza differed from his friend Meyer on this point. Both took accommodation to erroneous beliefs as a given in the Bible. However, Meyer proposed that philosophy was the best interpretive tool for distinguishing between literal or figurative readings. In contrast, Spinoza held that Scripture's history—not philosophy—was best poised to tell us when to interpret figuratively or literally.

The reverse was also true for Spinoza. Just as reason could not supersede the Bible, so too the Bible could not override reason. Spinoza feared that when the Bible was used to interpret philosophy, one would elevate the erroneous, accommodated beliefs over philosophical truth. In his view, the Bible only taught piety, so when the Bible was used in

---

[79] Spinoza, *Theological-Political Treatise*, 93.
[80] Spinoza, *Theological-Political Treatise*, 98.
[81] Spinoza, *Theological-Political Treatise*, 111.

conjunction with natural and philosophical truths, it forced the prophets to say things they never intended.⁸² These statements, limited by their historical context, could not stand up against universal truth.

On a final note, Spinoza promoted the continued use of accommodation in contemporary theology. As the Bible was adapted to the common understanding of its day, so too must it be accommodated to the present day. Spinoza wrote,

> Indeed everyone, as we have already said, must adapt these doctrines of faith to his own understanding and to interpret them for himself in whatever way seems to make them easier for him to accept unreservedly and with full mental assent. For, as we have pointed out, faith was once revealed and written according to the understanding and beliefs of the prophets and of the common people of their time, and in the same manner everyone in our day must adapt faith to their own views so that they may accept it without any mental reservation or hesitation.⁸³

The accommodated nature of Scripture necessitated that each generation adapt the teachings of the Bible to best suit the needs of present readers. For Spinoza, faith was a matter of piety and not philosophical truth, validated by one's obedience and not doctrine.⁸⁴ Thus, each reader was free to accommodate the Bible to his or her understanding and belief as long as it promoted piety and obedience.

With this understanding, one can see why Preus argues that Spinoza rid accommodation of the "Divine Intender" behind accommodated language.⁸⁵ The traditional understanding of accommodation held that a Divine Intender included deeper meaning and truth within the accommodated language of the Bible. The purpose of the Divine Intender was to use common notions and language to effectively communicate more complicated truth. Through Spinoza's removal of the Divine Intender and radicalized definition of accommodation, not only was there no deeper truth behind accommodated language, but also these accommodations carried no relevance for the modern reader. The accommodations were relevant for those during the time when the Bible was written

---

⁸²Spinoza, *Theological-Political Treatise*, 186.
⁸³Spinoza, *Theological-Political Treatise*, 183–184.
⁸⁴Spinoza, *Theological-Political Treatise*, 181–182.
⁸⁵Preus, *Spinoza and the Irrelevance of Biblical Authority*, 188.

and for no one else. Instead, modern readers had to accommodate the Bible for themselves.

As in the case with Meyer's publication, Cartesio-Cocceians were quick to dissociate themselves from Spinoza's *Tractatus Theologico-Politicus*. For example, in *Tractatus de Cultu Naturali, et Origine Moralitatis* (1680), van Velthuysen tried to distance himself from Spinoza. To his critics, the exegetical principles of Spinoza appeared similar to what van Velthuysen had been suggesting for years. The need for understanding the Bible's historical context and language were exegetical principles that both van Velthuysen and Spinoza shared. They both also held to a similar understanding of accommodation. Still, van Velthuysen attempted, inconsistently, to retain his and Wittichius's accommodation while rejecting Spinoza's.

It is true that van Velthuysen did not adhere to the fatalism that he had accused Spinoza of. He claimed that this fatalistic approach converted accommodation into lies.[86] However, van Velthuysen did not directly object to Spinoza's accommodation. Rather, he admonished Spinoza's determinism and what it meant for Spinoza's and van Velthuysen's accommodation. Without this determinism, Spinoza was left with a form of accommodation shared by Wittichius and van Velthuysen. However, Spinoza claimed that fatalism did not interfere with the accommodation of the Bible. As van Velthuysen would contend, Spinoza's doctrine of accommodation was based on the disparity between God and man. The exegetical use of the doctrine by Spinoza and van Velthuysen was contingent on their common separation of the moral elements from the natural matters in the Bible.

THE CULMINATION OF THE VOETIAN RESPONSE

Up to this point, we have been preoccupied with the heterodoxy of the Cartesio-Cocceians without examining the Voetian response. Certainly, the Voetians contributed their own share in polemical writings, quick to rebuff Cartesio-Cocceian innovations in hermeneutics and the redefinition of accommodation. Perhaps the most significant rejoinder to Cartesio-Cocceian hermeneutics came from Petrus van Mastricht (1630–1706), who sought to sustain Augustinian accommodation.

---

[86]Lambert van Velthuysen, "Epistola XLII," in *Spinoza Opera* (Heidelberg: Carl Winters, 1925), 4:210.

Born in Cologne, Mastricht spent his early career teaching and ministering outside the Netherlands. Then in 1677, Mastricht was appointed to succeed Voetius as professor of theology at Utrecht, a position he held until his death. While best known for his *Theologia Theoretico-Practica* (1682–1687), Mastricht's *Novitatum Cartesianarum Gangraena* (1677) is more relevant for our purposes.[87] The work is divided into two sections. The first part addresses Cartesianism and the philosophical system's impact on biblical interpretation. The much larger second section is a systematic treatment of the whole spectrum of theology.

In this work, Mastricht combatted Cartesian theology along with Meyer's *Philosophia S. Scripturae Interpres* and Spinoza's *Tractatus Theologico-Politicus*. Mastricht challenged the Cartesian foundation of Wittichius's and other Cocceians' hermeneutics. According to Mastricht, central to the Cartesio-Cocceian approach to Scripture was the role of philosophy in interpreting the Bible. By elevating Cartesianism, they made philosophy the principle judge of the Bible's meaning.[88] Cartesio-Cocceians thus divided philosophical truth from spiritual truth, resulting in a Bible that contained only spiritual truths and nothing else. This separation meant that the Bible related erroneous statements concerning natural science.[89]

As Voetius's successor at Utrecht, Mastricht made use of Voetius's understanding of accommodation. For Mastricht, Cartesians such as Wittichius argued that the Bible's description of the sun's motion spoke "according to the erroneous opinion of the common people" and depicted "things to us he knows are not true."[90] Similar to his refutation of Wittichius in 1655, Mastricht contended that Cartesio-Cocceian accommodation essentially made God into a liar who intentionally deceived not only the Israelites but all generations of Christians.[91]

---

[87] For Mastricht's discussion of accommodation in *Theologia Theoretico-Practica*, see 70–188.

[88] Peter van Mastricht, *Novitatum Cartesianarum Gangraena* (Amsterdam: Janssonio Waesbergios, 1677), 34–49, especially 36, 38.

[89] Mastricht, *Novitatum Cartesianarum Gangraena*, 9–10, 62–73, 96–105, 392–395.

[90] Mastricht, *Novitatum Cartesianarum Gangraena*, 62.

[91] Mastricht, *Novitatum Cartesianarum Gangraena*, 71–73, 102–103. See also Petrus van Mastricht, *Vindiciae veritatis et authoritatis Sacrae Scripturae in rebus philosophicis* (Utrecht: Johannis Waesberge, 1655), 13.

In contrast, Mastricht contended that all statements of God were "divine and infallible" according to the exact truth and not according to the erroneous perception of man.[92] This included the proper use of accommodation, which utilized nonscientific language yet remained absolutely accurate.[93] Additionally, this divine deception that the Cartesio-Cocceians promoted was not limited to matters of nature but extended—even more so—to "practical, moral matters" and to faith and doctrine.[94] According to Mastricht, while Spinoza was the chief culprit of the abuse of accommodation, there was no fundamental difference between Spinoza's position and that of Wittichius or Wolzogen.[95] Mastricht's understanding of Cartesio-Cocceian accommodation would be equally true of the last accommodationist in our discussion of seventeenth-century exegesis.

The Beginning of the End of Cartesio-Cocceian Accommodation

Balthasar Bekker's (1634–1698) *De Betoverde Weereld* (1691) was the culmination of Cartesio-Cocceian accommodation. Even more than Spinoza's *Tractatus Theologico-Politicus*, Bekker's four-volume work epitomized Cartesian dualism and its effect on Socinian accommodation. However, while Bekker may be rightly perceived as the zenith of Cartesio-Cocceian accommodation, his work also signaled its demise. As we will see in subsequent chapters, Socinian accommodation continued into the eighteenth century, albeit stripped of the Cartesian dualism associated with Bekker and his fellow Cocceians. We have already seen how Spinoza progressed past Cartesian dualism. I will argue that most early eighteenth-century German scholars who utilized Socinian accommodation appropriated a Spinozist or Wolffian variant rather than a Cartesio-Cocceian approach. Also, though a Wolffian form of Socinian accommodation was prevalent during the first half of the eighteenth

---

[92] Mastricht, *Novitatum Cartesianarum Gangraena*, 42.
[93] Mastricht, *Novitatum Cartesianarum Gangraena*, 8–12, 28–29, 45–46.
[94] Mastricht dedicates chapter 5 to accommodation in natural matters. Chapter 8 deals with "Practicis & Moralibus," and Chapter 9 addresses accommodation in doctrine and faith.
[95] Israel, *Radical Enlightenment*, 215.

century, Spinoza's radicalization of the doctrine existed throughout the century, especially in the second half of the eighteenth century.

Born the son of a Reformed minister in Friesland, Bekker followed his father's career path. After studying philosophy at Groningen and theology at Franeker, he served as a minister. However, Bekker soon faced criticism over the funeral oration he gave for his wife, a practice prohibited by the Reformed church. Not long after, Bekker gained the label of a Cartesian for the publication of *De philosophia cartesiana admonitio candida et sincera* (1668). His Cocceian leaning was also displayed in several of the theses in his doctoral disputations. Even more so, Bekker's catechism for adults further demonstrated his Cocceian theology.

In 1680, Bekker accepted a position in Amsterdam. In that same year and the two subsequent years, Amsterdam witnessed several comets. After the comets dissipated, Bekker addressed the superstition of comets as omens in *Ondersoek van de betekeninge der Kometen* (1683), presenting a Cartesio-Cocceian understanding of accommodation. The work added little original substance, simply rehashing arguments against the idea that comets were premonitions of future disaster. He argued that the superstition surrounding comets had more to do with erroneous common thinking than with scientific truth.

Despite facing little repercussion for his views in *Ondersoek van de betekeninge der Kometen*, Bekker's fate after the publication of *De Betooverde Weereld* was an entirely different matter.[96] Bekker completed the first two volumes in 1691, followed by the second two volumes in 1693. The first volume examined how various religions and cultures, particularly Catholicism, understood the spirit world. The second volume served as the core of his argument. This was where he worked out his dualism and Cartesio-Cocceian accommodation in the interpretation of the Bible's presentation of the spirit world. The less original third and fourth volumes analyzed demonic practices and the origin of supernatural accounts. Immediately after the publication of the first installment,

---

[96] In addition to attacks from the Voetians, Bekker received little support from the Cartesio-Cocceians, in part because some Cartesio-Cocceians alienated him after he criticized Cocceius's interpretation of the book of Daniel in *Uitlegging van den propheet Daniel* (Amsterdam: Daniel van den Dalen, 1688). Bekker was backed by Eric Walten (1663–1697), who shared a similar understanding of accommodation. see Eric Walten, *Aardige Duyvelary* (Rotterdam: Pieter van Veen, 1691), 27, 47; Eric Walten, *Brief Aan sijn Excellentie, de Heer Graaf van Portland* (Hague: Meyndert Uytwerf, 1692), 19–20.

Bekker received negative criticism and was released from his ministerial position.[97]

In Cartesio-Cocceian fashion, Bekker adhered to a Cartesian dualism that segregated natural science from spiritual truth within the Bible. According to Bekker, Scripture's intent was to instill faith and not scientific accuracy.[98] There was no better example of this misunderstanding than how we interpret passages that address the spirit world. When the Bible spoke of the spirit world, the modern reader had to realize that these accounts were adapted to the thinking of the ancient Near East.[99] Cartesian dualism stated that the immaterial nature of the spiritual world could not interact with the material world in the fashion depicted in the Bible. These accounts were ancient Israel's erroneous concepts of the spirit world.

This misconception arose in part from the incorrect translation of biblical terms. For instance, the Hebrew word *malach* could be translated "angel," but equally valid was the translation "messenger." To use the translation of "angel" misconstrued the nature of the spirit world.[100] In other words, the Bible was not teaching the existence of angels or their interaction with the material world but was instead recounting human activity with a divine mission.[101]

The second fault of modern interpreters was their lack of knowledge of the accommodated nature of Scripture. The Bible used adapted language to better communicate spiritual truths. Bekker stated, "The style

---

[97] See Melchior Leydekker's review, *Dissertatio historico-theologica, de vulgato nuper cl. Bekkeri volumine, et Scripturarum authoritate ac veritate, pro Christiana religione apologetica* (Utrecht: Clerck, 1692); Jacobus Koelman, *Wederlegging van B. Bekkers Betoverde Wereldt* (Amsterdam: Johannes Boekholt, 1692); Petrus Hamer, *Voorlooper tot de volstrekte wederlegginge van het gene de heeren, Orchard, Daillom en Bekker* (Dordrecht: Cornelis Wilgaarts, 1692); Johannes Molinaeus, *De Betoverde Werelt van D. Balthazar Bekker... Onderzogt en Wederlegst* (Rotterdam: Barent Bos, 1692); Johannes van der Waeyen, *De betooverde weereld van D. Balthasar Bekker ondersogt en weederlegt* (Franeker: Strik and Horreus, 1693).

[98] Balthasar Bekker, *De Betoverde Weereld* (Amsterdam: Daniel van den Dalen, 1691–1693), 2:54–55.

[99] Bekker, *De Betoverde Weereld*, 2:143–179.

[100] Bekker, *De Betoverde Weereld*, 2:43–52. The same can be said of the Hebrew word *satan*, which Bekker translated "opponent" or "enemy," not the proper name "Satan." Bekker, *De Betoverde Weereld*, 2:101–104.

[101] Bekker, *De Betoverde Weereld*, 1:85–90.

of great masters has been not only to leave people in errors for a time, but also to accommodate themselves to that language which in part arose out of such misunderstanding."[102] The Bible used the language of demon possession not based on facts but in conjunction with common notions, or more precisely, a lack of knowledge concerning mental illness. What modern medicine would accurately diagnose as mental illness, the biblical audience perceived as demon possession.[103] Rather than correcting ancient notions of the spirit world, the Holy Spirit bypassed these minor errors in order to better communicate the salvific message.

As disturbing as Bekker's conclusions on the spirit world were to the orthodox, his hermeneutics were cause for greater concern. Andrew Fix argues that "Bekker's Cartesian critique of the foundations of spirit belief was not nearly as dangerous to traditional religion as his exegetical methods were."[104] Bekker's use of accommodation in his exegesis was at the center of the debate within the Reformed church. Fix goes on to state, "It was to the outcome of this dispute, and not to the fate of Cartesianism in Holland, that Bekker's arguments against spirits were ultimately tied."[105] This assessment may be true to a degree, but it fails to understand the connection between Bekker's Cartesianism and his understanding of accommodation. Fix associates Bekker's accommodation with both Spinoza and Calvin, but he does not recognize the difference between their positions on the doctrine. I would argue that while Fix is correct to highlight Bekker's exegesis, the hermeneutic that guided Bekker in his exegesis and use of accommodation was based on Cartesian dualism. Bekker did not share Calvin's understanding of accommodation but continued the Cartesio-Cocceian accommodation of Wittichius, van Velthuysen, and Spinoza.

The influence of Bekker's work would continue well into the eighteenth century. In particular, Semler would go on to release a new edition of Bekker's *De Betoverde Weereld* and to affirm Bekker's stance on the spirit world. The argument that demon possession was nothing more than the accommodated language of a misguided culture about

---

[102] Bekker, *De Betoverde Weereld*, 2:287. Quoted in Andrew Fix, *Fallen Angels: Balthasar Bekker, Spirit Belief, and Confessionalism in the Seventeenth-Century Dutch Republic* (Dordrecht: Kluwer Academic, 1999), 63.

[103] Bekker, *De Betoverde Weereld*, 2:176.

[104] Fix, *Fallen Angels*, 10.

[105] Fix, *Fallen Angels*, 10.

mental illness became a common theme in eighteenth-century exegesis. However, for Semler and others, this was not due to a logical conclusion based on Cartesian dualism. Instead, we find a Spinozist accommodation or a call for a critical-historical method that had no need for such a philosophical basis. The Socinian core of Bekker's accommodation continued on into the eighteenth century, but the particularities of his Cartesianism dropped away.

Conclusion

Adhering to a Socinian doctrine in the seventeenth century was quite unattractive and detrimental to one's scholarship and vocational progress. Similarly, in the eighteenth century, association with Spinoza was considered tantamount to atheism or at the very least to pantheism. Though Socinianism, especially Socinian accommodation, continued beyond its namesake's lifetime into the seventeenth century, scholars were not free to admit their commonality with Socinus. As we have seen, Cartesio-Cocceians such as Wittichius, van Velthuysen, Wolzogen, Meyer, and Bekker advanced Socinian accommodation in principle but not in name. They shared with Socinus an understanding that the Holy Spirit accommodated not only to ancient Israel's limited capacity but also to their erroneous thinking.

In contrast with the Voetians and the Augustinian accommodation they shared with Calvin, the Cartesio-Cocceians combined a Socinian definition of accommodation with Cartesian philosophy. As Cartesians, they embraced a dualism that pitted spiritual truth against scientific truth. The Cartesio-Cocceian application of accommodation often dealt with matters of natural science, such as the Copernican theory, but also extended to doctrinal matters, such as the existence of angels and demons. The Cartesian variety of Socinian accommodation deemed errors within the biblical text an inevitable result of an ancient Near East writing. While rejecting the Cocceian reinterpretation, the Voetians maintained the importance of the doctrine by upholding Augustinian accommodation.

We have seen how Cartesio-Cocceian accommodation went through at least four major stages in the seventeenth-century Dutch Republic. First, the Cartesio-Cocceian camp solidified their position on accommodation. Due to the significance of Socinian accommodation in Cocceian hermeneutics, concerted effort was made to rally Cocceians around the Socinian doctrine. Though initially disagreeing with Wittichius, van Velthuysen was eventually persuaded of the doctrine, thus unifying the Cocceian camp against Augustinian accommodation.

Second, with the publication of Meyer's much-contested *Philosophia S. Scripturae Interpres*, Cartesio-Cocceians were put on the defense and forced to justify their hermeneutics. Allegations called into question the validity of exegesis based on philosophy. Rather than distancing themselves from these claims, however, Cartesio-Cocceians such as Wolzogen revealed their indebtedness to philosophical and Socinian hermeneutics while emphasizing the significance of Cartesian-Socinian accommodation. In addition, the controversy forced Maresius, previously a neutral, to side with the Voetians against Cartesio-Cocceian hermeneutics and especially Cartesio-Cocceian accommodation.

Third, Cartesio-Cocceian accommodation went through the wringer of Spinozist thought. As we have seen, both forms of Socinian accommodation resulted in similar interpretations, but Spinoza replaced the philosophical base of Cartesio-Cocceian accommodation with a historical method. Also, due to Spinoza's materialism, the boundaries of Socinian accommodation were stretched to new, expansive limits.

Finally, Cartesio-Cocceian accommodation culminated in Bekker's use of the doctrine. Advancing the most consistent expression of Cartesio-Cocceian accommodation, Bekker also symbolized the end of this particular variant of Socinian accommodation. The Cartesian dualism of the Cocceians would eventually be replaced by Spinoza's radicalization of the doctrine and, as we will see, by a Wolffian reinterpretation. We will witness all three forms of Socinian accommodation in the first half of the eighteenth century. While Cartesio-Cocceian accommodation had a very limited use, Spinozist accommodation increased in importance and underwent new developments throughout the accommodation debate.

Bibliography

Asselt, Willem J. van. "Scholasticism in the Time of High Orthodoxy (ca. 1620–1700)," in *Introduction to Reformed Scholasticism*, ed. Willem J. van Asselt, trans. Albert Gootjies, Reformed Historical-Theological Studies. Grand Rapids, MI: Reformation Heritage, 2011.

———. *The Federal Theology of Johannes Cocceius (1603–1669)*. Studies in the History of Christian Thought 100. Leiden: Brill, 2001.

Balserak, Jon. *Divinity Compromised: A Study of Divine Accommodation in the Thought of John Calvin*. Studies in Early Modern Religious Reforms 5. Dordrecht: Springer, 2006.

Battles, Ford Lewis. "God Was Accommodating Himself to Human Capacity." *Interpretation* 31, no. 1 (1977): 19–38.

Bekker, Balthasar. *De Philosophia Cartesiana Admonitio Candida & Sincera*. Wesel: Hoogenhuysen, 1668.

———. *De Philosophia Cartesiana Admonitio Candida & Sincera*. Wesel: Hoogenhuysen, 1668.

———. *Naakte Uitbeeldinge van alle de vier boeken der Betoverde weereld*. Amsterdam: Daniel van den Dalen, 1693.

———. *Uitlegginge van den Propheet Daniel*. Amsterdam: Daniel van den Dalen, 1688.

Bizer, Ernst. "Die reformierte Orthodoxie und der Cartesianismus." *Zeitschrift für Theologie und Kirche* 55, no. 3 (1958): 306–72.

Bois, Jacobus du. *Dialogus theologico-astronomicus*. Leiden: Petrus Leffen, 1653.

———. *Naecktheyt van de Cartesiaensche Philosophie: Ontbloot in een antwoort Op een Cartesiaensch Libel Genaemt Bewys, dat het gevoelen van die gene die leeren der Sonne-Stilstandt*. Utrecht: Johannes van Waesberge, 1655.

Bunge, Wiep van. "Balthasar Bekker's Cartesian Hermeneutics and the Challenge of Spinozism." *British Journal for the History of Philosophy* 1, no. 1 (1993): 55–79.

———. *From Stevin to Spinoza: An Essay on Philosophy in the Seventeenth-Century Dutch Republic*. Brill's Studies in Intellectual History 103. Leiden, Brill, 2001.

———. "Van Velthuysen, Batelier and Bredenburg on Spinoza's interpretation of the Scriptures." In *L'hérésie spinoziste: La discussion sur le Tractatus theologico-politicus, 1670–1677, et la réception immédiate du spinozisme*, edited by Paolo Cristofolini, 49–65. Amsterdam: APA-Holland University Press, 1995.

Dawes, Gregory W. *The Historical Jesus Question: The Challenge of History to Religious Authority*. Louisville: Westminster John Knox, 2001.

Descartes, René. *Philosophical Writings*. Translated by John Cottingham, Robert Stoothoff, and Dugald Murdoch. 3 vols. Cambridge: Cambridge University Press, 1984–1991.

Dibon, Paul. "Der Cartesianismus in den Niederlanden." In *Die Philosophie des 17. Jahrhunderts*. Vol. 2, *Frankreich und Nierderlande*, edited by Jean-Pierre Schobinger, 349–74. Grundriss der Geschichte der Philosophie. Basel: Schwabe, 1993.

———. "Die Republik der Vereinigten Niederlande." In *Die Philosophie des 17. Jahrhunderts*. Vol. 2, *Frankreich und Nierderlande*, edited by Jean-Pierre Schobinger, 42–86. Grundriss der Geschichte der Philosophie. Basel: Schwabe, 1993.

———. "Scepticisme et orthodoxie reformée dans la Hollande du Siècle d'Or." In *Scepticism from the Renaissance to the Enlightenment*, edited by Richard H. Popkin and Charles B. Schmitt, 55–81. Wolfenbüttler Forschungen 35. Wiesbaden: In Kommission bei O. Harrassowitz, 1987.

Fix, Andrew. *Fallen Angels: Balthasar Bekker, Spirit Belief, and Confessionalism in the Seventeenth-Century Dutch Republic.* Dordrecht: Kluwer Academic, 1999.

Funkenstein, Amos. *Theology and the Scientific Imagination: From the Middle Ages to the Seventeenth Century.* Princeton: Princeton University Press, 1986.

Hamer, Petrus. *Voorlooper tot de volstrekte wederlegginge van het gene de heeren, Orchard, Daillom en Bekker.* Dordrecht: Cornelis Wilgaarts, 1692.

Harris, Jay Michael. *How Do We Know This?: Midrash and the Fragmentation of Modern Judaism.* Albany: State University of New York Press, 1995.

Israel, Jonathan. *The Dutch Republic: Its Rise, Greatness, and Fall, 1477–1806.* Oxford: Clarendon, 1995.

———. *Radical Enlightenment: Philosophy and the Making of Modernity 1650–1750.* New York: Oxford University Press, 2001.

Koelman, Jacobus. *Wederlegging van B. Bekkers Betoverde Wereldt.* Amsterdam: Johannes Boekholt, 1692.

Lee, Hoon J. "'Men of Galilee, Why Stand Gazing Up into Heaven?': Revisiting Galileo, Astronomy, and the Authority of the Bible." *Journal of the Evangelical Theological Society* 53, no. 1 (2010): 103–16.

Leydekker, Melchior. *Der Goddelykheid en Waarheid der H. Schriften.* 2 vols. Utrecht: Ottho de Vries, 1692.

———. *Dissertatio historico-theologica, de vulgato nuper cl. Bekkeri volumine, et Scripturarum authoritate ac veritate, pro Christiana religione apologetica.* Utrecht: Clerck, 1692.

———. *Fax Veritatis, seu exercitationes ad nonnullas controversias quae hodie in Belgio potissimum moventur.* Leiden: Lugduni Batavorum, 1766.

Maresius, Samuel. *De Abusu Philosophiae Cartesianae.* Groningae: Tierck Everts, 1670.

———. *Disputationes Theologicae prior refutatoria libelli de philosophia Interprete Scripturae.* Groningen: Johannis Collenus, 1667.

Mastricht, Petrus van. *Novitatum Cartesianarum Gangraena, Nobiliores plerasque Corporis Theologici Partes arrodens et exedens.* Amsterdam: Jansson, 1676.

———. *Theologia Theoretico-Practica: Qua, per singula capita theologica, pars exegetica, dogmatica, elenchtica & practica, perpetua successione conjugantur.* 2 vols. Utrecht: Thomas Appels, 1699.

———. *Vindiciae veritatis et authoritatis Sacrae Scripturae in rebus philosophicis.* Utrecht: Johannis Waesberge, 1655.

Meyer, Lodewijk. *Philosophia Sive Scripturae Interpres.* Amsterdam: Eleutheropoli, 1666.

Molinaeus, Johannes. *De Betoverde Werelt van D. Balthazar Bekker... Onderzogt en Wederlegst*. Rotterdam, Barent Bos, 1692.

Muller, Richard A. "Reformation, Orthodoxy, 'Christian Aristotelianism,' and the Eclecticism of Early Modern Philosophy." *Nederlands Archief voor Kergeschiedenis* n.s., 81, no. 3 (2001): 306–25.

Preus, J. Samuel. "Prophecy, Knowledge and Study of Religion." Religion 28 (1998): 124–38.

———. *Spinoza and the Irrelevance of Biblical Authority*. Cambridge: Cambridge University Press, 2001.

Revius, Jacobus. *Analectorum theologicorum disputatio XXI*. Leiden: Johannis Nicolai van Dorp, 1647.

———. *Kartesiomanias pars altera, qua ad secundam partem rabiosae Assertionis Tobiae Andreae respondetur*. Leiden: Hieronymum de Vogel, 1655.

———. *Methodi Cartesianae consideratio theologica*. Leiden: Hieronymum de Vogel, 1648.

Schoock, Martin. *De Scepticismo*. Groningen: Henrici Lussinck, 1652.

Spinoza, Benedict de. "Letter 75." In *The Letters*. Translated by Samuel Shirley, with an introduction and notes by Steven Barbone, Lee Rice, and Jacob Adler. Indianapolis, IN: Hacket, 1995.

———. *Theological-Political Treatise*. Translated by Michael Silverthorne and Jonathan Israel. Cambridge: Cambridge University Press, 2007.

Velthuysen, Lambertus van. *Bewys, Dat het gevoelen van die genen, die leeren der Sonne Stilstandt, En des Aertycks Beweging niet strydich is met Godts-Woort*. Utrecht: Jaer onses Herren, 1655.

———. *Bewys, Dat noch de Leere van der Sonne Stilstant, En des Aertryx Bewegingh, Noch de gronden vande Philosophie van Renatus Des Cartes strijdig sijn met Godts Woort. Gesteld tegen een Tractaet van J. du Bois*. Utrecht: Jaer onses Herren, 1656.

Voetius, Gijsbertus. *Thersites heautontimorumenos. Hoc est, Remonstrantium hyperaspistes, catechesis, et liturgiae Germanicae, Gallicae, et Belgicae denuo insultans*. Utrecht: Abrahami ab Herwiick et Hermanni Ribbius, 1635.

Waeyen, Johannes van der. *De betooverde weereld van D. Balthasar Bekker ondersogt en weederlegt*. Franeker: Strik and Horreus, 1693.

Walten, Eric. *Aardige Duyvelary*. Rotterdam: Pieter van Veen, 1691.

———. *Brief Aan sijn Excellentie, de Heer Graaf van Portland*. Hague: Meyndert Uytwerf, 1692.

Willis, E. David. "Rhetoric and Responsibility in Calvin's Theology." In *The Context of Contemporary Theology: Essays in Honor of Paul Lehmann*, edited by Alexander J. McKelway and E. David Willis, 43–64. Atlanta: John Knox, 1974.

Wittichius, Christophorus. *Consensus veritatis in Scriptura divina et infallibili revelatae cum veritate philosophica a Renato Des Cartes detecta*. 2nd ed.

Leiden: Cornelii Boutesteyn & Cornelii Lever, 1682. Originally published in Neomagi: Wyngaerden, 1659.

———. *Dissertationes Duae, Quarum prior De S. Scripturae in rebus Philosophicis abusu examinat.* Amsterdam: Ludovicum Elzevirium, 1653.

Wolzogen, Lodewijk. *De Scripturarum Interprete adversus Exercitatorem Paradoxum.* Utrecht: Linde, 1668.

CHAPTER 3

Accommodation in Early Eighteenth-Century Germany

Enlightenment studies have progressed beyond antiquated depictions, which exaggerated the rationalistic and naturalistic elements of the period. The "age of reason" has been unfairly perceived as a triumph of rationalism, dispelling religious superstition and belief in the supernatural. While appreciated for his development of Enlightenment studies, Peter Gay's assessment has been rejected, or at the very least significantly modified, in light of a more holistic understanding that includes a diverse range of philosophical, theological, and scientific ideologies within Enlightenment thinking.[1] These voices had always existed within the century but had been marginalized because they did not fit modern perceptions of what the Enlightenment entailed.[2]

One example of this shift can be found in the scholarship of Jonathan Israel. Israel goes to great lengths to distinguish the ideologies of mainstream moderates from those of radical figures influenced by Spinoza.[3]

---

[1] Peter Gay, *The Enlightenment: An Interpretation* (New York: Knopf, 1966, 1969).

[2] In recent years, the concept of the Enlightenment as a European movement has also been challenged. Rather than centering the Enlightenment in Europe and then tracing its impact on subsequent enlightenments throughout the world, Sebastian Conrad argues that the Enlightenment should be perceived as a worldwide phenomenon. Sebastian Conrad, "Enlightenment in Global History: A Historiographical Critique," *American Historical Review* 117, no. 4 (2012): 999–1027.

[3] Jonathan Israel, *Radical Enlightenment: Philosophy and the Making of Modernity 1650–1750* (New York: Oxford University Press, 2001), 3–22.

Though Israel has shown the differences between the rationalism and naturalism advanced by the radicals—which in the past had been associated with the entire Enlightenment—and that held by the moderates, who did not possess such convictions, he still falls short of a complete assessment. In his efforts to legitimize and bring greater significance to the Radical Enlightenment, Israel neglects Christian Enlightenment figures, marginalizing them as enthusiasts.

On the other hand, numerous studies have sought to provide a balanced understanding by including Christian voices within the Enlightenment. Oswald Bayer has led the charge to overcome the misconception of Johann Georg Hamann's philosophical and theological thought. Combatting Isaiah Berlin's interpretation of Hamann as an irrationalist and opponent of the Enlightenment, Bayer contends in his groundbreaking biography that Hamann should be recognized as a radical *Aufklärer* (though not in the same sense of Israel's Radical Enlightenment) and as one who possessed an even deeper devotion to freedom than Kant.[4] David Sorkin offers several case studies discussing the intersection of religion and the Enlightenment.[5] Jonathan Yeager examines how the Scottish clergyman John Erskine disseminated not only Christian ideas but also Enlightenment developments throughout Great Britain and across the Atlantic to colonial America.[6] In writing about the understudied Baron d'Holbach, Mark Curran presents d'Holbach's Christian opponents as members of the Enlightenment.[7] Finally, the ongoing publication *Religion in the Age of Enlightenment* continues to further the practice of including religious voices within the

---

[4] Oswald Bayer, *Zeitgenosse im Widerspruch: Johann Georg Hamann als radikaler Aufklärer* (Munich: Piper, 1988). Also available in English as *A Contemporary in Dissent: Johann Georg Hamann as a Radical Enlightener*, trans. Roy A. Harrisville and Mark C. Mattes (Grand Rapids, MI: Eerdmans, 2012).

[5] David Sorkin, *The Religious Enlightenment: Protestant, Jews and Catholics from London to Vienna* (Princeton: Princeton University Press, 2008). Sorkin's understanding of religion in the Enlightenment is more restrictive than Jonathan Yeager's or Mark Curran's.

[6] Jonathan Yeager, *Enlightened Evangelicalism: The Life and Thought of John Erskine* (Oxford: Oxford University Press, 2011).

[7] Mark Curran, *Atheism, Religion and Enlightenment in Pre-revolutionary Europe*, Royal Historical Society Studies in History, New Series (Suffolk, UK: Boydell, 2012).

Enlightenment, providing a more robust understanding of the movement and its impact on modern society.[8]

This progression in Enlightenment studies has changed the way we speak of the eighteenth century as the age of reason or the century of revolutions—or even simply as the Enlightenment. While it is difficult to capture a whole century in a pithy title, the century did contain such elements. Many during the eighteenth century were involved in promoting rationalism and criticizing traditional authority and institutions. However, many also participated in deep spiritual awakening, witnessed by the numerous revivals throughout the century. What is true of the eighteenth century is that it was a time of transition. Over the eighteenth century, the world would see advances in science, medicine, industry, and philosophical and religious thought. This period brought innovation and modernization in a way never before witnessed.

This characterization of transition also held true for the doctrine of accommodation. Cartesian philosophy certainly stretched into the eighteenth century, but it was gradually eclipsed by Newtonian and Lockean empiricism in England and Leibnizian and Wolffian philosophy in Germany. As with philosophy, accommodation underwent similar changes. In the early years of the eighteenth century, scholars still spoke for and contended against the seventeenth-century Cartesio-Cocceian accommodation of Wittichius and Bekker, but this variant was soon replaced by Spinozist and Wolffian accommodation. Eighteenth-century scholars continued debating issues from the seventeenth century, but they also introduced new themes, which developed into a uniquely eighteenth-century interpretation. Heterodox accommodation was no longer contingent on a strict Cartesian dualism, becoming dissociated with Descartes and more directly linked to Socinus. Also, eighteenth-century Augustinian accommodation developed its Lutheran heritage rather than relying on Reformed orthodoxy. Despite these shifts, the dividing line remained between those who affirmed the Augustinian position, which upheld the Bible's authority and inerrancy, and those who held to an innovative understanding of accommodation to error, which could be indifferent to inerrancy or could even challenge outright the Bible's inerrancy and authority.

---

[8] *Religion in the Age of Enlightenment* is an annual publication edited by Brett C. McInelly.

Reshaping of the Accommodation Debate

Though we now begin to see how the discussion of accommodation in the eighteenth century was dominated by German scholars, the geographical shift away from the Netherlands occurred before the turn of the century. The Swiss Reformed theologian and philologist Johann Caspar Suicer (1620–1684) included an article on the patristic use of accommodation in his *Thesaurus Ecclesiasticus* (1682). As we will see, turning to the church fathers to legitimize one's position on accommodation would become a common practice in the eighteenth century. Trained in Zurich, Montauban, and Saumur, Suicer's first position was as a minister in Basadingen, but he eventually moved to Zurich, where he became a professor of Hebrew and later of Greek. It was here where he completed his celebrated work, which circulated throughout Switzerland, Germany, and the Netherlands.

In his article on Συγχαταβασις (*Synchatabasis*), Suicer described accommodation as God's adaptation of the "mysteries of our salvation" revealed in Scripture.[9] He divided the patristic understanding of accommodation into five categories. First, Suicer addressed issues related to God's condescension in general, specifically discussing the church fathers ' polemical practice of discrediting Jewish thought because it promoted the use of sacrifices and other ceremonies.[10] The second, and longest, section was devoted to accommodation in relation to Jesus. Here Suicer relied on Athanasius's endeavors to establish the full deity of Christ along with the accommodated nature of Christ's incarnation. During his earthly ministry and especially in his teaching, Jesus "accommodated according to his audience." In the third section, similar to the use of sacrifices, Suicer argued that the church fathers understood certain Old Testament laws, such as the allowance of multiple wives and divorce, as an accommodation to the weakness of the Israelites. The fourth section addressed the apostles' continued practice of the Sabbath, circumcision, and praying in the temple as an accommodation to their Jewish audience, but noted that Paul, at times, discontinued such practices because they were not expected in his ministry to the Gentiles. In the final section,

---

[9] Johann Caspar Suicer, *Thesaurus Ecclesiasticus* (Amsterdam: J. Henricum Wetstenium, 1682), 1067.

[10] Suicer, *Thesaurus Ecclesiasticus*, 1068.

Suicer advanced the notion of some early fathers that Satan used accommodation in his corruption of man.

Accompanying the geographical change that occurred in the eighteenth century was a theological shift from Reformed to Lutheran thought. Though the discussion of the doctrine in the previous century was controlled by Reformed scholars, in the eighteenth century the center of the doctrinal debate shifted to Lutheran circles. This was true not only for the first half of the century, discussed in this chapter, but also for the continuation of the accommodation debate in the latter half of the century. Lutherans of various strides, including the orthodox and Pietists, debated the proper understanding of accommodation.

This is not to suggest that seventeenth-century Lutherans were unfamiliar with the doctrine of accommodation. On the contrary, as Robert D. Preus states, "This doctrine of accommodation is either explicitly taught or at least inferred by all the Lutheran dogmaticians."[11] He characterizes seventeenth-century Lutheran accommodation as expressed by Johannes Andreas Quenstedt (1617–1688):

> Now insofar as they were instructed in and accustomed to a lofty or ordinary style of speaking and writings, the Holy Spirit chose to adjust and accommodate Himself to the natural endowments of these men and to express the same things through some in an ornate manner, through others in an inferior manner. The Holy Spirit accommodated Himself to the understanding and natural endowments of the holy writers in order that He might record mysteries according to the usual mode of speaking.[12]

Preus contends that post-Reformation Lutherans held the doctrine of accommodation in an apparent paradox with their understanding of inspiration. While their doctrine of inspiration may have appeared to void the biblical authors' voice in their writing, their doctrine of accommodation assured that "there is nothing docetic about Scripture."[13]

---

[11] Robert D. Preus, *Theology of Post-Reformation Lutheranism*, vol. 1, *A Study of Theological Prolegomena* (St. Louis, MO: Concordia, 1970), 289.

[12] Johannes Andreas Quenstedt, *Theologia Didactico-Polemica sive Systema Theologiae* (Leipzig: Thomam Fritsch, 1702), P. 1, C. 4, S. 2, q. 4 (I, 75). Quoted in Preus, *Theology of Post-Reformation Lutheranism*, 1:289.

[13] Preus, *Theology of Post-Reformation Lutheranism*, 1:291.

For post-Reformation Lutherans, the doctrine of accommodation did not compromise the biblical authors, nor did the authors introduce error of any kind into the biblical text. As Abraham Calov (1612–1686) wrote, "Not only must we hold to be true what is set forth in Scripture concerning faith and morals, but we must hold to everything that happens to be included therein."[14] The orthodox understanding of inerrancy thus extended to all matters in the Bible, not just those of faith and doctrine. Nor did they distinguish between inerrancy and infallibility, as some do in modern debates. Salomon Deyling (1677–1755) illustrated the Lutheran understanding of accommodation in relation to inerrancy and the scientific worldview when he stated,

> For Scripture sometimes conforms to the experiences of our senses or to the ideas of sense perception as they particularly affect us. Likewise Scripture speaks of the heavenly and earthly bodies in no other manner than as they represent themselves to our senses, inasmuch as whatever we know about heavenly bodies is made known to us through our senses. Such ways of speaking are usually called "observation"; and are distinguished from the physical reality itself. Let this not be construed as though we were saying that the divine Scripture accommodates itself to the comprehension of the masses, that is, to error, or that it speaks erroneous, as many, especially from the school of René Descartes foolishly and wrongly imagine. But there is nothing wrong with our saying and admitting that the Scriptures in some places did not speak of things scientifically but phenomenally, or according to the experience of our senses and as things were apprehended by the senses. . . . One errs only when one mistakes and substitutes appearance for reality. But the Spirit, who is the author of the Sacred Scriptures never does this, nor does He make any concession to commonly held error, but accommodates Himself only to our sense of sight.[15]

---

[14] Abraham Calov, *Systema Locorum Theologicorum* (Wittenberg: Sumptibus A. Hartmann, 1655), 1:462. Quoted in *Theology of Post-Reformation Lutheranism*, 1:341. See also Quenstedt, *Systema*, P. I, C. 4, S. 2, q. 5 Ekthesis (I, 112). There is a small debate over whether Calov shared the same understanding of accommodation with Quenstedt. Contra Hoenecke, Preus proves that this apparent difference was due to a neglect of the context of certain statements made by Calov. See Robert D. Preus, *The Inspiration of Scripture: A Study of the Theology of the Seventeenth-Century Lutheran Dogmaticians* (Edinburgh: Oliver and Boyd, 1955), 63.

[15] Salomon Deyling, *Observationum Sacrarum in qua Multa Scripturae Veteris ac Novi Testamenti Dubia Vexata Sovunutur* (Leipzig: S. H. F. Lanckisii, 1735), 1:397. Quoted in Preus, *Theology of Post-Reformation Lutheranism*, vol. 2, *God and His Creation*, 233–234.

It was this seventeenth-century understanding of Augustinian accommodation that was first passed on to early eighteenth-century Lutherans and was subsequently challenged throughout the century by Socinian accommodation.

EARLY EIGHTEENTH-CENTURY ACCOMMODATION

One of the earliest mentions of the doctrine can be found in Valentin Ernst Löscher's (1673–1749) *Praenotiones Theologicae* (1708). Löscher's father was professor of theology at Wittenberg.[16] He followed his father's career path leaving aside his ambitions for history. As an orthodox Lutheran, Löscher's dissertation was a critique of the advancement of Pietism. He continued his polemic against Pietism throughout his career, most famously in his dispute with Joachim Lange (1670–1744).[17] Löscher later became superintendent at Jüterbog from 1698 to 1701 and then at Delitzsch from 1701 to 1707. During his time at Delitzsch, Löscher founded and operated the first German theological journal, *Alles und Neues oder Unschuldige Nachrichten*. After being offered a chair as professor of theology at Wittenberg, Löscher eventually fulfilled his father's wish for him to teach at the same university where his father had taught. However, after a short, 2-year stint, Löscher left Wittenberg for the superintendent position at Dresden. He felt that Dresden, as a center of theological interaction, offered a greater opportunity to impact the church.

Before arriving in Jüterbog, Löscher spent some time in the Netherlands.[18] During his travels he became acquainted with other opponents of Cartesianism, including such scholars as Melchior Leydekker (1642–1721). Years earlier, in 1677, Leydekker had published his *Fax Veritatis*, in which he presented his full treatment of Cartesian philosophy and theology. The work consisted of ten *loci*, or central issues, that plagued Cartesian philosophy and the Cartesio-Cocceians,

---

[16] Hans Friese, *Valentin Ernst Löscher* (Berlin: Evangelische Velagsanstalt, 1964), 13–17. Also see Martin Greschat, *Zwischen Tradition und neuem Anfang: Valentin Ernst Löscher und der Ausgang der lutherischen Orthodoxie* (Witten: Luther, 1971).

[17] Friese, *Valentin Ernst Löscher*, 64–68.

[18] Friese, *Valentin Ernst Löscher*, 21–24.

including issues such as Cartesian doubt and its challenge against theological truth.[19]

Leydekker turned to accommodation in his second *locus*.[20] Ernst Bizer states that Cartesian accommodation was the unifying denominator and *proton pseudos* of "all the efforts of his opponents."[21] According to Leydekker, there was a contradiction between Cartesio-Cocceian accommodation, which stipulated errors in the Bible, and the true nature of the Bible, which contained no error.[22] The Cartesio-Cocceian understanding of accommodation suggested that God intentionally deceived humanity. Not only did God allow man to remain in error, he also actively taught false information. For Leydekker, Cartesio-Cocceian accommodation was a direct challenge to the authority of the Bible.[23]

Löscher continued Leydekker's and the seventeenth-century orthodox understanding in his *Praenotiones theologicae*. As Vernon P. Kleinig proposes, Löscher rooted the challenges to the Bible in his day in Cartesian doubt.[24] The primary detractor of biblical authority in the eyes of Löscher was none other than Spinoza and his use of accommodation. Spinoza was guilty of claiming that the apostles' doctrinal teachings were a reflection of the erroneous thinking of their time.[25] This rationalistic use of accommodation was not limited to Spinoza but was indicative of various attacks on scriptural authority.

In a similar work, Rostock theologian Zacharias Grapius (1671–1713) responded to the increasing danger of theological innovation in

---

[19] Melchior Leydekker, *Fax Veritatis, seu exercitationes ad nonnullas controversias quae hodie in Belgio potissimum moventur* (Leiden: Lugduni Batavorum, 1766), 1–6. Due to limited availability, I am using the 1766 edition and not the original 1677 edition.

[20] Leydekker, *Fax Veritatis*, 2:1, 24. In addition to this section, also see the fourteenth controversy in *locus* 3. In the latter section, Leydekker addressed Wolzogen's accommodation and the issue of divine error. Also see Leydekker's *Der Goddelykheid en Waarheid der H. Schriften* (Utrecht: Ottho de Vries, 1692), 1:197–214; 2:3–12, 191–222.

[21] Ernst Bizer, "Die reformierte Orthodoxie und der Cartesianismus," *ZTK* 55, no. 3 (1958):366.

[22] Leydekker, *Fax Veritatis*, 2:1, 24.

[23] Leydekker, *Fax Veritatis*, 2:2, 30.

[24] Vernon P. Kleinig, "Confessional Lutheranism in Eighteenth-Century Germany," *CTQ* 60, no. 1–2 (1996): 103.

[25] Valentin Ernst Löscher, *Praenotiones theologicae contra naturalistarum et fanaticorum omne genus atheos, deistas, indifferentistas, antiscripturarios* (Wittenberg: Gerdesius, 1708), 219.

Germany. In *Systema novissimarum controversiarum* (1709), Grapius challenged the claims of Bekker and the physician Anthonie van Dale (1638–1708). As the dean of Haarlem's medical college, van Dale popularized Bekker's ideology concerning demons and the spirit world.[26] Using his medical training, he discredited demon possession as physically impossible, thus negating the historical accounts found in the Bible. According to Grapius, however, such a naturalistic reading of the Bible undermined the authority of Scripture and contributed to the rise of heterodoxy.

In the first volume, Grapius addressed the issue of whether God could lie or deceive man for his own good. Grapius specifically challenged Wolzogen's understanding that while accommodation included the erroneous thinking of man, it should not be considered a fault on God's part. Approving of Leydekker's assessment, Grapius contended against Cartesian accommodation. As Hebrews 6:19 illustrates, God could not lie or depart from his truth. Also, what Wolzogen had proposed would be a violation of divine immutability.[27] Wolzogen's attempt to differentiate between divine accommodation that included error and a God who cannot err had failed. According to Grapius, such an accommodation would place the blame on God and not on the biblical author or the audience for which the accommodation was intended. Socinian accommodation implied that "Scripture sometimes speaks to the erroneous opinion of the people," which amounted to "blasphemy."[28] It would be a complete denial of God's perfect nature.

It was around this time that the association between Socinian accommodation and Cartesianism was dissipating. As we have seen, earlier eighteenth-century opponents of this form of accommodation often equated Cartesian philosophy with heterodox accommodation. For example, in the 1717 edition of *Historia Ecclesiastica cum Parallelismo Profanae*, Johann Wolfgang Jaeger repeated this argument, identifying as a Cartesian thought the notion that "Scripture often speaks about nature according to common opinion and appearance, not according to

---

[26] It was commonly understood that van Dale was continuing Bekker's argument against the spiritual world. Otto Mencke, *Acta Eruditorum* (Leipzig: Grosse and Gleditsch, 1692), 21.

[27] Zacharias Grapius, *Systema novissimarum controversiarum, seu theologia, recens controversa* (Rostock: Georg. Ludov. Fritschuum, 1719), 1:98.

[28] Grapius, *Systema novissimarum controversiarum*, 1:99.

accuracy and truth."[29] However, discussions on accommodation in the eighteenth century increasingly viewed not Cartesio-Cocceians as the main culprits but figures such as Spinoza and Wolff, who became pegged as the central proponents of Socinian accommodation.

Pietism and Accommodation

German Pietism was a late seventeenth- and early eighteenth-century renewal movement within Lutheranism. Dissatisfied by the scholastic dogmatism of orthodox Lutheranism, Pietism emphasized the inner subjective experiences of the Christian faith and the outward practical expressions of charity and love. The origins of the movement can be traced to Phillip Jakob Spener's (1635–1705) *Pia Desideria* (1675), in which he emphasized the need for individual study of the Bible and communal gathering for edification through the *collegium pietatis*. Though initially written as an introduction to a reissue of Johann Arndt's *True Christendom* (1605–1610), the work outgrew its original purpose and was published as a separate volume. Reflecting many of Arndt's principles, Spener's writings fueled the progression of the devotional gatherings, and Pietism quickly developed into a spiritual and intellectual movement not only in Germany but throughout Europe. Pietism would become characterized as a personal renewal movement that emphasized holiness and religious experience. It was not only a reaction against what was deemed stale formalism and the unfinished Reformation but also a response to the growing rationalism and naturalism within the Enlightenment.

Several points should be made about Pietism generally and accommodation specifically. First, Pietism has often been depicted as a negative movement focused on outward displays of piety rather than on Christian conviction or intellectual rigor, resulting in an individualistic, legalistic, and self-righteous system. Time has not been kind to Pietism's legacy. Across the disciplines, Pietism has gained a reputation for promoting otherworldliness, emotionalism, subjectivism, latitudinarianism, individualism, moralism, and perfectionism.[30] Simply put, Pietism

---

[29] Johann Wolfgang Jaeger, *Historia Ecclesiastica cum Parallelismo Profanae* (Hamburg: Samuelis Heylii, 1717), 2:106.

[30] These charges against Pietism have been identified and refuted by Roger E. Olson in "Pietism: Myths and Realities," in *The Pietist Impulse in Christianity*, ed. Christian T.

has been deemed a negative movement that is largely anti-intellectual. In his *Geschichte des Pietismus* (1880–1886), Albrecht Ritschl portrayed Pietism as a renewal of medieval monasticism and mysticism. Karl Barth described Pietism as a movement characterized by being individualistic and subjective. Some level of criticism is fair, as with any movement, but such caricatures fail to acknowledge the theological and hermeneutical advances Pietists made.

F. Ernest Stoeffler served as the leading voice for the few who endeavored to reverse this biased depiction of Pietism, particularly in its German variety.[31] His works *The Rise of Evangelical Pietism* (1965) and *German Pietism during the Eighteenth Century* (1973) are long-standing classics for Pietism studies in English. More recently, Pietism studies have made a much needed corrective, achieving a balanced understanding of the movement through Martin Brecht's multivolume work *Geschichte des Pietismus* (1993–2004).[32] These pivotal studies have led to a shift in Pietism research, witnessed in collected volumes such as Carter Lindberg's *The Pietist Theologians* (2004), Christian T. Winn, Gehrz Collins, Carlson Christopher, and Eric Holst's *The Pietistic Impulse in Christianity* (2011), and Douglas H. Shantz's *Introduction to German Pietism*.[33] A significant component of the changing historiography is the scholarship of Donald W. Dayton. Continually advancing Pietism studies, particularly in relation to Wesleyan and Pentecostal traditions, Dayton's research provides a fuller understanding of historical Pietism.

Second, primarily through the influence of Dayton, a segment of scholars posit that early Pietism countered the Princetonian and neo-evangelical doctrine of inerrancy. For Dayton, the doctrine of inerrancy

---

Footnote 30 (continued)
Collins Winn, Gehrz Collins, Carlson Christopher, and Eric Holst (Cambridge: James Clarke, 2011), 3–16.

[31] F. Ernest Stoeffler, *The Rise of Evangelical Pietism*, Studies in the History of Religions 9 (Leiden: Brill, 1965) and *German Pietism during the Eighteenth Century*, Studies in the History of Religions 24 (Leiden: Brill, 1973).

[32] Martin Brecht, *Geschichte des Pietismus* (Göttingen: Vandenhoeck & Ruprecht, 1993–2004).

[33] Carter Lindberg, ed. *The Pietist Theologians: An Introduction to Theology in the Seventeenth and Eighteenth Centuries* (Malden, MA: Blackwell, 2005); Winn, Collins, Christopher, and Holst, eds, *The Pietist Impulse in Christianity*; Douglas H. Shantz, *An Introduction to German Pietism: Protestant Renewal at the Dawn of Modern Europe* (Baltimore: Johns Hopkins, 2013).

is a product of Princetonian theology, which neo-evangelicals popularized in the 1940s, and is not a historical doctrine found in movements of the church such as Pietism.[34] Articulated in a journal article by A. A. Hodge and B. B. Warfield, the Princetonian doctrine upheld complete inerrancy in the original autographs.[35] Dayton acknowledges that early Pietists upheld a "radical biblicism" but contends that the Pietist tradition also "reject[ed] ... the orthodox and inerrantist tradition."[36] Issues of twentieth-century inerrancy are not the focus here; these matters continue to be debated, and strong arguments for the doctrine can be found elsewhere.[37] Rather, the task at hand is to examine the interplay between hermeneutics and Pietism during the Enlightenment in Germany, and these matters bear on modern discussions.

Finally, for our discussion of accommodation, the particular strand of Pietism with which we will be concerned does not stray outside the Lutheran variety described above. This is not to say that the term cannot be applied to certain movements within radicals, Puritanism, or the Reformed tradition.[38]

We begin with Dayton's twofold argument that Pietism not only opposed the orthodox Lutheran understanding of Scripture but was also in line with Enlightenment theology and interpretive methodology.

---

[34] See Stanley J. Grenz, "Nurturing the Soul, Informing the Mind: The Genesis of the Evangelical Scripture Principle," in *Evangelicals and Scripture: Tradition, Authority, and Hermeneutics*, ed. Vincent Bacote, Laura C. Miguélez, and Dennis L. Okholm (Downers Grove, IL: InterVarsity Press, 2004), 21–41.

[35] A. A. Hodge and B. B. Warfield, "Inspiration," *Presbyterian Review* 2, no. 6 (1881), 225–60.

[36] Donald W. Dayton, "The Pietist Theological Critique of Biblical Inerrancy," in Bacote, Miguélez, and Okholm, *Evangelicals and Scripture*, 81. In support of his claim, Dayton cites Fredrick Holmgren, "The Pietistic Tradition and Biblical Criticism," *CQ* 28 (1970): 49–59, and K. James Stein, *Phillip Jacob Spener: Pietist Patriarch* (Chicago: Covenant, 1986), 152. However, neither source provides evidence of early Pietism's rejection of biblical inerrancy.

[37] See works such as John D. Woodbridge, *Biblical Authority: A Critique of the Rogers/McKim Proposal* (Grand Rapids, MI: Zondervan, 1982); James K. Hoffmeier and Dennis R. Magary, eds., *Do Historical Matters Matter to Faith?: A Critical Appraisal of Modern and Postmodern Approaches to Scripture* (Wheaton, IL: Crossway, 2012).

[38] For more information on other forms of Pietism, see, Stoeffler, *The Rise of Evangelical Pietism*; Lindberg, ed., *The Pietist Theologians*; Brecht, *Geschichte des Pietismus*. Also, for the earliest assessment of Pietism, see Johann Heinrich Callenberg, *Neueste Kirchenhistorie* (1689).

Acknowledging that many scholars see the Pietist and orthodox doctrine of Scripture as standing in unison, Dayton nonetheless emphasizes the discontinuity between the two. He describes the two traditions saying, "Orthodoxy tended to locate the doctrine of Scripture in theological prolegomena as the transcendent grounding of speculative reason; Pietism was more inclined to see in the Scriptures the charter of the church and consider it under a different theological locus."[39] The orthodox doctrine of Scripture elevated the Bible in a hypertranscendent fashion, whereas Pietism was willing to engage the Bible in a manner natural to the text.

The differing approaches to Scripture result in at least three outcomes.[40] First, in understanding important biblical passages instructive to exegesis, the orthodox interpretation "emphasized the once-for-all givenness and absoluteness of the process of biblical inspiration," while Pietism "emphasized the ongoing process of inspiration in the church and the present work of the Holy Spirit in making the Scriptures alive and vital today."[41] Second, in opposition to the hypertranscendent view of Scripture held by the orthodox, Pietism embraced biblical-critical methods of interpretation. Finally, in a "mutually supporting" fashion, Pietism and the Enlightenment often stood in opposition to orthodoxy.[42]

Despite these outcomes, Dayton argues, "contemporary categories of thought" blind us to seeing the discontinuity between Pietists and orthodoxy, and the continuity between Pietism and the Enlightenment.[43] Specifically, Dayton emphasizes the issue of biblical criticism as the connection to the Enlightenment and the breaking point

---

[39] Donald W. Dayton, "The Use of Scripture in the Wesleyan Tradition," in *The Use of the Bible in Theology: Evangelical Options*, ed. Robert K. Johnston (Atlanta: John Knox, 1985), 131.

[40] Dayton, "The Use of Scripture," 131.

[41] Dayton, "The Use of Scripture," 131.

[42] Dayton repeats this argument in his essay on the Pentecostal tradition, where he states, "With regard to the orthodoxy, it is important to notice that pietism shared with the Enlightenment many points in a critique of orthodoxy, in many ways seeing itself as an *alternative* way of 'completing' the Reformation." Donald W. Dayton, "The Limits of Evangelicalism: The Pentecostal Tradition," in *The Variety of American Evangelicalism*, ed. Donald W. Dayton and Robert K. Johnston (Knoxville: University of Tennessee, 1991), 50.

[43] Dayton, "Pietist Theological Critique," 82.

from orthodoxy. As the "pioneers" of biblical criticism, Pietists were open to a historical and contextual study of the Bible and to appropriating Enlightenment thought in their hermeneutics.

Within his case for continuity between Pietism and the Enlightenment, which both opposed orthodox hermeneutics, Dayton acknowledges an inconsistency on the part of Pietists. At times Pietists wavered in their "self-conscious opposition to orthodoxy."[44] Dayton goes on to provide the example of the *neuPietismus* of the nineteenth and twentieth centuries, when we witness great continuity with American fundamentalism. According to Dayton, such inconsistencies can be attributed to the mediation of Pietism through the Puritan and Reformed traditions, which softened the distinct lines between German Pietism and Lutheran orthodoxy. If the trajectory of the original Pietists in Germany continued, we would have clearly seen the disparity between pietistic and orthodox exegesis.

By taking a look at the Enlightenment in Germany, we arrive at a rather different understanding of Pietism than the one expressed by Dayton. One of August Hermann Francke's (1663–1727) brightest students was the often misunderstood Joachim Lange (1670–1744). After studying at Leipzig under Franke, Lange continued his pietistic training at Halle. He was called as a professor of theology at Halle in 1709 after serving as the rector at a Berlin gymnasium. A prolific writer, Lange served as the leading spokesman for Pietism, often involved in polemic battles, such as the prolonged debate with Löscher between 1707 and 1722.[45]

Perhaps due to his polemics, Lange has gained a negative reputation in today's reading of history. Löscher is often praised as a natural descendant of Luther's theology and one of the greatest theologians during this period, while Lange has been incorrectly viewed as a controversialist, provoking dissent within Lutheranism. As a victim of this misunderstanding of Pietism, Lange's role as Halle Pietism's chief

---

[44] Dayton, "Pietist Theological Critique," 85.

[45] For more on this debate, see Stoeffler, *German Pietism during the Eighteenth Century*, 63–71. Also see Hans Martin Rotermund, *Orthodoxie und Pietismus: Valentin Ernst Löschers "Timotheus Verinus" in der Auseinandersetzung mit der Schule August Hermann Franckes*, Theologische Arbeiten 13 (Berlin: Evangelische Verlagsanstalt, 1959). The controversy did not end in mutual understanding or even progress much from where it started. Rather, Löscher decided not to respond to Lange's final work on the topic. Instead of exerting so much energy on each other, the rise of Wolffian philosophy became the greater and more urgent threat to both orthodox and pietistic interests.

theologian has been eclipsed in modern perception, which depicts the theologian in a negative light. Nonetheless, while Lange certainly disagreed with Löscher and his form of orthodox Lutheranism, which served as a constant hindrance for the promotion of Pietism, the larger threat to Christianity was the rise of Leibnizian and Wolffian philosophy.

Gottfried Wilhelm Leibniz (1646–1716) served as a diplomat, mathematician, and philosopher. In reaction to but also benefiting from Cartesian and Spinozist philosophy, Leibniz's system sought to use a system of logic and mathematics to order the world. He developed the concept of an infinite amount of singular units called monads in his work *Monadologie* (1714). While each unit was independent, they were related to other monads, having a direct cause and effect on each other. It was his hope that such an understanding of reality and existence could bypass Cartesian dualism and avoid the pitfall of Spinozist monism.

Leibnizian philosophy gained much notoriety when it was popularized by Christian Wolff (1679–1754). Wolff was appointed professor of mathematics and natural philosophy at Halle in 1706 by the recommendation of Leibniz. It was at Halle that he developed his interpretation of Leibnizian philosophy. Wolff deemphasized the role of monads but elevated the importance of universal and logical law. His modified philosophical system had clear inclinations toward Leibnizianism, and it became the main medium for understanding and appropriating Leibnizian philosophy.

An ardent critic of Wolff, Lange eventually succeeded in securing a ban on all teaching and promotion of Wolffian philosophy in May 1723. Shortly thereafter, in November of the same year, Wolff was dismissed from his position and took a position in Marburg. In 1733, King Friedrich Wilhelm reassessed the imperial ban and offered Wolff his former position at Halle. At first, Wolff declined the king's offer, but after Wilhelm officially exonerated Wolff and his philosophical system in 1739, he accepted a position at Halle.

In harmonizing the Bible's presentation of the universe with the heliocentric universe, Leibniz turned to the common understanding that the Bible "accommodated itself to the opinions of mankind."[46]

---

[46] Gottfried Wilhelm Leibniz, "Preface," in *Phoranomus seu de potentia et legibus Naturae*, in *Opuscules et fragments inédits de Leibniz*, ed. Louis Couturat (Paris: Felix Alcan, 1903), 590–93.

His use of accommodation was not unlike Galileo Galilei (1564–1642), who expressed his views in a letter to the Grand Duchess Christina.[47] While not denying the accuracy of the Bible, scientists gravitated toward accommodation because it enabled them to maintain both their Christian confession and what they knew to be proven by science. Scripture remained fully accurate, but modern science contributed to its interpretation, especially in passages that could be attributed to accommodation.

Wolff extended the discussion of how to integrate accommodation with science in his *Philosophia rationalis* (1728). Agreeing with Leibniz, he promoted the use of logic and reason in the interpretation of Scripture.[48] Science and the Bible could not contradict each other since reason and revelation shared the "same author."[49] Hence, in the interpretation of the Bible, we must use reason and science to understand passages in context. For example, in interpreting the episode of the sun standing still in the book of Joshua, it was a matter not of the Bible being wrong but rather of how best to understand the passage. Wolff argued that the phenomenological reading was the proper interpretation of Joshua.[50]

This was also true of Moses's description of the creation of the universe and the "two great lights" (Gen. 1:16). While science has taught us that the moon does not emit its own light, the description found in Genesis was only a phenomenologically accommodated description of the moon. Wolff was not making a case against the inerrancy of the Bible but stating that the Bible was written according to the way humans understand the world around them.[51] Similarly to Galileo, Wolff was not accusing the Bible of having errors but was using accommodation to say that science was a suitable tool for the interpretation of the Bible.

---

[47] For more on Galileo's use of accommodation, see Hoon J. Lee, "'Men of Galilee, Why Stand Gazing Up Into Heaven?': Revisiting Galileo, Astronomy, and the Authority of the Bible," *JETS* 53, no. 1 (2010): 103–16.

[48] Christian Wolff, *Philosophia Rationalis Sive Logica: Methodo Scientifica Pertractata Et Ad Usum Scientiarum Atque Vitae Aptata; Praemittitur Discursus Praeliminaris De Philosophia In Genere* (Leipzig: Rengeriana, 1728), 692.

[49] Wolff, *Philosophia rationalis*, 703.

[50] Wolff, *Philosophia rationalis*, 695.

[51] Wolff, *Philosophia rationalis*, 700.

Though not directly correlated to Spinozism, Wolffian philosophy did share a common understanding of the universe. According to Lange, Wolff's mechanistic worldview had a certain affinity with Spinoza's fatalism.[52] While Wolff did not adhere to Spinoza's pantheism or monism, his understanding of natural law looked very much like Spinoza's concept of reality. In Lange's view, Wolff, Spinoza, and Spinoza's promoter Frederik van Leenhof (1647–1712) were the greatest threats.[53] Leenhof followed Spinoza in claiming that the Bible's accommodation to the times of its writing resulted in a text full of factual and ideological errors.[54] All three adhered to a form of accommodation that challenged the authority of the Bible, albeit in different ways. Contending against Spinoza's understanding that the Bible was to render its reader obedient rather than scientifically accurate, Lange rejected Spinoza's form of accommodation. He denied Spinoza's understanding that the Bible contained errors because it was an "accommodation to the ability of common man."[55]

By 1734 Lange was prohibited from criticizing Wolffian philosophy in his teaching and writing. The imperial decree that once banned Wolffian philosophy was rescinded, not only reestablishing the philosophical system but also welcoming Wolff back to Halle. However, a new publication allowed Lange to reignite the fight with Wolffian philosophy. In 1735, Johann Lorenz Schmidt (1702–1749) published his rationalistic translation of the Bible, which came to be known as the Wertheim Bible. Accompanying the translation was an introduction where he explained his philosophical system, relying heavily on Wolffian philosophy. As Paul Spalding states, "Schmidt's Wolffian presuppositions caused him to posit God as the omniscient and omnipotent 'Autonomous Being,' the first cause of the world and all its interrelated phenomena, who wills the perfection of everything. Armed with this philosophical construct from

---

[52] Joachim Lange, *Modesta disquisitio novi philosophiae systematis de Deo, Mundo et homine* (Halle: Orphanotropheum, 1723), 45. Jena theologian Volkmar Conrad Poppo argued similarly that Leibnizian/Wolffian mathematical rationalism led to a mechanistic world, which opened the door to Spinozist fatalism. Volkmar Conrad Poppo, *Spinozismus detectus, oder vernünfftige Gedanken von dem wahren Unterscheid der philosophischen und mathematischen Methode oder Lehr-Art* (Weimar: Mumbachen, 1721), 5.

[53] Lange, *Modesta disquisitio*, 44. Also see Joachim Lange, *Bescheidene und ausführliche Entdeckung der falschen und schädlichen Philosophie in dem Wolffianischen Systemate metaphysico* (Halle: Wäysenhauses, 1724), 476.

[54] Israel, *Radical Enlightenment*, 406–435.

[55] Lange, *Modesta disquisitio*, 45.

outside the Bible, Schmidt did all he could to deconstruct the language about God within the Bible."[56] The work was seen by many as an extension of Wolffian philosophy to biblical interpretation. The Wertheim Bible was opposed by Lange in his *Der Philosophische Religionsspötter* (1735), but it also received approval by Siegmund Jakob Baumgarten (1706–1757). Later during the *Wolfenbüttel Fragments* controversy, Lessing intentionally misled others by suggesting that Schmidt was its author, due to Schmidt's association with the city and the common themes found in the Wertheim Bible and the *Fragments*.

Though dependent on Wolffian philosophy, Schmidt's use of accommodation went beyond Wolff's own position. In his preface, Schmidt contended that accommodated errors of the common people were allowed to remain within the text of the Bible.[57] Schmidt's discussion of phenomenological language in the Bible was similar to Wolff's, but he also applied the doctrine to theological matters, jeopardizing the core doctrines of Christianity. For instance, in his notes of Genesis 1:26 and 3:22, Schmidt argued that the Trinity was an accommodation to the polytheistic mindset of ancient Israel.

Aiding Lange's cause was fellow Pietist Johann Jacob Rambach (1693–1735). Born in Halle, Rambach studied both at the city's university and at Jena. In 1727, he replaced Francke as professor of theology, though he stayed for only a short period, leaving Halle for Giessen in 1731. As a Pietist, Rambach naturally gravitated toward Puritan influences in his life and scholarship; in fact, he edited the works of Puritan scholars such as Thomas Goodwin (1600–1680), Richard Baxter (1615–1691), and Isaac Watts (1674–1748). Rambach greatly contributed to pietistic systematic theology and also to the mystical interpretation of Scripture.[58]

---

[56] Paul S. Spalding, *Seize the Book, Jail the Author: Johann Lorenz Schmidt and Censorship in Eighteenth-Century Germany* (West Lafayette, IN: Purdue University Press, 1998), 69.

[57] Johann Lorenz Schmidt, *Die göttlichen Schriften vor den Zeiten des Messie Jesus* (Wertheim: Johann Georg Nehr, 1735), 8.

[58] For Rambach's mystical hermeneutics, see Benjamin T. G. Mayes, "The Mystical Sense of Scripture according to Johann Jacob Rambach," *CTQ* 72, no. 1 (2008): 45–70; Klaus Wetzel, *Johann Jakob Rambach in Halle und Gießen: Impulse für eine geistliche Ausrichtung von theologischer Arbeit und Theologiestudium* (Wuppertal: Verlag und Schriftenmission der Evangelischen Gesellschaft, 1987), 22–24.

In 1729, Rambach published his *Hypothesis de Scriptura sacra ad erroneos vulgi conceptus adcommodata*, in which he addressed the various hermeneutical issues surrounding the doctrine of accommodation. In the first of two sections, he gave a descriptive summary of those who use accommodation in a heterodox fashion, and in the second section, he refuted them. Rambach began by providing some brief details about Cartesian accommodation, especially concerning Wittichius, and how some such as du Bois and Schoock maintained historical accommodation *and* biblical authority.[59] Rambach recounted many of the issues of accommodation and cosmology, discussing in detail matters such as the creation narrative of Genesis and how the Copernican theory related to the Bible's description of the sun.[60] Though Spinoza was the main culprit, Rambach also identified Bekker's use of accommodation as one to be rejected, equating Bekker's understanding of demon possession with Spinoza's explicit challenge to the Bible.[61] In addition, he highlighted Socinians as misusers of the doctrine of accommodation. In his view, the Socinian interpretation that Christ and the apostles taught false doctrine as an accommodation to their Jewish audience not only violated the doctrine but also defied the Bible's authority.[62]

Rambach reserved his harshest criticism for Spinoza and the *Tractatus Theologico-Politicus*. Repeating much of our discussion of the *Tractatus Theologico-Politicus*, Rambach recounted how Spinoza considered matters such as descriptions of nature, anthropomorphic language, and Mosaic Law as accommodations to ancient Israel's erroneous thinking.[63] Rambach noted that these uses of accommodation all stood on the foundation of Spinoza's concept that the Bible is instructive only in matters of piety and morality.[64] Thus, Spinoza epitomized the

---

[59] Johann Jacob Rambach, *Hypothesis de Scriptura sacra ad erroneos vulgi conceptus adcommodata* (Halle: Henckel, 1729), 8.

[60] Rambach, *Hypothesis de Scriptura sacra*, 10–12, 15.

[61] Rambach, *Hypothesis de Scriptura sacra*, 20.

[62] Rambach, *Hypothesis de Scriptura sacra*, 32. Also see Rambach's earlier work, *Institutiones Hermeneuticae Sacrae, variis observationibus copiosissimisque exemplis biblicis illustratae* (Jena: Hartungius, 1723), 613. For further information on the *Hermeneuticae Sacrae*, see Wetzel, *Johann Jakob Rambach in Halle und Gießen*, 9–10.

[63] Rambach, *Hypothesis de Scriptura sacra*, 22, 35, 26, respectively.

[64] Rambach, *Hypothesis de Scriptura sacra*, 29–30. Rambach also identified Leenhof as a contemporary proponent of Spinoza's philosophy and accommodation. Rambach, *Hypothesis de Scriptura sacra*, 30.

type of accommodation Rambach warned against in the first section of *Hypothesis de Scriptura sacra ad erroneos vulgi conceptus adcommodata*, and he exemplified the reasons why Rambach offered his work as a study of the different understandings of accommodation.[65]

The second section is a more constructive effort of interpreting the Bible in light of Augustinian accommodation. The bulk of the section examines various texts illustrating how Cartesian or Spinozist accommodation was misapplied. Rambach did not dispute the importance of science and the continued advancement of our understanding of the natural world. For Rambach, Scripture never intended to give an exhaustive presentation of physical science, and yet, because the two share one author, they never contradict each other.[66] Where the Bible described physical matters in a fashion that appeared to contradict science, Rambach found harmony in a phenomenological description.[67] He argued that everything the Bible affirmed, including scientific matters, was entirely accurate.[68] In an ironic twist, while scholars such as Wittichius and Spinoza thought they were improving hermeneutics, they were in fact using a simplistic, "absolute" understanding of the text without a sophisticated comprehension of exegesis.[69] By overlooking the nature of communication and language, his opponents not only failed to see how Christ and the apostles used accommodation in order to illuminate great spiritual truths through everyday topics such as fishing but also proposed a heretical interpretation through the distortion of the biblical concept of accommodation.[70]

---

[65] Also see Rambach, *Institutiones Hermeneuticae Sacrae*, 121–28.

[66] Rambach, *Hypothesis de Scriptura sacra*, 60.

[67] For more on how Rambach interpreted the Genesis description of the sun and moon as the two great lights, see Rambach, *Hypothesis de Scriptura sacra*, 52. For Rambach's interpretation of the rising and setting of the sun, see Rambach, *Hypothesis de Scriptura sacra*, 44.

[68] Rambach, *Hypothesis de Scriptura sacra*, 46.

[69] Rambach, *Hypothesis de Scriptura sacra*, 54.

[70] Rambach, *Hypothesis de Scriptura sacra*, 43–44.

Foreshadowing Later Developments in the Accommodation Debate

Though accommodation in eighteenth-century Germany had a link to seventeenth-century Dutch accommodation, the later German use of accommodation also developed in other directions. The early years of the eighteenth century served as a transitional period during which certain characteristics of seventeenth-century Dutch accommodation were lost and new distinctions of eighteenth-century accommodation were formed. However, not all these new developments continued into the second half of the eighteenth century. For instance, while Wolffian philosophy featured heavily during the early eighteenth century, only remnants of the philosophical system were associated with accommodation during the second half of the century. Instead, accommodation became coupled with new strides in the historical-critical method. Though Semler, who would become the main progenitor of Socinian accommodation, was greatly influenced by Baumgarten, who in turn was influenced by Wolffian philosophy, the Wolffian influence did not feature in Semler as prevalently as Spinozist thought did. As it was not yet suitable for scholars to openly reveal their appreciation of Spinoza even in the late eighteenth century, many refrained from speaking of their approval of the controversial figure. Nevertheless, later eighteenth-century Socinian accommodation showed more of an affiliation to Spinoza and Socinus than to Wolff.

In anticipation of these developments, we turn to several works that foreshadow what is to come in later chapters. In Rambach's work on accommodation, we have already seen how discussion of accommodation progressed into publications dedicated specifically to the doctrine. Now we turn to a much overlooked work by Christoph Friedrich Calsov, where he called attention to the recent attacks on Scripture. In 1737, he published his *Antiscripturariis, speciatim Werthemiensi*, in which he resisted the "enemies of sacred scripture."[71] He argued that these critics feigned to profess the authority of Scripture when in truth they despised the very nature of what Scripture stood for.

---

[71] Christoph Friedrich Calsov, *Antiscripturariis, speciatim Werthemiensi* (Jena: Ritter, 1737), 2.

In categorizing those who were antiscriptural, Calsov situated his opponents as either atheists or naturalists.[72] Later critics of Socinian accommodation often demonstrated the connection between specific violators of accommodation with larger ideologies, whether it was Spinoza and atheism or the rationalism and naturalism of the Enlightenment. Chief among these detractors of divine truth was Spinoza. Though Calsov did couple Cartesianism's role in the erosion of biblical authority with Spinoza, in his view it was Spinoza who played the bigger part and who continued to influence modern hermeneutics. It was Spinoza's understanding of accommodation that reduced the Bible to the "false and erroneous thinking of the common people."[73]

Toward the middle of the eighteenth century, Christian Ernst Windheim (1722–1766) published a work that foreshadowed similar works that appeared later in the accommodation debate. In his short study *De erroribus vulgi in libris sacris non probatis* (1748), Windheim contended against the understanding that accommodation of Scripture included the erroneous thinking of the common people. Spending much of his career as professor of oriental languages at Erlangen, Windheim was well aware of the significance accommodation played in the interpretation of the biblical text, especially of the Old Testament. Prior to his time at Erlangen, Windheim studied at Halle and Helmstedt, and then, upon the completion of his education, he briefly served as an associate professor of philosophy at Göttingen. It was during his time at Göttingen that he published his work on accommodation.

For Windheim, the dividing question over accommodation was whether it could be proven that biblical accommodation included error.[74] As opposed to those who saw errors in the Bible, Windheim argued that what appeared to be errors was the accommodated language of common speech. His understanding of accommodation distinguished between the "usual way of speaking" and error.[75] Just as one would speak of the rising and setting of the sun, one was not wrong to speak of the sun in phenomenological fashion. Understanding the way one spoke in an "ordinary" manner was a more natural reading of the Bible than

---

[72] Calsov, *Antiscripturariis*, 3, 4.

[73] Calsov, *Antiscripturariis*, 15. Also see Calsov, *Antiscripturariis*, 17.

[74] Christian Ernst Windheim, *De erroribus vulgi in libris sacris non probatis* (Göttingen: Vandenhoeck, 1748), 6.

[75] Windheim, *De erroribus vulgi*, 9.

attributing error to the biblical authors. Also, if accommodation included errors in the text, then other truths of Christianity would be compromised. Scripture would be placed on a bed of uncertainty, constantly unsure of whether a biblical principle or doctrine was divine revelation or an accommodated error.[76]

As already argued, Semler was a central figure in the accommodation debate. But before we can address Semler's use of the doctrine, we must examine his mentor. In the middle of Lange's conflict with Wolff, Lange accused his fellow professor at Halle, Siegmund Jacob Baumgarten (1706–1757), of using Wolffian philosophy. Baumgarten was raised in the Pietist tradition under his father, who had studied with Francke at Leipzig. After graduating with a degree in theology at Halle in 1726, he was encouraged to lecture at Halle, first in an unofficial capacity, then as a lecturer in 1732, and finally as a professor in 1734. It was during the transition from lecturer to professor that he faced the most opposition as an adherent of the Wolffian system.[77]

Baumgarten's theology and methodology reflected pietistic inclinations yet was governed by Wolffian principles.[78] David Sorkin argues that "Baumgarten built his theology around the Pietist notion that Christianity's true end was the union of man with God."[79] However, Baumgarten rejected the pietistic and orthodox shared understanding of union with God, which viewed conversion as a relatively instantaneous work of the Holy Spirit. This is not to say that the Spirit does not work within the individual before one's conversion or continue to sanctify the person afterward. Baumgarten, on the other hand, contended for a lifelong conversion experience concurrent with the process of sanctification. This extended process of conversion was dependent on the right understanding of both natural and revealed theology. Martin Schloemann

---

[76] Windheim, *De erroribus vulgi*, 14.

[77] Baumgarten lost the favor of Pietists who once supported him. During the same period, Francke's son, who had gained considerable control of the University of Halle, partnered with Halle's other leading Pietist, Lange, in opposing Baumgarten.

[78] Lutz Danneberg, "Siegmund Jacob Baumgartens Biblische Hermeneutik," in *Unzeitgemäße Hermeneutik: Verstehen und Interpretation im Denken der Aufklärung*, ed. Axel Bühler (Frankfurt: Klostermann, 1994), 107–108. Also see Martin Schloemann, *Siegmund Jacob Baumgarten: System und Geschichte in der Theologie des Überganges zum Neuprotestantismus* (Göttingen: Vandenhoeck & Ruprecht, 1974), 59–66, 66–79, for Baumgarten's relationship with Pietism and Wolffian philosophy, respectively.

[79] Sorkin, *The Religious Enlightenment*, 129.

avers that Baumgarten's understanding of union with God is essentially an extension of Wolffian mathematics to theology.[80] As Wolff's mathematical method established a logical causal sequence, so too man's union with God followed this mathematical and logical procedure.

In his hermeneutics Baumgarten emphasized the comprehensive understanding of the author. This extended beyond a study of the original languages and historical context to include the Wolffian distinction between the content of the Bible and the actual text of the Bible. But as Schloemann argues, while maintaining Wolff's bifurcation, Baumgarten also elevated the significance of history in biblical interpretation, which made the subject matter of Scripture more important than the text itself. That is, rather than seeing both text and subject in unity, the subject matter of the Bible was more associated with divine revelation than the text was.[81] Hans Frei argues that Baumgarten's Wolffian distinction between the text and subject served as a transitional period in biblical hermeneutics. This shift in hermeneutics resulted in a "nontheological, general hermeneutics of the Bible" and a "reading of the Bible as well as any other book in the ordinary conceptual way and by classification of its content as well as procedure."[82] Similarly, Emanuel Hirsch describes Baumgarten's transitional hermeneutics as "faith based on the Bible to a faith based on revelation," by which he meant that "the Bible in reality was nothing more than a once given record."[83]

Baumgarten balanced his new understanding of the biblical text and Christian doctrine with the use of accommodation. Certain texts, especially passages that address nature and science, reflected the thinking of ancient Israel rather than divine truth.[84] The Spirit wrote in accommodated language, whereas the Bible used the language of appearances and misunderstanding. Due to the accommodated nature of the Bible, knowledge of the historical context became critical to the

---

[80] Sorkin, *The Religious Enlightenment*, 133. Schloemann, *Siegmund Jacob Baumgarten*, 79–95.

[81] Hans W. Frei, *The Eclipse of Biblical Narrative: A Study in Eighteenth and Nineteenth Century Hermeneutics* (New Haven, CT: Yale University Press, 1974), 89.

[82] Frei, *The Eclipse of Biblical Narrative*, 91, 99.

[83] Emanuel Hirsch, *Geschichte der neuern evangelischen Theologie* (Gütersloh: Mohn, 1951), 2:378.

[84] Siegmund Jacob Baumgarten, *Ausführlicher Vortrag der Biblischen Hermeneutik* (Halle: Johann Justinus Gebauer, 1769), 317–319.

interpretation of the Bible.[85] God "condescended" through divine inspiration according to the "common way" of thinking.[86] The significance of history within Baumgarten's hermeneutic already revealed a shift away from Wolff, and this new progression became even more actualized in Baumgarten's student. In appropriating Baumgarten, Semler emphasized the role of history in biblical interpretation while distancing himself from his teacher's use of Wolffian mathematics.

JOHANN GEORG HAMANN AND TRIUNE CONDESCENSION

Before we take a look at the accommodation debate of the second half of the eighteenth century, one final discussion is needed. Johann Georg Hamann (1730–1788) explicated his approach to accommodation in the *London Writings*, and while he published this work in 1758, the *London Writings* grew out of his personal writings immediately after his conversion and thus did not deal directly address the accommodation debate. Fortunately, these writings have been saved, providing a foundation for his later works against naturalism and rationalism. The *London Writings* not only established the foundation of Hamann's literary career but also outlined his doctrine of accommodation, which was critical to his thought. As John Betz states, "his radical intuition of divine condescension, as lyrically expressed in these writings, is the source of his profoundly anti-Gnostic sensibility, informing everything from his aesthetics (including his view of creation and language) to his late 'metacritique' of pure reason; consequently, these writings are indispensable to understanding everything he subsequently wrote."[87]

The enigmatic figure of Hamann has been condemned as incomprehensible and at the same time praised as the "forerunner of almost every theological trend of the last 150 years."[88] While neither is an accurate portrayal of Hamann, scholars continued to see his writings as a source

---

[85] Danneberg, "Siegmund Jacob Baumgartens Biblische Hermeneutik," 106. Baumgarten, *Ausführlicher Vortrag der Biblischen Hermeneutik*, 143–145.

[86] Baumgarten, *Ausführlicher Vortrag der Biblischen Hermeneutik*, 144.

[87] John R. Betz, *After Enlightenment: The Post-Secular Vision of J. G. Hamann* (Malden, MA: Wiley-Blackwell, 2009), 38.

[88] Martin Seils, *Theologische Aspekte zur gegenwärtigen Hamann-Deutung* (Göttingen: Vandenhoeck and Ruprecht, 1957), 105.

of great insight and remain puzzled by his cryptic prose.[89] Recognizing his genius, Hamann's friend Christoph Berens and Immanuel Kant (1724–1804) set out to convince Hamann of the folly of his conversion and to encourage him to return to rationalistic thinking. In a completely unexpected turn, this experience ignited within Hamann, who was originally content with living a quiet life, a lifelong passion for writing against rationalistic extremes. Beginning with his *Socratic Memorabilia* (1759), in which Hamann felt the need to reciprocate Berens's and Kant's call to conversion, he went on to write what has been called the "first and best critique of Kant" in *Metacritique of the Purism of Reason* (1784).[90]

Before Hamann initiated the first linguistic turn and coined the term *metacritique*, before Herder and Jacobi considered themselves disciples of Hamann, before Goethe called him the "brightest mind of his day" and Kierkegaard claimed him as the greatest humorist, Hamann wrote a private reflection in the wake of hitting rock bottom and finding salvation through reading the Bible.[91] These seven pieces of varying

---

[89] For some examples of modern appropriations of Hamann's thought, see the works of Oswald Bayer for Lutheran theology, John Milbank for radical orthodoxy, Hans Urs von Balthasar for Catholic theology, and John Betz for postmodern theology. Gotthold Ephraim Lessing, widely known as a polyhistorian, once noted, "I would not presume to understand Hamann in every respect; at least I would not be able to be sure whether I understood him. His writings seem to be tests of manhood for those who claim to be polyhistorians. They truly require a little knowledge of everything." Letter to Johann Gottfried Herder, January 25, 1780, in *Lessings Werke*, ed. Julius Petersen, et al. (Berlin: Bong, n.d.), 18:332.

[90] John R. Betz, "Enlightenment Revisited: Hamann as the First and Best Critic of Kant's Philosophy," *Modern Theology* 20, no. 2 (2004): 291–301. Having arranged the publication of Kant's *Critique*, Hamann was among the first, including Kant himself, to receive the completed work. He immediately wrote several versions of his critique of the volume. After sending his review to a select few and receiving many subsequent requests to publish it from scholars such as Jacobi and Herder, Hamann ultimately decided not to publish the work. He felt that such an outright criticism would betray Kant's friendship and demonstrate ungratefulness toward Kant's generosity, who had made financial contributions to his son's education.

[91] Hamann joined his friend Christoph Berens's family business and was sent to London on some venture. Though the details of his commission are unclear, we know that he was unsuccessful. Hamann remained in London for some time, compounding debt and misery. After a period of depression, he began studying the Bible, whereupon he was spiritually convicted and embraced biblical faith. When he returned to the Berens business, his employers were not disappointed in his failed mission, since the likelihood of success had always been slim, but they deeply disapproved of his conversion. This resulted in a falling out and the calling off of Hamann's engagement to Catharina Berens, Christoph's sister.

length where known collectively as the *London Writings* and were written between March and July of 1758. They centered on the study of the Bible but also included personal narrative, a commentary on hymns, and a response to Isaac Newton's understanding of prophecy. Of the various works, *Biblische Betrachtungen eines Christen* is most relevant for our study.

For Hamann, the doctrine of accommodation or condescension was a Trinitarian doctrine. He stated,

> How has God the Father humbled himself when he not only formed a lump of clay, but even enlivened it with his breath? How has God the Son humbled himself! He became a man, the most humble of men; he took the form of a servant; he became the most unfortunate of men; he was made sin for us. In the eyes of God he was the sinner of all men. How has God the Holy Spirit humbled himself when he became a historian of the smallest, the contemptible, and most insignificant events on earth in order to reveal to men in their own language, in their own history, in their own ways the counsels, the mysteries, and the ways of the Godhead?[92]

Whereas others have associated accommodation with Scripture or with Christ's condescension, Hamann saw three distinct forms of condescension. In addition to the widely recognized condescension of the second person of the Trinity in his incarnation, ministry on earth, and death on the cross, Hamann perceived divine accommodation in both Scripture and creation as well.[93]

Central to Hamann's Trinitarian doctrine of accommodation was the relationship between accommodation and the concept of God as author. He began the work with the exclamation, "God an author!—The inspiration of this book is just as great a humiliation and condescension of God as the creation of the Father and the incarnation of the Son."[94] Oswald Bayer argues that Hamann "rejects the metaphysical and theistic

---

[92] Johann Georg Hamann, *Sämtliche Werke*, ed. Josef Nadler (Vienna: Herder, 1949–57), 1:91 (henceforth abbreviated as N.

[93] As part of the *London Writings*, in *Betrachtungen über Newtons Abhandlung über die Weissagungen* Hamann described the Holy Spirit's condescension in the Bible in the language of incarnational condescension: "As Christ bore the form of a servant [Knechtsgestalt] in flesh, so too did the Spirit take on flesh through man's words." N 1:315.

[94] N 1:5.

predicate for God as 'Originator' and replaces it with the title of the actively speaking 'Author.'"[95] While "Originator" is a "limiting concept" that can be reduced to a "scheme of causality," the "transcendental-philosophical and transcendental-theological efforts" are supplanted by a "vocative" and active God who addresses "the creature through the creature."[96] By perceiving God as a Trinitarian deity, who not only is the originator of all but the author of all, Hamann established divine condescension as central to all Christian truth and revelation.[97]

Early in the *Biblische Betrachtungen* Hamann described accommodation as follows:

> God condescended as much as possible to accommodate to human inclinations and concepts, indeed, even prejudices and weaknesses. This excellent characteristic of philanthropy, of which holy Scripture is full of, is ridiculed by weak minds, who prefer human wisdom or a satisfaction of their curiosity. No wonder if they are deceived by their own belief and if the Spirit of Scripture is rejected with as much indifference, indeed, if the Spirit seems just as mute and useless as the savior did to Herod.[98]

According to Hamann, there is a limit to God's accommodation. The Holy Spirit's condescension was described "as much as possible," indicating a certain point at which it was no longer possible or beneficial. Betz couples the doctrine of accommodation with the doctrine of inerrancy to establish the parameters for each other. The two are mutually dependent in Hamann's hermeneutic.[99] Hamann proposed that divine revelation was communicated to the creature through the creature.

While Betz's proposal has much to offer, he remains ambiguous on whether Hamann's accommodation actually affirmed inerrancy. He

---

[95] Bayer, *A Contemporary in Dissent*, 60–61.

[96] Bayer, *A Contemporary in Dissent*, 61.

[97] Another aspect of Hamann's Trinitarian doctrine of accommodation is the unity of revelation. In *Kleeblatt Hellenistischer Briefe* (1762) he wrote, "It belongs to the unity of divine revelation that the Spirit of God himself, through the human pen of holy men who were led by him, lowered himself and emptied himself of his majesty, just as the Son of God did through taking upon himself the form of a servant, and as the entire creation is a work of the highest humility." N 2:171.

[98] N 1:10–11.

[99] John R. Betz, "Glory(ing) in the Humility of the Word: The Kenotic Form of Revelation in J. G. Hamann," *Letter & Spirit* 6 (2010): 170–171.

writes, "Hamann's understanding of kenosis bears a certain similarity to doctrines of accommodation that have been current in theology at least since the nineteenth century."[100] However, without mentioning the more prevalent understanding of accommodation found in the Lutheran orthodoxy and Pietism of Hamann's day, Betz associates Hamann's understanding with Charles Gore (1853–1932), an English theologian of the nineteenth century whose doctrine of accommodation differed from the Augustinian definition of accommodation.[101]

In more explicit language, Gwen Griffith Dickson denies that Hamann held to the Augustinian understanding of accommodation. Dickson writes, "The Bible, whatever the source of its inspiration, is written by human authors, and it is addressed to human beings to evoke a very 'human' and personal response. Perfection (were it even possible) would be *inappropriate* in these circumstances; indeed, such a perfection would be a 'certainly very imperfect' way for a perfect God to communicate with humanity."[102] It seems that for Dickson accommodation and inerrancy are mutually exclusive categories. This reasoning is based not on Hamann's belief but on Dickson's own understanding of accommodation and inerrancy. Though it can be argued that Hamann did not clearly define his understanding of inerrancy, such an expectation would be anachronistic, and we have seen that many who upheld Augustinian accommodation also maintained the inerrancy of the Bible. Also, Dickson mistakes Hamann's understanding of dual authorship with modern literary criticism and bypasses centuries of biblical interpretation that maintained the same understanding.[103] Whereas Dickson understands Hamann's doctrine of accommodation and human authorship as somewhat innovative, it is more contextually accurate to see it as in keeping with seventeenth and early eighteenth-century Lutheran accommodation.

Hamann's understanding of accommodation was limited to the manner in which the Holy Spirit reveals. He wrote,

---

[100] Betz, "Glory(ing) in the Humility of the Word," 162.

[101] Betz, "Glory(ing) in the Humility of the Word," 162. See Charles Gore, "The Holy Spirit and Inspiration," in *Lux Mundi: A Series of Studies in the Religion of the Incarnation* (London: John Murray, 1904).

[102] Gwen Griffith Dickson, *Johann Georg Hamann's Relational Metacriticism*, Theologische Bibliothek Töpelmann 67 (Berlin: de Gruyter, 1995), 132. Italics original.

[103] Dickson, *Relational Metacriticism*, 171.

> The Holy Spirit has become a historian of human foolishness, indeed, even sinful deeds in order to fool Achish like David. . . . The Holy Spirit is not satisfied to speak and write like a man—but as less than a man—as a foolish, raving madman—but he seems this way only in the eyes of God's enemies—he paints the doors of the gates with signs that no Achish could make any sense of, signs that one took for the handwriting of an idiot—what is more, he lets his spittle run down on his beard, to contradict and pollute himself. He has [told] the lies of an Abraham, the bloodguilt of Lot.[104]

As David humiliated himself to trick Achish, so too God humiliated himself in giving the Bible. Though perfect, the Holy Spirit became the historian of such small and sinful acts. Later in the *London Writings*, Hamann marveled at how the Holy Spirit chose to incorporate "small, contemptuous events into the history of heaven and of God."[105] Rather than presenting a philosophical manifesto, God had chosen to use such humble things as the narrative of Abraham's and Lot's sins to communicate God's truth to man.

Also, Hamann recognized a negative reaction to the accommodated nature of the Bible. Commenting on Jeremiah 32, he described the Scriptures as "discarded rags and worn-out clothes."[106] Just as the prophet was humbled in appearance, so too did the Holy Spirit condescend in the visible text of the Bible. It was no wonder that some rejected God's truth since they despised the appearance of the condescended revelation of God.[107] The Bible was rejected because its accommodated nature appeared as "mute and useless as the savior did to Herod."[108] On the one hand, Hamann thought it ridiculous to expect Moses to use "Aristotelian, Cartesian, or Newtonian concepts" or "philosophical language."[109] On the other hand, speaking against rationalism, Hamann advanced the Bible's humbleness as a testament to the rejection of gospel truth by the world. Just as the truths of Christianity were

---

[104] N 1:99.
[105] N 2:43.
[106] N 1:176. Also see N, 2:169.
[107] N 1:10.
[108] N 1:11.
[109] N 1:12.

denigrated as superstition and enthusiasm, so too the Bible was considered unworthy of great philosophical thought.

Turning to 2 Corinthians 4, Hamann argued that God's deliberate decision to use "earthen vessels" was to demonstrate his might through the "meekest and lowliest."[110] The accommodated language of the Bible was more like Jesus's "colt whereon man had never ridden, the foal of an ass, than like those proud stallions."[111] Scripture's accommodation was a "pedagogue, which leads to Christ"; "God! How did pride come into the human heart? The entire Scripture was written in a way whereby you humbled yourself in order to teach us humility."[112]

God's decision to use "the foolish, the shallow, the ignoble, to put to shame the strength and ingenuity of all profane writers" did not negate that the Scriptures were "beams of heavenly glory" but instead accentuated for Hamann the bankruptcy of naturalistic and rationalistic thinking. This camouflage or, better yet, embodiment in human word was a portrayal of the splendor of Scripture. Commenting on Psalm 6, he wrote, "The Spirit of God clothes himself in our own voices so that with wonder we see rising up out of our own stony hearts his address to us, his counsel, his wisdom."[113] Hamann described the effect of God's accommodated revelation in the Bible and the power of his truth in humble form, stating, "there is no greater creation than the transformation of human concepts and impressions into heavenly and divine mysteries; this omnipotence [transforms] human language into the thoughts of the Cherubim and Seraphim."[114] God's accommodated revelation in the Bible was a cyclical movement of the greatness of God's word transformed into the lowliness of man's word, so that the lowliness of man may be transformed to receive and inherit the greatness of God.

Though not part of Hamann's *London Writings,* a passage from his *Aesthetica in nuce* (1762) contains much of Hamann's mature hermeneutics and the development of many themes discussed in *Biblische*

---

[110] N 2:171. For further development of this thought, see *Kleeblatt Hellenistischer Briefe* in N 2:167–184. This work together with Hamann's more noted work *Aesthetica in Nuce* (1762) form a critique of Johann David Michaelis's (1717–1791) hermeneutics.

[111] N 2:171.

[112] N 1:100.

[113] N 1:151.

[114] N 1:190.

Betrachtungen. One passage from the *Aesthetica* largely summarizes our discussion to this point:

> The book of creation contains examples of universal concepts that GOD wished to reveal to the creature through the creature; the books of the covenant contain examples of secret articles that GOD wished to reveal to mankind through mankind. The unity of the author is reflected in the dialect of his works;—in all one tone of immeasurable height and depth! A proof of the most glorious majesty and of the most self-emptying! A wonder of such infinite quiet that makes GOD seem like nothing, so that as a matter of conscience, one is forced either to deny his existence or be cattle; but at the same time of such infinite power, which fills all in all, that one does not know how to save oneself from his most intimate activity![115]

Conclusion

As we move into the second half of the eighteenth century, we should take note of at least three observations. First, in this chapter we have seen how the debate over accommodation progressed from the Cartesio-Cocceian position to a Spinozist and Wolffian understanding. Though Wolff himself did not use the doctrine as extensively as others, biblical scholars developed the Wolffian system in a more thorough manner. Also, while naming Spinoza as a source of support was as unfavorable as calling oneself a Socinian, Socinian accommodation through Spinozist philosophy continued to spread in German academia. The demise of Cartesio-Cocceian accommodation reflected a common shift in the Enlightenment, as Cartesian thought was replaced by other philosophical systems, such as Wolffian philosophy and eventually Kantian criticism.

Second, we have seen how the dispute over accommodation in the Dutch Republic crossed geographical and confessional boundaries. The conversation migrated to Germany and transitioned from Reformed circles to a primarily Lutheran discussion. Though both eighteenth-century Augustinian and Socinian accommodation benefited from the seventeenth-century Dutch dispute, it was mainly the Socinian form that held a direct historical connection, specifically through its Spinozist variety.

---

[115] N 2:204.

Eighteenth-century German Augustinian accommodation developed out of post-Reformation theology. Rather than depending on Voetians, Augustinian accommodationists emphasized a trajectory from Luther through seventeenth-century Lutherans. This theological lineage was supported by the orthodox and Pietists alike. Though the two parties disagreed over much during the eighteenth century, orthodox and Pietists agreed on Augustinian accommodation. Putting aside their differences, they combatted Socinian accommodation expressed through Wolffian and Spinozist thought.

Third, in the first half of the eighteenth century, we find precursors of the accommodation debate that quickly ensued. The frequency of works dealing with accommodation would drastically increase. Dealings with the doctrine would begin to take form in full-length monographs. More scholars extended the use of accommodation beyond cosmology to matters of doctrine. Some of these elements already appeared in the early eighteenth century through the works of Rambach, Calsov, and Windheim, but they increased dramatically in the second half of the eighteenth century. So we turn now to the accommodation debate.

Bibliography

Baumgarten, Siegmund Jacob. *Ausführlicher Vortrag der Biblischen Hermeneutik.* Halle: Johann Justinus Gebauer, 1769.
———. *Auslegung des Buches Hiob.* Halle: Johann Andreas Bauer, 1740.
———. *Evangelische Glaubenslehre.* Halle: Gebauer, 1759–1760.
———. *Untersuchung Theologischer Streitigkeiten.* Halle: Gebauer, 1762–1764.
Bayer, Oswald. *A Contemporary in Dissent: Johann Georg Hamann as a Radical Enlightener.* Translated by Roy A. Harrisville and Mark C. Mattes. Grand Rapids, MI: Eerdmans, 2012.
———. *Zeitgenosse im Widerspruch: Johann Georg Hamann als radikaler Aufklärer.* Munich: Piper, 1988.
Betz, John R. *After Enlightenment: The Post-Secular Vision of J. G. Hamann.* Malden, MA: Wiley-Blackwell, 2009.
———. "Enlightenment Revisited: Hamann as the First and Best Critic of Kant's Philosophy." *Modern Theology* 20, no. 2 (2004): 291–301.
———. "Glory(ing) in the Humility of the Word: The Kenotic Form of Revelation in J. G. Hamann." *Letter & Spirit* 6 (2010): 141–179.
Bizer, Ernst. "Die reformierte Orthodoxie und der Cartesianismus." *Zeitschrift für Theologie und Kirche* 55, no. 3 (1958): 306–72.

Brecht, Martin, ed. *Geschichte des Pietismus*. 4 vols. Göttingen: Vandenhoeck & Ruprecht, 1993–2004.
Calov, Abraham. *Systema Locorum Theologicorum*. Wittenberg: Sumptibus A. Hartmann, 1655.
Calsov, Christoph Friedrich. *Antiscripturariis, speciatim Werthemiensi*. Jena: Ritter, 1737.
Conrad, Sebastian. "Enlightenment in Global History: A Historiographical Critique." *American Historical Review*, 117, no. 4 (2012): 999–1027.
Danneberg, Lutz. "Siegmund Jacob Baumgartens Biblische Hermeneutik." In *Unzeitgemäße Hermeneutik: Verstehen und Interpretation im Denken der Aufklärung*, edited by Axel Bühler, 88–157. Frankfurt: Klostermann, 1994.
Dayton, Donald W. "The Limits of Evangelicalism: The Pentecostal Tradition." In *The Variety of American Evangelicalism*, edited by Donald W. Dayton and Robert K. Johnston, 36–56. Knoxville: University of Tennessee Press, 1991.
———. "The Pietist Theological Critique of Biblical Inerrancy." In *Evangelicals and Scripture: Tradition, Authority and Hermeneutics*, edited by Vincent Bacote, Laura C. Miguélez, and Dennis L. Okholm, 76–89. Downers Grove, IL: InterVarsity Press, 2004.
———. "The Use of Scripture in the Wesleyan Tradition." In *The Use of the Bible in Theology: Evangelical Options*, edited by Robert K. Johnston, 121–136. Atlanta: John Knox, 1985.
Deyling, Salomon. *Observationum Sacrarum in qua Multa Scripturae Veteris ac Novi Testamenti Dubia Vexata Sovunutur*. Leipzig: S. H. F. Lanckisii, 1735.
Dickson, Gwen Griffith. *Johann Georg Hamann's Relational Metacriticism*. Theologische Bibliothek Töpelmann 67. Berlin: de Gruyter, 1995.
Frei, Hans W. *The Eclipse of Biblical Narrative: A Study in Eighteenth and Nineteenth Century Hermeneutics*. New Haven, CT: Yale University Press, 1974.
Friese, Hans. *Valentin Ernst Löscher*. Berlin: Evangelische Velagsanstalt, 1964.
Gay, Peter. *The Enlightenment: An Interpretation*. New York: Knopf, 1966, 1969.
Grapius, Zacharias. *Systema novissimarum controversiarum, seu theologia, recens controversa*. 4 vols. Rostock: Georg. Ludov. Fritschuum, 1719.
Grenz, Stanley J. "Nurturing the Soul, Informing the Mind: The Genesis of the Evangelical Scripture Principle." In *Evangelicals and Scripture: Tradition, Authority, and Hermeneutics*, edited by Vincent Bacote, Laura C. Miguélez, and Dennis L. Okholm, 21–41. Downers Grove, IL: InterVarsity Press, 2004.
Greschat, Martin. *Zwischen Tradition und neuem Anfang: Valentin Ernst Löscher und der Ausgang der lutherischen Orthodoxie*. Witten: Luther, 1971.
Hamann, Johann Georg. *Briefwechsel*. Edited by Walther Ziesemer and Arthur Henkel. 7 vols. Wiesbaden: Insel, 1955–1975.
———. *Sämtliche Werke*. Edited by Josef Nadler. 6 vols. Vienna: Herder, 1949–1957.

Hirsch, Emanuel. *Geschichte der neuern evangelischen Theologie: im Zusammenhang mit den allgemeinen Bewegungen des europäischen Denkens.* Gütersloh: Mohn, 1952.

Hodge, A. A. and B. B. Warfield, "Inspiration," *Presbyterian Review* 2 (1881), 225–260.

Holmgren, Fredrick. "The Pietistic Tradition and Biblical Criticism." *The Covenant Quarterly* 28 (1970): 49–59.

Israel, Jonathan. *Radical Enlightenment: Philosophy and the Making of Modernity 1650–1750.* New York: Oxford University Press, 2001.

Jaeger, Johann Wolfgang. *Historia Ecclesiastica cum Parallelismo Profanae.* 2 vols. Hamburg: Samuelis Heylii, 1709, 1717.

Kleinig, Vernon P. "Confessional Lutheranism in Eighteenth-Century Germany." *Concordia Theological Quarterly* 60, no. 1–2 (1996): 97–125.

Lange, Joachim. *Bescheidene und ausführliche Entdeckung der falschen und schädlichen Philosophie in dem Wolffianischen Systemate metaphysico.* Halle: Wäysenhauses, 1724.

———. *Modesta disquisitio novi philosophiae systematis de Deo, Mundo et homine.* Halle: Orphanotropheum, 1723.

Lee, Hoon J. "'Men of Galilee, Why Stand Gazing Up into Heaven?': Revisiting Galileo, Astronomy, and the Authority of the Bible." *Journal of the Evangelical Theological Society* 53, no. 1 (2010): 103–116.

Leibniz, Gottfried Wilhelm. *Phoranomus seu de potentia et legibus Naturae.* In *Opuscules et fragments inedits de Leibniz.* Edited by Louis Courturat. Paris: Alcan, 1903.

Leydekker, Melchior. *Der Goddelykheid en Waarheid der H. Schriften.* 2 vols. Utrecht: Ottho de Vries, 1692.

———. *Fax Veritatis, seu exercitationes ad nonnullas controversias quae hodie in Belgio potissimum moventur.* Leiden: Lugduni Batavorum, 1766.

Lindberg, Carter, ed. *The Pietist Theologians: An Introduction to Theology in the Seventeenth and Eighteenth Centuries.* Malden, MA: Blackwell, 2005.

Löscher, Valentin Ernst. *Praenotiones theologicae contra naturalistarum et fanaticorum omne genus atheos, deistas, indifferentistas, antiscripturarios.* Wittenberg: Gerdesius, 1708.

Mayes, Benjamin T. G. "The Mystical Sense of Scripture according to Johann Jacob Rambach." *Concordia Theological Quarterly* 72, no. 1 (2008): 45–70.

Olson, Roger E. "Pietism: Myths and Realities." In *The Pietist Impulse in Christianity*, edited by Christian T. Collins Winn, Gehrz Collins, Carlson Christopher, and Eric Holst, 3–16. Cambridge: James Clarke, 2012.

Poppo, Volkmar Conrad. *Spinozismus detectus, oder vernünfftige Gedanken von dem wahren Unterscheid der philosophischen und mathematischen Methode oder Lehr-Art.* Weimar: Mumbachen, 1721.

Preus, Robert D. *The Inspiration of Scripture: A Study of the Theology of the Seventeenth-Century Lutheran Dogmaticians*. Edinburgh: Oliver and Boyd, 1955.

———. *Theology of Post-Reformation Lutheranism*. 2 vols. St. Louis, MO: Concordia, 1970–1972.

Quenstedt, Johannes Andreas. *Theologia Didactico-Polemica sive Systema Theologiae*. Leipzig: Thomam Fritsch, 1702.

Rambach, Johann Jakob. *Hypothesis de Scriptura sacra ad erroneos vulgi conceptus adcommodata*. Halle: Henckel, 1729.

———. *Institutiones Hermeneuticae Sacrae, variis observationibus copiosissimisque exemplis biblicis illustratae*. Jena: Hartungius, 1723.

Rotermund, Hans Martin. *Orthodoxie und Pietismus: Valentin Ernst Löschers "Timotheus Verinus" in der Auseinandersetzung mit der Schule August Hermann Franckes*. Theologische Arbeiten 13. Berlin: Evangelische Verlagsanstalt, 1959.

Schloemann, Martin. *Siegmund Jacob Baumgarten: System und Geschichte in der Theologie des Überganges zum Neuprotestantismus*. Göttingen: Vandenhoeck & Ruprecht, 1974.

Schmidt, Johann Lorenz. *Die göttlichen Schriften vor den Zeiten des Messie Jesus*. Wertheim: Johann Georg Nehr, 1735.

Seils, Martin. *Theologische Aspekte zur gegenwärtigen Hamann-Deutung*. Göttingen: Vandenhoeck & Ruprecht, 1957.

Sorkin, David. *The Religious Enlightenment: Protestants, Jews and Catholics from London to Vienna*. Princeton, NJ: Princeton University Press, 2008.

Spaulding, Paul. *Seize the Book, Jail the Author: Johann Lorenz Schmidt and Censorship in Eighteenth-Century Germany*. West Lafayette, IN: Purdue University Press, 1998.

Stein, K. James. *Phillip Jacob Spener: Pietist Patriarch*. Chicago: Covenant, 1986.

Stoeffler, F. Ernest. *German Pietism during the Eighteenth Century*. Studies in the History of Religions 24. Leiden: Brill, 1973.

———. *The Rise of Evangelical Pietism*. Studies in the History of Religions 9. Leiden: Brill, 1965.

Suicer, Johann Caspar. *Thesaurus Ecclesiasticus*. Amsterdam: J. Henricum Wetstenium, 1682.

Wetzel, Klaus. *Johann Jakob Rambach in Halle und Gießen: Impulse für eine geistliche Ausrichtung von theologischer Arbeit und Theologiestudium*. Fundierte theologische Abhandlungen 5. Wuppertal: Verlag und Schriftenmission der Evangelischen Gesellschaft, 1987.

Windheim, Christian Ernst. *De erroribus vulgi in libris sacris non probatis*. Göttingen: Vandenhoeck, 1748.

Wolff, Christian. *Philosophia rationalis*. Leipzig: Rengeriana, 1728.

Woodbridge, John D. *Biblical Authority: A Critique of the Rogers/McKim Proposal*. Grand Rapids, MI: Zondervan, 1982.

Yeager, Jonathan. *Enlightened Evangelicalism: The Life and Thought of John Erskine*. Oxford: Oxford University Press, 2011.

CHAPTER 4

The Beginning of the Accommodation Debate, 1761–1789

As we enter into the years of the accommodation debate, we quickly see the changing nature of the discussion from the formative stages leading up to the debate. This progression is not a break from either the Dutch or the early Enlightenment disputes. Both stages are critical to the accommodation debate of 1761–1835. The two-party line continued from the Dutch disputes, into the German Enlightenment, and existed throughout the accommodation debate.

Nevertheless, there are significant differences between the accommodation debate and these earlier stages. First, a much larger number of works dealt directly with the doctrine, an increase that also represented a wider variety of participants. Second, whereas previous works used the doctrine for a broader objective, the volumes from this time tended to treat accommodation as the main focus. With monographs dedicated specifically to the doctrine, the level of dialogue developed further than in preceding periods, exploring in great depth the implications of accommodation for hermeneutics and theology. Third, these works appeared in a concentrated period, more often than not, in direct response to each other. The progression of the debate generated work after work in quick succession, resulting in numerous publications within the same year.

To preserve the historical development of the accommodation debate, I have arranged the chapter divisions chronologically rather than thematically. In this chapter, we will begin with the first phase of the debate from 1761 to 1789. While the latter date may seem arbitrary, it provides a break before the subsequent flurry of works published in the 1790s.

In the following chapter, we will see that there is good reason to group them together as the middle phase of the debate. The final phase began in 1800 and continued into the 1830s.

Within the period of the present chapter, we will explore the accommodation debate by seeing how the doctrine was used to address various issues in the monographs. In addition, we will examine other literature such as theological lexicons. Two phenomena within the eighteenth century feature heavily in our discussion, specifically rationalism and historical criticism. We will see how these movements combined with Socinian accommodation. However, it will also be argued that rationalism was not the defining character of Enlightenment theology and that the historical criticism of scholars such as Semler was not the only historical approach to the Bible. Finally, we will assess the central question of the debate, namely, to what extent did Jesus and the apostles use accommodation in their teaching?

HERMENEUTICS, THEOLOGY, AND ACCOMMODATION

Liberal theology has often been associated with the historical criticism of the eighteenth century.[1] Gottfried Hornig, who attempted to bridge Semler's hermeneutics with Luther, argued that as father of historical criticism, Semler was pivotal not only to the interpretive method but also to modern liberal theology.[2] For Hornig, hermeneutics and historical criticism were the central factors in developing liberal theology. On the other hand, emphasizing the doctrinal and philosophical roots of liberal theology, Gary Dorrien contends that Kant's system of criticism implemented the needed changes in theology and then subsequently in hermeneutics for liberal theology to develop.[3] Both positions are defended by scholars and by no means prove to be mutually exclusive. The accommodation debate adds an additional layer of intricacy when recognizing

---

[1] Jonathan Israel has built a case for the origin of historical criticism and liberal theology in the previous century through the scholarship of Spinoza. See Jonathan Israel, *Radical Enlightenment: Philosophy and the Making of Modernity 1650–1750* (New York: Oxford University Press, 2001).

[2] See Gottfried Hornig, *Die Anfänge der historisch-kritischen Theologie* (Göttingen: Vandenhoeck & Ruprecht, 1961).

[3] Gary J. Dorrien, *Kantian Reason and Hegelian Spirit: The Idealistic Logic of Modern Theology* (Malden, MA: Wiley-Blackwell, 2012).

the importance of Socinian accommodation to the rise of both historical criticism and liberal theology. It is not simply a matter of whether hermeneutics first influenced theology or vice versa.

We begin this chapter with two case studies of how one's understanding of accommodation can greatly impact larger issues such as hermeneutics and theology. Due to the direct correlation between accommodation and biblical authority, the implications of accommodation extend beyond specific doctrines such as inerrancy. Accommodationists have used the doctrine in formative ways to define their theological and exegetical system.

Johann August Ernesti

As our first case study, how are we to understand Johann August Ernesti's (1707–1781) grammatical method of interpretation in conjunction with his understanding of accommodation? Emanuel Hirsch has typified Ernesti's hermeneutics as "purely profane-scientific biblical exegesis."[4] Fostering a rationalistic approach to the Bible, Ernesti and Semler are often coupled as the progenitors of higher criticism. On the other hand, John H. Sailhamer argues that to align Ernesti with what Sailhamer identifies as ill-advised strands of higher criticism would be to reflect modern hermeneutics and not Ernesti's grammatical position.[5] For Sailhamer, Ernesti stood as an example for evangelical hermeneutics, as a grammatical approach that combined Enlightenment thinking with philology and lower criticism. These two vastly different understandings of Ernesti may be hard to harmonize, but I suggest that by deciphering his stance on accommodation, we gain a better grasp of Ernesti's hermeneutics.

Ernesti studied at Wittenberg and Leipzig, staying in Leipzig to serve in various capacities until 1759, when he received a position in theology at the university. During his time at Leipzig, Ernesti gained a reputation as the leading biblical scholar at the university, renowned for his use

---

[4] Emanuel Hirsch, *Geschichte der neuern evangelischen Theologie: im Zusammenhang mit den allgemeinen Bewegungen des europäischen Denkens* (Gütersloh: Mohn, 1952), 4:11.

[5] John H. Sailhamer, *The Meaning of the Pentateuch: Revelation, Composition, and Interpretation* (Downers Grove, IL: IVP Academic, 2009), 100–148. Also see John H. Sailhamer, "Johann August Ernesti: The Role of History in Biblical Interpretation," *JETS* 44, no. 2 (2001): 193–206.

of philology. Among his long list of students were Christoph Friedrich von Ammon (1766–1850), Wilhelm Abraham Teller (1734–1804), and Johann August Heinrich Tittmann (1773–1831), all of whom played roles in the accommodation debate. Karl Friedrich Bahrdt (1741–1792), a student of Christian August Crusius (1717–1775), once remarked that the brightest students at Leipzig studied under Ernesti, while the less gifted chose Crusius.

Though showing evidence of Wolffian influence, Ernesti rejected Baumgarten's distinction between the subject or content of the Bible and the text of the Bible. At the same time, as John Sandys-Wunsch states, "Ernesti's approach to the Bible and how to interpret it was conditioned by his negative reaction to the growing esteem given to the new philosophy where it was thought possible to combine the certainty of mathematics with the usefulness of moral suasion and reasonable behavior."[6] Against Baumgarten's Wolffian hermeneutics and certain trends of hermeneutics found in pietistic exegesis, Ernesti sought to develop hermeneutics that mirrored the study of ancient texts characteristic of his day.[7] As argued in the *Institvtio Interpretis Novi Testamenti* (1761), this meant that the biblical text had no other meaning than the grammatical-historical reading.[8] The literal sense was the grammatical sense, which was also the historical sense, summed up by what Ernesti meant when he used the term *usus loquendi*. Utilizing a philological approach, Ernesti found the meaning of a passage in the *res* or *thing* of the text. The words of the text provided the meaning of the *thing*, and the grammatical and historical background provided the meaning of the words.

The question remains, how are we to understand Ernesti's grammatical hermeneutic in relation to the greater implications of his hermeneutic for doctrines such as biblical authority? As I have stated, it seems that Ernesti's position on accommodation addresses this very dilemma. We begin with his concession that there were limits to the method of interpretation he wished to establish. With the introduction of "novel

---

[6] John Sandys-Wunsch, "Early Old Testament Critics on the Continent," in *Hebrew Bible / Old Testament: The History of Its Interpretation*, vol. 2, *From the Renaissance to the Enlightenment*, ed. Magne Saebø (Göttingen: Vandenhoeck and Ruprecht, 2008), 977.

[7] Johann August Ernesti, *Institvtio Interpretis Novi Testamenti* (Leipzig: Weidmanni, 1761), 11.

[8] Ernesti, *Institvtio Interpretis Novi Testamenti*, 11.

concepts" in the Bible, "new words and phrases" were inserted into the text.[9] In other words, due to the mistaken understanding of the nation of Israel, certain concepts and ideas described in the Bible resulted from accommodation to these false views. While Ernesti's statement is only a brief remark, it has great consequences for how to understand his hermeneutics. Ernesti made it clear that he was not addressing figurative or allegorical texts.[10] Nor was this innovation a result of the ingenuity of the biblical writers, for they lacked the cognitive skills required for such an undertaking. Rather, these accommodations were "supernaturally communicated" to the biblical authors. Ernesti included subjects such as demon possession and miracles within this accommodation. However, Ernesti did not explain his statement, leaving the relationship between accommodation and matters such as demon possession and miracles ambiguous. It seems that August Tholuck (1799–1877) was correct in associating Ernesti with Semler, Teller, and Griesbach.[11]

While Sailhamer might be correct in attempting to separate Semler's historical method from Ernesti's, their differences are not as drastic as Sailhamer proposes. Sailhamer's distinction between Ernesti's philological approach, mostly adhering to a lower criticism, and Semler's hermeneutics, representative of modern higher criticism, was not one that Ernesti's students held as rigidly. More importantly, Ernesti's understanding of accommodation appears more similar than dissimilar to Semler's. Hence, Lutz Danneberg is quite accurate when tracing the Socinian definition from Ernesti to Friedrich Schleiermacher (1768–1834).[12] This is not to say that evangelical scholarship cannot borrow from Ernesti's hermeneutics, as Sailhamer contends, but rather, it shows

---

[9] Ernesti, *Institvtio Interpretis Novi Testamenti*, 47–48. The 1765 edition added the word "accommodata" for greater emphasis. *Institvtio Interpretis Novi Testamenti* (Leipzig: Weidmanni, 1765), 51–52.

[10] Earlier in the work, Ernesti briefly mentioned the relationship between allegory and accommodation. *Institvtio Interpretis Novi Testamenti*, 9. For his remarks on the mythical approach in conjunction with accommodation, see *Institvtio Interpretis Novi Testamenti*, 159–160.

[11] August Tholuck, *A Commentary on the Epistle to the Hebrews*, trans. James Hamilton (Edinburgh: Thomas Clark, 1842), 2:185.

[12] Lutz Danneberg, "Schleiermacher und das Ende des Akkomodationsgedankens in der *hermeneutica sacra* des 17. und 18. Jahrhunderts," in *200 Jahre "Reden über die Religion,"* ed. Ulrich Barth and Claus-Dieter Osthövener (Berlin: Walter de Gruyter, 2000), 194–201.

that Ernesti's use of accommodation puts him closer to someone like Semler than Sailhamer claims.

Gotthilf Traugott Zachariae

By deciphering Ernesti's definition of accommodation, we come to a better understanding of his hermeneutic. As we now turn to the first full-length monograph dedicated to the doctrine, we gain a greater appreciation for the impact of accommodation on one's theology. Gotthilf Traugott Zachariae (1729–1777) was the son of a Lutheran pastor in Tauchardt, Thuringia. Rather than follow his father's clerical career, Zachariae chose instead the path of an academic. He matriculated at the University of Königsberg in 1747, several years after Kant and just 1 year after Hamann. Having completed 2 years at the university, Zachariae decided to continue his education at the University of Jena.

On his way there, he detoured to Halle without ever fulfilling his plans for Jena. At Halle, Zachariae's greatest influence was Baumgarten, under whose care Zachariae's education continued to flourish. He went on to take positions in Bützow and Göttingen, eventually earning a chair at Kiel. It was during his final years at Göttingen that Zachariae completed his celebrated work, *Biblische Theologie oder Untersuchung des biblischen Grundes der vornehmsten theologischen Lehren* (1771–1775). This groundbreaking work on biblical theology was republished in several subsequent editions, the last of which included a fifth volume added by Johann Karl Volborth in 1786.

Before Zachariae's illustrious career at Göttingen, his seminal work on biblical theology, and his short time at Kiel due to his untimely death, Zachariae wrote his *Theologische Erklärung der Herablassung Gottes zu den Menschen* (1762/1763) as a recently hired professor of theology at Bützow.[13] Zachariae's exposition of accommodation in this work is in line with Baumgarten's understanding and use of the doctrine.[14] As

---

[13] Due to the limited availability of the original published work, I am working from the 1776 edition of *Theologische Erklärung der Herablassung Gottes zu den Menschen* included in Zachariae's *Philosophisch-Theologische Abhandlungen als Beilagen zur Biblischen Theologie*, ed. Christian Gottlieb Perschke (Lemgo: Meyer, 1776), 541–800.

[14] For a brief example of another of Baumgarten's student and the use of accommodation, see Johann Gottlieb Töllner, *Grundriß einer erwiesenen Hermeneutik der heiligen Schrift* (Züllichau: Waisenhaus, 1765), 103, 136.

we will see, while Semler often connected the doctrine to his teacher, Baumgarten, his use of accommodation was actually a fully developed Socinian definition in its modern use, unlike the ambiguous position of Baumgarten. This is not to say that the two are mutually exclusive. As I argued in the previous chapter, Baumgarten's position falls under the Socinian definition, though it is a slightly inconsistent version that attempted to ignore the implications of Socinian accommodation. Zachariae's understanding of the doctrine aligned him with the Socinian definition, especially as expressed by Baumgarten.[15]

Despite Zachariae's desire to uphold orthodoxy and the authority of the Bible, he perhaps unknowingly undermined his own mission. Zachariae's biblical theology attempted to order the biblical doctrines through a logical and historical structure. Although Zachariae affirmed traditional doctrines, his biblical theology became dependent on a rationalistic foundation.[16] Combining his rationalistic hermeneutic with a Baumgartenian accommodation resulted in an inconsistent adherence to Socinian accommodation and the desire to uphold the authority of the Bible. Similar to Ernesti's dilemma with his grammatical approach to the Bible, Zachariae's use of the doctrine failed to offer a coherent, orthodox biblical theology.

Hans Frei describes Zachariae as follows:

> He locates the meaning of biblical stories at once in their ostensive reference and in their ideal reference clothed in sensuous form—the narratives are simultaneously factual accounts and allegories. Not only is it exceedingly difficult to maintain both ideal and ostensive reference for the same statement, but the position obviously violates also the doctrine of single meaning to which Zachariä wants to adhere.[17]

Frei goes on to argue that Zachariae's use of accommodation "forced the narrative into a didactic, non-narrative interpretive framework."[18] However, Frei utilizes Zachariae's *Biblische Theologie* without the benefit

---

[15] For Ernesti's thoughts on Zachariae's work, see Johann August Ernesti, *Neue theologische Bibliothek: Darinnen von den neuesten theologischen Büchern und Schriften Nachricht gegeben wird*, vol 4 (Leipzig: Bernard Christoph Breitkopf, 1760-1771), 432–453.
[16] Frei, *The Eclipse of Biblical Narrative*, 168.
[17] Frei, *The Eclipse of Biblical Narrative*, 170.
[18] Frei, *The Eclipse of Biblical Narrative*, 171.

of the *Theologische Erklärung der Herablassung Gottes zu den Menschen*. This omission overlooks not only the specific work that provides Zachariae's full discussion of accommodation but more importantly the correlation between Zachariae's use of accommodation and his theology. By beginning with the *Theologische Erklärung der Herablassung Gottes zu den Menschen*, which predated his *Biblische Theologie* by a decade, we gain a better understanding of how the doctrine impacted his theology. Contributing to his mature biblical theology was his earlier use and understanding of accommodation.

Within Zachariae's definition was the common understanding that God's act of accommodation was "condescension to the despised and weak," to "their own weaknesses and oversight."[19] While accommodation may have been a necessity, it was also an act of love. In his desire to communicate not only divine truth but also knowledge of his majesty and salvation, God condescended to man with love.[20] Repeating the illustration of a teacher instructing his student or an adult communicating to a child, Zachariae expounded the need for an infinite God to condescend to the level of worldly creatures.[21] For example, the description of the sun found in the Old Testament was the accommodated language of "visual expressions" and not scientific language.[22] Such use of language could provide only an inadequate description of the divine, and this inadequate, accommodated language had to suffice for how humanity could know God.[23]

Up to this point, Zachariae's definition coincided with the historical position. However, similar to Spinoza, Zachariae also utilized the Socinian understanding as a supporting doctrine to the overall purpose of the Bible. That is, Scripture was not intended for a systematic revelation of divine truth; rather, it was for the purpose of fostering voluntary obedience and worship. This objective presented itself within the text in a particular way, which often incorporated the thinking of ancient Israel. As a means to this end, the accommodated language of the Bible contained errors and doctrinal misgivings. Zachariae juxtaposed the

---

[19] Zachariae, *Theologische Erklärung*, 544–545.

[20] Zachariae, *Theologische Erklärung*, 544, 570.

[21] Zachariae, *Theologische Erklärung*, 553–557. Zachariae also connected the role of a teacher to Jesus's instructions through parables. Zachariae, *Theologische Erklärung*, 635.

[22] Zachariae, *Theologische Erklärung*, 639.

[23] Zachariae, *Theologische Erklärung*, 626.

4 THE BEGINNING OF THE ACCOMMODATION DEBATE, 1761–1789

objective of obedience against the Bible's authority to give the illusion that Socinian accommodation was the only form of accommodation that could exist with Scripture's purpose of salvation.[24]

According to Zachariae, the practice of accommodation to error was a necessity; otherwise, man would not be able to understand divine things.[25] This necessity carried over not only into *how* God communicated but also into *what* he communicated. Addressing the use of anthropomorphic language when describing God, Zachariae justified such terminology based on the facilitation of communicating truth through the erroneous concepts of common man.[26] The Israelites were allowed to continue in their misunderstanding of God's characteristics because through these errors God's true being was revealed. Zachariae also contended that the similarity of Jewish Old Testament laws to those of their neighbors was no coincidence; God accommodated to ancient Israel by incorporating laws and principles with which they were already familiar. These laws were original to neither God nor Israel but were pasted into the Bible from previous cultures. God had to establish within them his teaching, which would benefit from the preexisting ideas but would also show to be true long after the folly of Levitical laws was revealed.[27]

However, Zachariae argued, such use of accommodation did not violate God's perfection or cause any sort of "internal change" within God.[28] The accommodation described by Zachariae was not an active deception on the part of God but a passive omission of truth.[29] For instance, though any divine statement or promise is guaranteed truth, God chose to use oaths and covenants for the sake of man. In his interactions with Abraham, God struck a covenant out of consideration for Abraham's expectations—the use of a covenant reassured Abraham.[30]

---

[24] Zachariae, *Theologische Erklärung*, 609, 616, 630.
[25] Zachariae, *Theologische Erklärung*, 577.
[26] Zachariae, *Theologische Erklärung*, 634.
[27] Zachariae, *Theologische Erklärung*, 642. Zachariae also addressed other issues such as the Old Testament practice of polygamy (670–688), divorce (688–696), Christ's incarnation and ministry on earth (764–777), doctrinal matters such as grace (777–787), and the church (787–790).
[28] Zachariae, *Theologische Erklärung*, 560.
[29] Zachariae, *Theologische Erklärung*, 560.
[30] Zachariae, *Theologische Erklärung*, 618.

Covenants did not compromise God's holiness or instruct humans to believe an error. Zachariae contended that God's perfection would not be violated by an accommodation of matter. He stated that the accommodated language of the Bible "can never be contrary to the highest perfections of God."[31] More explicitly, Zachariae claimed that "God cannot lie out of condescension to mankind."[32] Similarly to Baumgarten, for Zachariae, if the error arose from ancient Israel, whether in regards to factual accuracy or doctrinal truth, the Bible could continue to teach these matters as truth while maintaining divine integrity.

It was this Socinian understanding of accommodation that would inform Zachariae's later biblical theology. By examining Zachariae's *Theologische Erklärung der Herablassung Gottes zu den Menschen*, we gain a better perspective on the progression of Zachariae's theology and ultimately of its influence on his *Biblische Theologie*. Rather than beginning with Zachariae's well-known *Biblische Theologie* and working back to understanding his position on accommodation, by beginning with the historically prior work, we not only examine a monograph on the issue of accommodation but also witness how the doctrine became an intricate factor in Zachariae's larger theology.

WILHELM TELLER, CHRISTOPH OETINGER, AND THE BATTLE OF THE LEXICONS

The publication of theological and biblical lexicons was not a recent innovation in the second half of the eighteenth century. Lexicons had an established precedence, with many already in circulation. The distinguishing characteristic of the two lexicons we will be examining was not their innovation as lexicons but rather their use of accommodation. Wilhelm Abraham Teller (1734–1804) was born in Leipzig, where he received his education under Ernesti. Having established himself as a rationalist after several years in Helmstedt, he moved to Berlin, where he met other rationalists such as Johann Joachim Spalding (1714–1804).

---

[31] Zachariae, *Theologische Erklärung*, 578. Zachariae repeated this claim while condemning certain church fathers who maintained a contrary position. Zachariae, *Theologische Erklärung*, 587, 588.

[32] Zachariae, *Theologische Erklärung*, 590. For the issue of Christ and his lack of knowledge concerning eschatological issues, see Zachariae, *Theologische Erklärung*, 587–603.

During his time in Berlin, Teller disseminated a rationalistic theology through his regular contributions to the *Allgemeine Deutsche Bibliothek* and as the editor of the *Magazin für Prediger*.[33]

Teller's *Wörterbuch des Neuen Testaments zur Erklärung der christlichen Lehre* was first published in 1772 and would go on to a total of six editions. Since the scope of the *Wörterbuch* extends beyond our purposes, we will limit our attention to Teller's presentation of a distinctly rationalistic and Socinian definition of accommodation. Central to the objective of the *Wörterbuch* was the concept that the accommodated language of the Bible had to be translated into modern language and concepts. However, these accommodations were an issue not merely of manner but also of matter.

Though interspersed throughout his work, Teller's exposition of the doctrine is most explicit in the preface of the various editions. In explaining the foundation of the work and its subsequent methodology, Teller presented a Socinian accommodation as manifested by Semler.[34] In agreement with Semler, Teller contended that Jesus's "pictorial representations" were an accommodation to ancient Israel's expectations. The apostles portrayed Jesus as a sacrificial lamb not because Jesus served as the atonement for humankind's sins or appeased God's wrath but because the concept of sacrifice was ingrained in the minds of the Israelites.[35] The Bible was written during a time when the masses could not comprehend divine truth in a more spiritual way, hence the necessity for "condescension."[36] The Israelites' limited capacity drastically shaped not only the way the Bible was written but also the specifics of what was written. Thus, the modern reader had to recognize the accommodated passages and bring to light the deeper truths hidden within the erroneous adaptations to ancient Israel. It was the task of the modern

---

[33] For more concerning Teller's role as a rationalist in the theological discussions of the Enlightenment, see Martin Bollacher, "Wilhelm Abraham Teller: Ein Aufklärer der Theologie," in *Über den Prozess der Aufklärung in Deutschland im 18. Jahrhundert*, ed. Hans Erich Bödeker and Ulrich Hermann (Göttingen: Vandenhoeck & Ruprecht, 1987), 39–52.

[34] Wilhelm Abraham Teller, *Wörterbuch des Neuen Testaments zur Erklärung der christlichen Lehre* (Berlin: Mylius, 1780), 17. Due to the limited availability of the original published work, I am working from the 1780 edition, which includes the original preface.

[35] Teller, *Wörterbuch des Neuen Testaments*, 24–25.

[36] Teller, *Wörterbuch des Neuen Testaments*, 18.

interpreter to decipher accommodated passages and to conceptualize the Bible according to rational and universal principles, making poignant the need for a modern lexicon.

As Teller's *Wörterbuch* gained popularity, a rival lexicon was published as an orthodox alternative to the rationalism of Teller. Friedrich Christoph Oetinger's (1702–1782) *Biblisches und Emblematisches Wörterbuch* (1776) was a direct response to Teller's work, as stated in the subtitle: *dem Tellerischen Wörterbuch und Anderer falschen Schrifterklärungen entgegen gesezt.*[37] Born in Göppingen, Oetinger became familiar with pietistic thinking while at Halle and, more significantly, through Bengel in Württemberg.[38] Oetinger faulted Teller for his rationalistic theology that discredited the supernatural and implemented a heterodox hermeneutic.[39]

Again, while the full scope of Oetinger's work is beyond the aims of this chapter, we can examine how he argued for historical accommodation against the Socinian definition promoted by Teller.[40] For Oetinger, accommodation never included error within the biblical text. He freely acknowledged the particularities of Jewish notions or "Jewish word games" within the Bible. As a historically situated text, the Bible would naturally reflect the words and thoughts of the authors and the time in which they wrote. However, these accommodations never violated the

---

[37] Also see Georg Heinrich Lang, *Zur Beförderung des nützlichen Gebrauches des Wilhelm Abraham Tellerischen Wörterbuchs des neuen Testaments*, 4 vols (Anspach: Benedict Friederich Haueisen, 1778–1785). Karl Viktor Hauff, *Bemerkungen über die Lehrart Jesu mit Rücksicht auf jüdische Sprache- und Denkungsart* (Offenbach: C.L. Brede, 1788), 37–47.

[38] For more on Württemberg Pietism, see Martin Brecht, "Der württembergische Pietismus," in *Geschichte des Pietismus*, ed. Martin Brecht (Göttingen: Vandenhoeck & Ruprecht, 1995), 2:225–295; F. Ernest Stoeffler, *German Pietism during the Eighteenth Century*, Studies in the History of Religions 24 (Leiden: Brill, 1973), 88–130.

[39] For a treatment of Oetinger's philosophy, see Guntram Spindler, ed., *Glauben und Erkennen: Die Heilige Philosophie von Friedrich Christoph Oetinger* (Metzingen: Franz, 2002).

[40] For further discussion on the comparison of the two lexicons, see Gottfried Hornig, "Wilhelm Abraham Tellers *Wörterbuch* des Neuen Testaments und Friedrich Christoph Oetingers *Emblematik*," *Das achtzehnte Jahrhundert* 22(1998): 76–88; Priscilla Hayden-Roy, "Sensate Language and the Hermetic Tradition in Friedrich Christoph Oetinger's *Biblisches und Emblematisches Wörterbuch*," in *Subversive Sublimities: Undercurrents of the German Enlightenment*, ed. Eitel Timm, 58–69 (Columbia, SC: Camden House, 1992).

authority or inerrancy of the Bible.[41] Condescending to a lower level of comprehension did not necessitate that these adapted teachings used errors. Oetinger argued that Teller's use of accommodation "drains" the Bible of its supernatural characters and "distorts" the text of the Bible into something altogether different from what the biblical authors sought to communicate.[42] Teller had unnecessarily stipulated that accommodation had to include the use of error, which resulted in a misinterpretation of the Bible. What was used to communicate higher truths through a method suitable to ancient Israel was distorted into an opportunity to read contrary elements into the nature of the Bible.

HISTORICAL INTERPRETATION AND ACCOMMODATION

Semler and Socinian Accommodation

We turn now to the relationship between the doctrine of accommodation and the historical-critical approach to interpreting Scripture, and to do so, we must discuss the influential figure of Johann Salomo Semler (1725–1791). Born in Saalfeld to a pietistic family, Semler was raised to follow his father's steps into clerical ministry. Despite his upbringing, Semler had little desire for either his father's career path or his religious faith. His time at Halle only confirmed this early conviction. Coming under the close guidance of Baumgarten, Semler continued his trajectory of forfeiting Pietism and developing in rationalistic thought. Nonetheless, Semler returned to Halle as a professor, made possible by Baumgarten, after positions in Koburg and Altdorf. He quickly established himself as a leading scholar in biblical exegesis, theology, and ecclesiastical history. Even within his lifetime, Semler was hailed as a pioneer in historical-critical methods of biblical interpretation, earning the title "father of historical criticism and German rationalistic theology." His vast corpus addressed a wide range of theological and exegetical issues, of which the *Abhandlung von freier Untersuchung des Kanons* (1771–1775) received the widest readership.

---

[41] Friedrich Christoph Oetinger, *Biblisches und Emblematisches Wörterbuch, dem Tellerischen Wörterbuch und Anderer falschen Schrifterklärungen entgegen gesezt* (Hildesheim: Georg Olms, 1776), 6.

[42] Oetinger, *Biblisches und Emblematisches Wörterbuch*, 67.

Gottfried Hornig argues that Semler's historical-critical method introduced the significance of looking beyond the text of the Bible, deciphering what is truth and what is reflective of myth or pre-Christian religious ideology.[43] Semler's historical-critical method emphasized understanding the cultural and historical setting in order to provide an accurate interpretation. As a result, it suggested that how the Bible addressed issues such as "heaven, hell, realm of the dead, Satan, and demons" was not accurate but merely "pre-Christian, Eastern mythology."[44] The modern reader must discover the meaning of the passage by understanding not only the words of the text but also how the historical setting shaped and changed this meaning. Semler wrote,

> The most important thing, in short, in hermeneutical skill depends upon one's knowing the Bible's use of language properly and precisely, as well as distinguishing and representing to oneself the historical circumstances of a biblical discourse; and on one's being able to speak today of these matters in such a way as the changed times and circumstances of our fellow-men demand. ... All the rest of hermeneutics can be reduced to these two things.[45]

However, Hornig's study oversteps the evidence when he attempts to relate Semler's historical-critical approach to Luther's exegesis, a focus captured by his subtitle, *Johann Salomo Semlers Schriftverständnis und seine Stellung zu Luther*. But as Frei shows, Luther's approach differed in that Luther's guiding principle was found within the Bible while Semler looked to extrabiblical sources.[46] Luther posited the authority of the Bible within itself as God's revelation while Semler challenged the Bible's authority with historical sources.

As stated previously, Semler has long been deemed the prime promoter of Socinian accommodation by both historical and Socinian accommodationists. This was just as true for eighteenth-century figures

---

[43] Gottfried Hornig, *Die Anfänge der historisch-kritischen Theologie* (Göttingen: Vandenhoeck & Ruprecht, 1961), 225.

[44] Johann Salomo Semler, *Vorbereitung zur Theologischen Hermeneutik* (Halle in Magdeburg: Hemmerde, 1760), 1:235.

[45] Semler, *Vorbereitung zur Theologischen Hermeneutik*, 160. Quoted in *The Eclipse of Biblical Narrative*, 247.

[46] Frei, *The Eclipse of Biblical Narrative*, 111.

involved in the accommodation debate as it is for modern scholars such as Hornig.[47] So Hornig argues that as the father of historical criticism, Semler used the doctrine of accommodation as a central component to his hermeneutics.[48] Neither Hornig nor Semler claims that his use of the doctrine was original to him. On the contrary, Hornig shows how Semler acknowledged earlier practices of accommodation by the patristic fathers, seventeenth-century Lutherans, and Spinoza. Like Spinoza, Semler contended that the historical elements within the text represented the erroneous concepts of ancient Israel.[49]

In addition to these influences, Hornig contends that Baumgarten was the most significant influence on Semler's approach to the doctrine. He argues that one can see the early influence of Baumgarten's accommodation on what would become Semler's mature thought in the edited version of his teacher's *Untersuchung Theologischer Streitigkeiten* (1762–1764).[50] However, while drawing attention to the historical association between Semler and Baumgarten, Hornig proposes that Semler actually broke from Baumgarten's accommodation. Semler's use of the doctrine departed from his teacher in that Semler limited the Bible's authority to salvific issues only. I contend that this is less of a departure and more of a progression. We have seen how Baumgarten used a Socinian definition of accommodation but attempted to avoid acknowledging the logical conclusion that the Bible contains errors in science and doctrine. Baumgarten wanted to hold in balance an accommodation to error with the Bible's full authority. Both scholars employed a Socinian definition; however, Baumgarten was simply less forthcoming about the implications the doctrine had on the Bible's inerrancy and authority. In contrast, rather than attempting to maintain an inconsistent position, Semler applied the same Socinian accommodation not only

---

[47] Hornig, *Die Anfänge der historisch-kritischen Theologie*, 212. Lutz Dannenberg argues the same in "Schleiermacher und das Ende des Akkommodationsgedankens in der hermeneutica sacra des 17. Und 18. Jahrhunderts," in *200 Jahre "Reden über die Religion": Akten des 1. Internationalen Kongresses der Schleiermacher-Gesellschaft*, ed. Ulrich Barth and Claus-Dieter Osthövener, Schleiermacher-Archiv 19 (Berlin: de Gruyter, 2000), 199.

[48] Albert Schweitzer argues that the doctrine of accommodation is the dividing point between Semler and Reimarus. Albert Schweitzer, *The Quest for the Historical Jesus*, trans. by W. Montgomery (London: Adam and Charles Black, 1910), 26.

[49] Semler, *Vorbereitung zur Theologischen Hermencutik*, 224. Dannenberg, "Schleiermacher und das Ende des Akkommodationsgedankens," 199.

[50] Hornig, *Die Anfänge der historisch-kritischen Theologie*, 217.

to natural science but also to doctrine, fully acknowledging the compromises on biblical inerrancy and authority that accompanied Socinian accommodation. Semler used the same definition as his teacher but more consistently acknowledged the consequences that accommodation to error had on biblical authority.

Hornig's distinction between Semler and previous Socinian accommodationists is further weakened by Semler's familiarity with Cartesio-Cocceian accommodation. Semler published German editions of both Meyer's *Philosophia S. Scripturae Interpres* and Bekker's *Die Betoverde Weereld*, acquainting himself well with Cartesio-Cocceian accommodation. Furthering the historical connection between Semler's accommodation and Socinian accommodation is Semler's well-established familiarity with Spinoza's *Tractatus Theologico-Politicus*. In addition to translating seventeenth-century Dutch sources, Semler also translated Hugh Farmer's (1714–1787) *An Essay on the Demoniacs of the New Testament* (1775) only 1 year after it was published. Farmer's argument centered on the use of Socinian accommodation to interpret New Testament demon possession as the erroneous conception of ancient Israel and their ignorance of mental illness. While Semler and Farmer differed on the existence of miracles—Farmer was more open to the supernatural described in the Bible—they both agreed on the nonexistence of demons and the accommodated language that accompanied this erroneous understanding. These historical connections were often noted by fellow accommodationists.[51]

Not only does Hornig attempt to distance Semler's use of accommodation from preceding Socinian accommodationists, but he also argues that Semler resolved the inconsistencies within seventeenth-century Lutheran accommodation. In further distinguishing Semler's use from previous practices, Hornig contends that Semler essentially proved seventeenth-century orthodox Lutheran accommodation to be false. However, as shown in the previous chapter, seventeenth-century Lutherans aligned the doctrine of accommodation with verbal inspiration, maintaining an inerrant Bible—a correlation affirmed by Robert Preus and Hornig alike. Yet Preus and Hornig differ in their

---

[51] See Johann August Ernesti, *Neue theologische Bibliothek: darinnen von den neuesten theologischen Büchern und Schriften Nachricht gegeben wird*, vol. 3. (Leipzig: Bernard Christoph Breitkopf. 1760–1771), 778–808. Friedrich Samuel Bock, *Lehrbuch für die neueste Polemik* (Halle: Johann Jacob Gebauer, 1782), 53–55.

understanding of the merits of verbal inspiration. While Preus contends that inerrancy and accommodation were held in unison as mutual supports for each doctrine, Hornig claims that inerrancy led to the downfall of seventeenth-century Lutheran accommodation.

An inerrant Bible and its authority in all areas could not hold up against the new methods of biblical interpretation. With the rise of historical criticism and inroads in philology, verbal inspiration was shown to be an antiquated position by eighteenth-century scholars such as Semler. In equating verbal inspiration with the Holy Spirit as the single author of Scripture, Hornig argues that new critical methods proved the human element in the Bible and thus excluded the possibility of verbal inspiration. In this telling of the story, the demise of verbal inspiration was followed by the dissolution of seventeenth-century historical accommodation, which was so closely related to it. However, as the accommodation debate shows, while Semler's promotion of Socinian accommodation became quite prolific, it hardly brought an end to historical accommodation. As seen throughout the entirety of the debate and its nineteenth-century resolution, historical accommodation remained a viable option in the development of hermeneutics.

Before we examine the objections of historical accommodationists, we should note that not all critics of Semler associated his accommodation with Socinus. Johann David Michaelis (1717–1791) credited Semler with reviving the doctrine that originated with the church fathers.[52] Michaelis began his discussion of accommodation in conjunction with his treatment of the New Testament use of the Old Testament. The question he asked was whether the New Testament author was borrowing from the Old for his own purposes or was using the Old Testament text as proof of a fulfilled prophecy. According to Michaelis, just as a lawyer would quote the *corpus juris* or a teacher the classics, so we should not be surprised to see New Testament authors quote the Old, especially drawing from the Septuagint.[53] As writers quoted classical authors by using the phrase "to speak in the words of Cicero" or "as Cicero expresses it," so too New Testament authors used phrases such as "as is

---

[52] Johann David Michaelis, *Einleitung in die göttlichen Schriften des Neuen Bundes*, vol. 1/1 (Göttingen: Vandenhoek & Ruprecht, 1788), 228.

[53] Michaelis, *Einleitung*, 223–224.

spoken by the prophet Isaiah" to indicate a borrowing of words for their own purpose.[54]

Michaelis claimed that Semler's use of accommodation forced such passages into an irreconcilable juxtaposition of error and divine inspiration.[55] Similar to Baumgarten, Michaelis attempted to uphold biblical authority while maintaining that the Bible included accommodations to error. However, rather than understanding Jesus's words as truth statements, Michaelis identified Jesus's use of Isaiah in Matthew 15:7–9 as an accommodation to his audience.[56] While Michaelis did not apply the doctrine of accommodation to all New Testament passages that cited the Old Testament as a fulfillment of prophecy, he did apply it to passages like Matthew 15:7–9 and John 13:18.[57] Despite his objection to Semler, Michaelis's position distanced him from the historical position. Aligning himself with the very one he criticized, Michaelis defined accommodation as a "borrowing of an image," which often included error, in order to more effectively represent it.[58]

Proponents of Historical Accommodation

While Semler's historical method produced interpretations that explained away supernatural elements within the Bible, Gottlob Christian Storr (1746–1805) used his historical method to give weight to the supernatural. Born in Stuttgart, Storr spent his early years in his birth city and in Denkendorf before entering the University of Tübingen in 1766, where he studied theology. After several years of travel, Storr returned to Tübingen as a lecturer and remained there, going on to serve as professor of philosophy and eventually professor of theology. During his illustrious career at Tübingen, Storr established himself as a leading supernaturalist and founder of the Ältere Tübinger Schule, an orthodox consortium combatting rationalistic theology. Of his numerous students, Johann Friedrich Flatt (1759–1821) and Friedrich Gottlieb Süsskind (1767–1829) are perhaps his best known.

---

[54] Michaelis, *Einleitung*, 226.
[55] Michaelis, *Einleitung*, 228.
[56] Michaelis, *Einleitung*, 237.
[57] Michaelis, *Einleitung*, 239.
[58] Michaelis, *Einleitung*, 237.

Storr addressed general hermeneutical issues in other works but devoted his *De sensu historico* (1778) to the topic of accommodation. Storr perceived Semler's historical method as a prime example of rationalistic hermeneutics and the violation of the Bible's authority. He argued that Semler's form of accommodation distorted the text to include supposed error.[59] Semler justified the existence of errors within the biblical text as a pedagogical necessity. As the biblical authors sought to bring their audience and readers from "childhood to adulthood," the inclusion of erroneous thought patterns, conceptions, and ideology was a necessary means to a greater end.[60] Hence, Semler's definition of accommodation resulted in false opinion and reasoning within the biblical text.[61] This is not to suggest that Storr negated all forms of accommodation; rather, he adhered to a historical and orthodox use of the doctrine.[62]

In agreement with Semler, Storr acknowledged the importance of understanding the historical circumstances of the narrative and the particularities of the biblical text.[63] All language is economical and related to its historical context. In understanding the text's context, the interpreter can gain a better understanding of the linguistic and historical issues in order to approach the surer meaning of the text. This is what Storr intended through his historical interpretation of the Bible. Semler's approach, however, elevated the historical nature of the Bible over its authority. Hence, heterodox accommodation imputed errors into the text that were not actually there.[64] Semler's use of Socinian accommodation made it impossible to decipher between truth and what was merely an accommodation to error.[65]

Storr's hermeneutic was not merely a literalistic reading of the Bible. Whereas a literalistic reading of Acts 27:27 would presume that the

---

[59] Gottlob Christian Storr, *De sensu historico*, in *Opuscula Academica ad Interpretationem Librorum Sacrorum Pertinentia* (Tubingen: Joannis Georgii Cottae, 1796), 1:8–9, 19–27.
[60] Hauff affirmed Storr's position. Hauff, *Bemerkungen über die Lehrart Jesu*, 101, 231.
[61] Storr, *De sensu historico*, 20.
[62] Storr, *De sensu historico*, 6–8.
[63] Storr, *De sensu historico*, 8.
[64] Storr, *De sensu historico*, 16–19.
[65] See Hauff, *Bemerkungen über die Lehrart Jesu*, 97–98, 114–117. In this passage, Hauff argued similarly to Storr against Semler's understanding of demonology. For a review of the work see, Johann Gottfried Eichhorn, *Allgemeine Bibliothek der biblischen Litteratur* (Leipzig: Weidmann, 1787–1801), vol. 4, 306–316.

sailors thought that land was actually moving and approaching the boat, Storr argued that such phenomenological language was merely a colloquial way of communicating.[66] The sailors did not actually believe that the land was moving toward the boat, but rather, the language they used was a way to say that they were approaching the land. In instances where the demon possessed were called "lunatics," as in Matthew 4:24, this did not imply that Jesus and the apostles thought that their condition was related to the moon, an argument later repeated by Karl Viktor Hauff.[67] Rather, they used the colloquial term for its commonality and not because they believed in such erroneous superstition.

Storr could agree with Semler and Farmer that the possibility of diagnosing mental illness with demon possession during New Testament times was very probable. However, Storr contended that when the Bible spoke of someone as being possessed, then the reader should accept that the person was actually taken over by an evil spirit. Storr was not being simplistic or literalistic when taking the Bible at face value. Nor was he ignoring historical conditions. Rather, Storr was affirming Jesus and the biblical authors as truthful. In a time when little was known of mental illness, it would be safe to assume that such cases of mental illness could easily be confused for demon possession. However, the real possibility of misdiagnosis did not exclude the equally possible case of demon possession. Whereas Semler's use of Socinian accommodation eliminated demon possession altogether, the historical position as Storr continued it acknowledged both the historical and supernatural context of the Bible. So when Jesus commanded the demons to exit a human body and allowed them to enter a herd of swine, this was, for Storr, a literal demon possession and not a case of mental illness.[68] In other words, Storr freely admitted that ancient Israelites could mistakenly identify mental illness as demon possession, but when Jesus, an apostle, or a biblical author claimed someone was possessed by a demon, then

---

[66] Storr, *De sensu historico*, 51–52.

[67] Hauff, *Bemerkungen über die Lehrart Jesu*, 306–307.

[68] Storr, *De sensu historico*, 53–55. Swiss theologian Johann Jakob Hess (1741–1828) also made reference to the relationship between accommodation, demoniacs, and the herd of swine in *Geschichte der drey letzten Lebensjahre Jesu* (Zurich: Orell, Geßner, Füeßlin, 1773), 1:343–346. Though originally published in 1768, due to the limited availability of the original work, I have used this later edition.

that individual was actually possessed and not merely ill. There was no historical or contextual reason to assume otherwise.

Storr also shared with Semler the understanding that accommodation was a common tool for the pedagogical objectives of the biblical authors. Jesus's use of parables often featured accommodated language and concepts as a "mode" for communicating truth. Storr held that his accommodation of manner and not matter never violated biblical inerrancy but rather stood in line with the notion that Scripture contained only true ideas.[69] He extended this argument to passages that included expressions originating from sources other than divine revelation, such as that found in Titus 1:13. Storr explained the juxtaposition of accommodation and biblical inerrancy by stipulating that accommodated passages were never "colored by Judaism" but were simply the "true opinions of the sacred teachers."[70] Pedagogy did not necessitate error, and true accommodation did not compromise the integrity of divine revelation.

Included within the historical definition of accommodation was the concept that accommodation carried a passive element. For instance, in condescending to their audience, Jesus and the apostles often used "milk" rather than "solid food" by not immediately opposing all errors.[71] Whereas Semler would see this admission as an indication of error, Storr was quick to defend the Bible's authority and inerrancy. Matters of "milk" did not necessitate error by any means.[72] Also, where people in biblical narratives held to erroneous ideas, Storr emphasized the need to distinguish between the author and protagonist not opposing error and actually promoting and instructing the error.[73] For instance, Jesus never corrected the Samaritan woman's acceptance of only the Pentateuch as sacred Scripture.[74] Nor did Paul feel the need to correct every Jewish objection, as in the case of Timothy's circumcision.[75] However, in both cases, neither Jesus nor Paul instructed others in error.

---

[69] Storr, *De sensu historico*, 36.
[70] Storr, *De sensu historico*, 33.
[71] Storr, *De sensu historico*, 23–27.
[72] Also see Hauff, *Bemerkungen über die Lehrart Jesu*, 291.
[73] Storr, *De sensu historico*, 24–25.
[74] Storr, *De sensu historico*, 25.
[75] Storr, *De sensu historico*, 56.

We see many of Storr's ideas manifested in Carl Traugott Eifert's (1740–1787) *Untersuchung der Frage: Könnte nicht die mosaische Erzählung vom Sündenfalle buchstäblich wahr, und durch den Fall ein erbliches Verderben auf die Menschen gekommen seyn?* (1781).[76] Little is known of the Burgscheidungen-born preacher. What is clear is the similarity between the hermeneutics of Eifert and Storr. For Eifert, it was unthinkable for an omniscient God to speak untruthfully.[77] His understanding of inerrancy carried over to the teachings of Jesus and the apostles. Thus Jesus and the apostles "could never teach error" in doctrine or otherwise.[78] This is not to say that Jesus and the apostles were unmindful of their audience. On the contrary, they spoke in an accommodated manner but never included error within their teaching.[79]

As with Storr, Eifert included phenomenological language within this accommodation of manner. When the Bible referred to the rising and falling of the sun, it was speaking not in error but rather according to the colloquial description of day and night.[80] Eifert repeated the example of the demon-possessed man and the herd of swine to show the missteps of heterodox accommodation. He agreed with Farmer and Semler that demon possession could have been mistaken for mental illness. However, mirroring Storr, Eifert argued that if Jesus or the apostles explicitly identified a case of demon possession, then it was not an accommodation to Jewish misunderstanding but an actual case of demon possession.[81] The possibility of a naturalistic explanation did not exclude the supernatural interpretation.

Also in agreement with Storr, Eifert did not interpret Scripture in a literalistic fashion. He wrote, "So many of the sayings of Jesus, which, if they would be taken literally in the Jewish sense, would certainly

---

[76] For a varying interpretation of Genesis 1–3 by someone involved in the accommodation debate, see Johann Balthasar Lüderwald, *Die allegorische Erklärung der drey ersten Capitel Mosis* (Helmstädt: Johann Heinrich Kühnlin, 1781).

[77] Carl Traugott Eifert, *Untersuchung der Frage: Könnte nicht die mosaische Erzählung vom Sündenfalle buchstäblich wahr, und durch den Fall ein erbliches Verderben auf die Menschen gekommen seyn?* (Halle: Hemmerde, 1781), 193.

[78] Eifert, *Untersuchung der Frage*, 194.

[79] Eifert, *Untersuchung der Frage*, 253.

[80] Eifert, *Untersuchung der Frage*, 197.

[81] Eifert, *Untersuchung der Frage*, 244–245, 288.

give erroneous doctrines."[82] He recognized, though, that to take these sayings literalistically would distort the meaning of the text and lead one to gravely misinterpret certain passages. In acknowledging the importance of the historical context and the linguistic peculiarities of the Bible, Eifert believed that we can gain a fuller interpretation of Scripture. However, a historical interpretation does not exclude the supernatural within human history. In fact, a historical interpretation gives light to the supernatural dimension of God's work throughout biblical times and to the divine instruction contained in Scripture.

Accommodation played a critical role in the historical method Eifert proposed. Knowing that God chose to communicate through human means, the interpreter then needed a proper understanding of accommodation to aid him in interpreting the biblical language clothed in human words and concepts. Storr and Eifert demonstrated through historical accommodation not only the compatibility of human and divine words but also the fruitfulness of understanding God's approach through condescension.

ACCOMMODATION IN THE TEACHING MINISTRY OF CHRIST AND THE APOSTLES

As we have already seen, the accommodation debate centered at various times on different issues. In the seventeenth century, much of the debate encompassed matters of cosmology. While cosmology remained a concern in the eighteenth century, it no longer commanded the same level of attention. Also, while the Old Testament featured more prominently in the seventeenth century, in the eighteenth century the New Testament became the more significant battleground.[83] In this last

---

[82] Eifert, *Untersuchung der Frage*, 208.

[83] As I have argued, the accommodation debate of the eighteenth century moved from the Dutch Republic to Germany. This is not to say the Dutch failed to continue their discussion from the seventeenth century. Both Jodocus Ezn Heringa and Johann Christian Bang published on the teaching ministry of Jesus and the apostles on behalf of the Society for the Defense of the Christian Religion in 1789. It is evident that the Dutch closely followed the German debate, as these two scholars made specific mention of various German authors, including Semler, who appeared as the prime culprit of Socinian accommodation. See Jodocus Ezn Heringa, *Verhandeling, ten betooge, dat Jesus en zyn Apostelen zich doorgaans niet geschikt hebben, naar de verkeerde denkbeelden van hunne Tydgenooten* (The Hague, 1789), and Johann Christian Bang, *Verhandeling, waarin ondersogt wordt, in hoe*

section we will discuss a central issue during the eighteenth century. We began this chapter with a study of Ernesti and Zachariae as examples of how a system of hermeneutics or theology can be greatly impacted by one's position on accommodation. Now we will examine how exegetical interpretations are directly connected to either the historical or the Socinian definition of accommodation. Specifically, this section will focus on this question: to what extent did Jesus and the apostles use accommodation in their teaching ministry?[84] As Hauff contended, Jesus's teaching included a "wise condescension."[85] Naturally, a teacher is effective in his task when he adapts his lessons in a manner his audience understands. However, are there limitations to this adaption, as in using only "ordinary, simple language," or is the teacher free to draw on any possible means of instruction?[86]

Footnote 83 (continued)

verre Jesus en zyne Apostelen zich geschikt hebben naar de vatbaarheid der Jooden in het vorstellen der Christelijke leere (Amsterdam, 1789). Bang's work also appeared in Latin while Heringa's was translated into German. Jodocus Ezn Heringa, *Über die Lehrart Jesu und seiner Apostel mit Hinsicht auf die Religionsbegriffe ihrer Zeitgenossen* (Offenbach: Weiss & Brede, 1792). For Johann Gottfired Eichhorn's remarks on Heringa, see *Allgemeine Bibliothek der biblischen Litteratur* 3 (1790): 316–329. In direct opposition to Heringa and Bang, Paulus van Hemert (1756–1825) defended Socinian accommodation in *Oratio de prudenti Christi, apostolorum, atque evangelistarum consilio, sermones suos ac scripta, ad captum atque intellectum vulgi, quantum illud fieri potuit, accommodantium* (Amsterdam: Schalekamp, 1790). Known for his propagation of Kantian philosophy in the Netherlands, van Hemert argued similarly to Kant when he advanced a rational faith that was aided by accommodations to mankind's limited capacities, especially during biblical times and in the teachings and text of the Bible. The work would be translated several years later into German. See Johann Gottfried Eichhorn, *Allgemeine Bibliothek der biblischen Litteratur* 7–8 (1787–1801):7:767–773, 8:319–327.

[84] This issue also spurred other related topics such as how to understand the relationship between Christ's and the apostles' teaching ministry and the teaching role of clergymen. For example, Georg Detharding discussed how accommodation impacted the "minister of the Word of God" in *Commentatio theologica de accommodatione verbi divini ministri ad captum vulgi* (Göttingen: Dieterich, 1782). Rather than emphasizing hermeneutical issues, Detharding examined the similarities of divine accommodation and the clergy's teaching.

[85] Hauff, *Bemerkungen über die Lehrart Jesu*, 3.

[86] Hauff, *Bemerkungen über die Lehrart Jesu*, 6.

Accommodation and the New Testament Use of the Old Testament

Encompassed within this question about accommodation in New Testament teaching is the issue of what modern readers are to make of the New Testament use of the Old Testament. We briefly addressed the issue when discussing how Michaelis treated it, but the topic would receive greater consideration later in the debate. At times, readers of the New Testament could become perplexed by the way the authors seemed to distort the meaning of the Old Testament. It could appear that while the Old Testament authors had a clear intent in their words, New Testament authors procured the text for their own purposes. This seemingly arbitrary use of the Old Testament was not limited to only the apostles but was followed by Jesus himself.

Though discussion of New Testament accommodation was most spirited during the 1780s, it was anticipated as early as the 1760s by Samuel Friedrich Unselt (1742–1790).[87] Unselt was born in Gdansk and went on to complete his studies at Leipzig. Returning to his native city, Unselt began his career as a rector at St. John's and shortly after went on to serve at St. Mary's. He left his role as rector to serve as a pastor in Praust. His final position was in Güttland. While little is known about Unselt, we do have his *Dissertatio Philologica De locorum Veteris Testamenti in Novo accommodatione orthodoxa* (1766), written during his time at Leipzig.

Central to Unselt's understanding of the Old Testament in the New was the doctrine of accommodation. After providing a brief summary of "orthodox" or historical accommodation, Unselt addressed what he called "heterodox" accommodation.[88] Among the promoters of such heterodoxy were Socinus and those who followed his hermeneutics. Unselt described Socinian and heterodox accommodation as "the most dangerous" to and destructive of the "divinity of our Savior" and the "truth of the Christian religion."[89] The remaining portion of the work is

---

[87] Karl Ludwig Bauer also has a short discussion of New Testament use of the Old Testament. See Karl Ludwig Bauer, *Logica Paullina, vel notatio rationis, qua utatur Paullus Apostolus in verbis adhibendis, interpretando, definiendo, enuntiando, argumentando, et methodo univers* (Halle Magdeburg: Orphanotrophei, 1774), 142–143.

[88] Samuel Fridericus Unselt, *De locorum Veteris Testamenti in Novo accommodatione orthodoxa* (Leipzig: Breitkopf, 1766), 2–9.

[89] Unselt, *De locorum Veteris Testamenti*, 7.

a discussion of 12 pairs of Scripture passages, each pair consisting of one passage from the Old Testament and one from the New.[90] Rather than taking time to refute various heterodox scholars, Unselt sought to take a more constructive approach by displaying the exegetical ramifications of orthodox accommodation.

Decades later, Georg Christoph Pisanski (1725–1790) returned to Unselt's work on the Old Testament in the New Testament to develop his own approach to the topic. Born in Johannisburg in East Prussia, Pisanski attended the University of Königsberg. Unlike Zachariae, Pisanski stayed in Königsberg much longer. Though Pisanski left the university in 1748, he remained in the city, first as an instructor at a local gymnasium and later as rector. While in this latter position, he began to lecture at the university, eventually earning an associate professorship in theology. His best-known work is his *Preußische Literärgeschichte* (1790), an impressive assessment of Prussian literary history. Pisanski is also noted for his *Antihephästion* (1776), a critique of fellow Königsberg theologian Johann August von Starck's (1741–1816) deistic *Hephästion* (1775). Pisanski explicitly referenced Unselt's work as foundational to his own, and while this may have been due to their common heritage, Pisanski nonetheless followed Unselt's historical position on accommodation.[91]

The question of how the New Testament writers used the Old Testament was again the main issue of the work. For example, how were modern readers to make sense of the use of Isaiah 22:22 in Revelation 3:7? The New Testament passage seemed to ignore the original context and intent of the Isaiah passage. Isaiah 22 addressed the condemnation of Israel. As God continued to unleash his wrath on the nation, he promised to dethrone Shebna from power and raise up Eliakim in his stead to rule in a just and godly way. However, Eliakim would also come to an end and fail to maintain a godly reign.

---

[90] The pairs of passages include Matt. 21:13 and Jer. 7:11; Luke 1:46–49 and Ps. 31:7; Luke 23:30 and Hos. 10:8; Acts 13:41 and Hab. 1:5; Rom. 2:24 and Isa. 52:5; Rom. 8:33 and Isa. 50:8, 9; Rom. 8:36 and Ps. 44:23 (Heb.; 44:22 Eng.); Rom. 11:8 and Deut. 29:4; 1 Cor. 5:13 and Deut. 13:5, 17:7, 19:19, 24:7; 1 Cor. 10:20 and Deut. 32:17; 1 Cor. 15:32 and Isa. 22:13; Heb. 13:6 and Ps. 118:6.

[91] Georg Christoph Pisanski, *Adversaria De Accommodationibus Veteris Testamenti In Novo Obviis* (Göttingen: Wedeliane, 1781), 4.

In Revelation 3 we find John's address to the church in Philadelphia. Following the format of the other addresses in Revelation, John took a moment to praise the church for its steadfast perseverance. These two passages appear to have different contexts and purposes, yet John quoted directly from Isaiah. So how are we to understand John's use of the key of David and the opening and closing of the door as symbolic of Eliakim and Christ's power? Pisanski proposed that the New Testament use of the Old Testament modeled a proper use of accommodation.[92] John in Revelation was saying that Eliakim was a historical type of Christ and that Christ was the one who completed what Shebna could not. It was more than a mere analogy or comparison but not a specific prophecy. Rather, this instance of the New Testament use of the Old Testament, which exhibited real meaning between the two, could be understood as an accommodation of the Old Testament by the New Testament author in that John. However, accommodation of this sort was based on a true connection between the two texts and was not arbitrary or merely a similarity in language or concept. In contrast to true accommodation, Pisanksi offered 2 Samuel 17:23 and Acts 1:18 or Psalm 105:18 and Acts 16:24 as examples of improper accommodation.[93] For example, while both Psalm 105:18 and Acts 16:24 spoke of someone's feet being fastened in fetters, the Acts passage showed no clear reliance on the psalm and was thus not a true accommodation.

In the New Testament use of the Old, Pisanski was also careful to differentiate between prophecy and accommodation. Prophecy had the element of a direct verbal prediction that would come to pass. Jesus's quoting of Malachi 3:1 in Matthew 11:10 concerning John the Baptist as the one to come and prepare the way was an example of fulfilled prophecy.[94] Isaiah's prediction of the rise and fall of Eliakim was also a prophecy. But Eliakim as a foreshadow of Christ's rule was an accommodation on John's part. As we will see, others would refute Pisanksi's position, claiming that true prophecy did not exist and that the fulfillment of prophecy was merely an accommodation to what was expected and not a prediction of the future.

---

[92] Pisanski, *Adversaria De Accommodationibus*, 12.
[93] Pisanski, *Adversaria De Accommodationibus*, 20, 30.
[94] Pisanski, *Adversaria De Accommodationibus*, 16–18.

While Pisanski was most concerned with exegetical matters, he did take time to address the misuse of accommodation, identifying Socinus as the originator of such misuse.[95] As seen in *Defensio Animadversionum Adversus Gabrielem Eutropium* (1618), Socinus attributed the Trinity partially to an accommodation to certain expectations of Christ. Pisanski adamantly denounced the way Socinus used accommodation to promote his anti-Trinitarian doctrine, and in the same way, Pisanski condemned scholars who denied the resurrection by calling it an accommodation to misplaced expectations of sacrifice.[96] While he did not name anyone specifically, it is easy to see how Pisanski's denouncement applied to someone like Semler.

Though Pisanski continued where Unselt had left off, others such as Johann Balthasar Lüderwald (1722–1796) departed from the historical position. Lüderwald was born in Fahrland and studied in Helmstädt, where he attended the lectures of Johann Lorenz Mosheim (1693–1755). In 1747, Lüderwald was ordained a Lutheran pastor. Apart from his work on accommodation, Lüderwald's scholarly contribution was limited to a minor role in the *Wolfenbüttel Fragments* controversy.[97]

In his *Gedanken von dem Unterscheid der Lehre und des Lehrvortrags im Christenthum in Absicht auf seine nationellen Vorzüge* (1781), Lüderwald argued for the "sensual presentation" of truth within the Bible.[98] This was apparent in the teaching of Jesus and the use of parables seen in Matthew 13:13 and Mark 4:33. Contrary to Hauff and other Augustinian accommodationists, for Lüderwald, this naturally led to the principle that Jesus appropriated the thinking of those during his time and adjusted to any existing thought or understanding.[99] Lüderwald viewed this as an admirable step that Jesus and the apostles took. By condescending to the level of their audience, they became more efficient teachers, providing the truth of salvation and not being

---

[95] Pisanski, *Adversaria De Accommodationibus*, 51.

[96] Pisanski, *Adversaria De Accommodationibus*, 38.

[97] Johann Balthasar Lüderwald, *Die Wahrheit Gewissheit der Auferstehung Jesu Christi* (Helmstädt: Kühnlin, 1778).

[98] Johann Balthasar Lüderwald, *Gedanken von dem Unterscheid der Lehre und des Lehrvortrags im Christenthum in Absicht auf seine nationellen Vorzüge* (Helmstädt: Kühnlin, 1781), 7.

[99] Hauff, *Bemerkungen über die Lehrart Jesu*, 266. Lüderwald, *Gedanken von dem Unterscheid*, 9.

hindered by needless adherence to mere accuracy. Accommodation signified the "improvement or transformation" of error, and the end result of such teaching justified the method.[100] Regardless of what erroneous concept was accommodated, it was the deeper spiritual truth that mattered most. Such an understanding of accommodation stipulated a Bible that contained many errors, which Lüderwald freely admitted.[101] However, it was necessary for God to communicate his revelation. Lüderwald compared it to the composition of metal: just as the various mineral elements do not compromise the overall integrity of the finished metal, so too the inclusion of errors in the Bible do not compromise the message of the gospel.

With innovations to the definition of accommodation also came changes in orthodox doctrines. For instance, Lüderwald altered the understanding of Jesus's atonement on the cross. The Old Testament approach to sacrifice was nothing more than an accommodation to the practices of ancient Israel.[102] God did not demand sacrifice for salvation but merely used this motif to offer salvation within a preexisting system of thought. In New Testament times, then, Jesus took on this accommodation by becoming a sacrifice for all. While God did not necessitate Jesus's death, he chose this method in order to communicate his message through the expectations of Israel. Thus, when Jesus was described as the sacrificial lamb, that did not mean readers should actually understand him as a sacrificial lamb; rather, that was merely a tool used by the apostles to describe Jesus in a way that their audience would comprehend.[103] Lüderwald's accommodation negated the authority and power of Christ's death on the cross and limited it to the possible effectiveness of a pictorial illustration.

While Pisanski differentiated between prophecy and accommodation by maintaining that prophecy resulted from a historical prediction that was fulfilled only after the initial prediction, Lüderwald made no

---

[100] Lüderwald, *Gedanken von dem Unterscheid*, 13.

[101] Lüderwald, *Gedanken von dem Unterscheid*, 17.

[102] Lüderwald, *Gedanken von dem Unterscheid*, 23. The same held true for the common Old Testament language of the fear of God. It was never God's desire for man to fear him. Ancient Israelites took it upon themselves to project this expectation on God, perhaps by following the practices of neighboring pagan religions. Hence the *fear of God* motif was used as an accommodation to erroneous expectations. *Gedanken von dem Unterscheid*, 32.

[103] Lüderwald, *Gedanken von dem Unterscheid*, 27, 28.

such distinction. Instead, Lüderwald applied the doctrine of accommodation to New Testament statements such as the one linking John the Baptist with the new Elijah in Matthew 11. When Jesus identified John as the fulfillment of Elijah, he did it because the Jews expected it and not because it was an actual prediction. While Pisanski excluded any sort of accommodation in John the Baptist's role as the new Elijah, Lüderwald stated that Jesus's identification of John the Baptist was an accommodation to the false expectations of his audience.[104]

Related to Lüderwald's use of accommodation was the concept of progressive revelation. For Lüderwald, the Old Testament authors used an abundance of anthropomorphic language that the New Testament authors did not. Old Testament writers attributed characteristics such as emotions to God due to their misunderstandings of his being. This was a convenient method of revealing himself to a nation that was insufficiently spiritual to understand otherwise.[105] However, the New Testament authors had progressed beyond their ancestors. Rather than using spiritually immature anthropomorphic terms, they were able to describe God in more accurate language. They neither have to use such accommodated verbiage in their teaching, nor did God have to allow them to remain with such misunderstandings.

Franz Volkmar Reinhard, Accommodation, and the Kingdom of God

Under the broad category of accommodation in New Testament teaching was the changing nature of God's kingdom from the Old Testament to the New. Political theory, a subject that occupied many Enlightenment thinkers, was yet another debated issue in the use of accommodation in New Testament teaching. Amid the numerous conflicts and changes in politics during the eighteenth century, there was no shortage of works on political thought. Eighteenth-century interpretations of the kingdom of God were not impervious to such discussions on political theory. Thus, the question posed by scholars such as Franz Volkmar Reinhard (1753–1812) centered on the role of an earthly

---

[104] Lüderwald, *Gedanken von dem Unterscheid*, 15. Lüderwald also repeated Semler's understanding of accommodation in passages related to demon possession. *Gedanken von dem Unterscheid*, 10.

[105] Lüderwald, *Gedanken von dem Unterscheid*, 11.

4 THE BEGINNING OF THE ACCOMMODATION DEBATE, 1761–1789

kingdom within God's plan for a kingdom of heaven. Did Jesus intend to establish an earthly kingdom in which he would rule as any other king?

Born in Vohenstrauß, Reinhard made his way through his studies and earned a chair in theology at the University of Wittenberg in 1780. After 10 years at the university, he became the rector at Wittenberg. Shortly thereafter, Reinhard accepted a position at Dresden, where he became the court preacher for the city. In addition to his preaching ministry, Reinhard also made important contributions to the *quest for the historical Jesus* movement. Though a supernaturalist, Reinhard was also an adherent to Enlightenment rationalism.

During his early years as a professor of theology at Wittenberg, Reinhard published his *Versuch über den Plan, welchen der Stifter der christlichen Religion zum Besten der Menschheit entwarf* (1781). He argued that God never intended to establish an earthly kingdom. But since ancient Israel expected an earthly kingdom, Jesus appeased the Jewish people by accommodating a material understanding of kingdom into his plan for a universal and rational kingdom of spiritual truth.[106] Rather than abandoning the primitive understanding of a material kingdom, Jesus accommodated these expectations into his universal and moral kingdom. Reinhard's blend of supernaturalism and rationalism gained a wide audience and popularity; this work would go on to be published in five German editions and one English translation.

Reinhard understood God's earthly kingdom as a condescension to Jewish understanding. He described Jesus's teaching on the kingdom as a strategic accommodation to the perception of his people.[107] This adjustment to the thought of ancient Israel was a pedagogical step that rooted new teaching within existing circumstances. By taking on Jewish

---

[106] The use of accommodation in defining the nature of God's kingdom was not unique or original to Reinhard. In 1775, Christian Friedrich Schmidt (1741–1778), nephew of Christian August Crusius, articulated an earthly kingdom based on the condescension of God's kingdom of heaven. Christian Friedrich Schmidt, *Iudaeorum qui Christi tempore vixerunt de eodem varias opiniones accommodata ad Loca N. T. enarrar et ad Solemnem Doctoris Theologi Inaugurationem* (Wittenberg: Litteris Caroli Christiani Dürrii, 1775).

[107] Franz Volkmar Reinhard, *Versuch über den Plan, welchen der Stifter der christlichen Religion zum Besten der Menschheit entwarf* (Wittenberg: Samuel Gottfried Zimmermann, 1784), 17. Due to the unavailability of the first edition, I am using the second edition (1784).

laws, customs, and understandings, Jesus created the opportunity to instruct the Jews in spiritual truth. It would have been a disservice to Jesus's ministry had he corrected every misunderstanding.[108] By working within the framework of their misconceived material kingdom, Jesus was able to communicate a kingdom of morality and true worship. However, Jesus accommodated to Jewish nationalistic expectations not to usher in a material kingdom but to inform his hearers through their particular historical setting and limited capacity that their notion of kingdom would be replaced by a kingdom of universal morality and truth.

Reinhard's use of accommodation extended beyond the nature of Jesus's kingdom to include his role as ruler and savior of his kingdom. For Reinhard, Jesus's death did not offer any atonement for humankind's sin but was only an accommodation to the Jewish understanding of sacrifice.[109] As Reinhard explained, "A principal reason why he delivered himself into the hands of his enemies, and receded from the scene of the world by so early and disgraceful a death, was as soon as possible to destroy forever the idea that it was his object to establish an earthly kingdom, and to give a different direction to the thoughts, desires, and efforts of his disciples and friends."[110] Jesus's death dashed any expectations for a material kingdom and forced the apostles into the realization that Jesus's intentions were never for an earthly kingdom but for a spiritual one. It is unclear whether Reinhard's use of accommodation was directly linked to Hugo Grotius's governmental theory of atonement. What is clear is that Reinhard related Jesus's atonement to the understanding of the kingdom of heaven and that accommodation played a critical role in establishing the difference between Israel's and Jesus's understanding of kingdom.

---

[108] Reinhard, *Versuch über den Plan*, 17, 25.

[109] The idea that Jesus's sacrificial atonement was merely an accommodation to the Jewish understanding of sacrifices was shared by Karl Friedrich Bahrdt in *Briefe über die Bibel im Volkston* (Halle: Johann Friedrich Dost, 1782). Albert Schweitzer described Bahrdt's approach as a necessary accommodation of "superstitions" and "folly" so that eventually they would learn of rational truth. Albert Schweitzer, *The Quest of the Historical Jesus: A Critical Study of its Progress from Reimarus to Wrede*, trans. by W. Montgomery (London: Adam and Charles Black, 1910), 40. Against this position see Hauff, *Bemerkungen über die Lehrart Jesu*, 272–274.

[110] Reinhard, *Versuch über den Plan* (1804), 62.

The following year Reinhard published his *Utrum et quando possint oratores divini in administrando mundere suo demittere se ad vanas hominum opiones* (1782). In many ways the work was an attempt to give historical support to the form of accommodation he used in *Versuch über den Plan*. The bulk of the work is a discussion of the patristic use of accommodation. To give further support to his study, he situated it as an extension of Suicer's entry on accommodation in his *Thesauro*.[111] A common practice of accommodationists was to look to ancient writers for support of their argument. The bulk of Reinhard's and Beyer's works is a discussion of the patristic use of accommodation, providing a more developed study than Suicer.[112] This practice was not limited to only the church fathers. Others such as Georg Theophil Pappelbaum looked to Cicero and Latin antiquity for historical support of accommodation.[113]

Reinhard's main argument was that the church fathers held to a Socinian accommodation as expressed in *Versuch über den Plan*. Admittedly, both Greek and Latin fathers argued that Jesus and the apostles did not deceive or lie when they used accommodation. However, at the same time, Reinhard stated that Jesus and the apostles accommodated to the erroneous thinking of their audience. While there could be errors in the Bible, which modern exegesis had to decipher, they were not acts of deception. Reinhard repeated Storr's example of Timothy's circumcision to show how Paul accommodated to the erroneous ceremonial practices of his audience.[114] Storr had shown that Paul's use of accommodation did not enact any sin or error but rather submitted to cultural demands in order to minister effectively. That is, while circumcision was no longer necessary, it was not wrong for Timothy to become circumcised, just as it would not be wrong for people in the modern age to become circumcised. But Reinhard applied Storr's defense and the

---

[111] Franz Volkmar Reinhard, *Utrum et quando possint oratores divini in administrando mundere suo demittere se ad vanas hominum opiones*, in *Opuscula academica* (Leipzig: Hinrichs, 1808), 1:487. Also see his *System der christlichen Moral* (Wittenberg: Zimmermann, 1791–1792), 1:243–251.

[112] For further discussion of the term *oikonomia*, see Jeremias Friedrich Reuss, *Disquisitio theologico-hermeneutica de oeconomia, qua in docendo ipse etiam dominus usus esse dicitur* (Tübingen: Fues, 1773). Central to the work is a criticism of Semler's use of accommodation.

[113] Georg Theophil Pappelbaum, *De Christo sapienter ac licite simulante et dissimulante* (Stargard: Joannis Ludouici Kunstii, 1763).

[114] Reinhard, *Utrum et quando possint oratores divini*, 1:491.

use of the doctrine by the church fathers to say that their understanding of accommodation maintained the authority of Scripture while admitting that certain passages contained erroneous accommodations to ancient Israel. Reinhard argued that his position was in keeping with the fathers, recognizing the erroneous human elements within the text while upholding the Bible's authority.

Reinhard clearly upheld a Socinian understanding of accommodation, though he did not apply it to the extent of Socinus or Semler. While using the language of historical accommodation, Reinhard demonstrated the incompatibility of orthodox and heterodox accommodation and illustrated, perhaps unwittingly, the relationship between heterodox accommodation and rationalistic hermeneutics.[115]

Clarity and Confusion in an Intensifying Debate

By the 1780s, the different party lines over the issue of accommodation were a well-established fixture. Evident in Franz Peter Schaefer's *De Christo et Apostolis in tradenda religione ad hominum captum sese demittentibus* (1787), the various accommodationists could be grouped by their understanding of whether there was an accommodation to error or not. While little is known of Schaefer other than this dissertation at the University of Mainz, his work defined heterodox accommodation clearly and explicitly grouped Semler, Teller, Johann Bernhard Basedow (1724–1790), and Gotthelf Samuel Steinbart (1738–1809) as adherents of Socinian accommodation. For Schaefer, accommodation entailed divine condescension to man but without error.[116] He acknowledged the occasional nature of the Bible and the unique manner in which God's revelation was embodied in the words and thoughts of ancient Israelites. However, God's accommodation was an accommodation of only manner and not matter.[117]

While Schaefer condemned all promoters of heterodox accommodation, he identified Semler as the primary culprit for the extensive use of

---

[115] A decade later Reinhard would rework his understanding of accommodation in the area of ethics. See Franz Volkmar Reinhard, *System der christlichen Moral* (Wittenberg: Zimmermann, 1791–1792), vol. 3, 233–253.

[116] Franz Peter Schaefer, *De Christo et Apostolis in tradenda religione ad hominum captum sese demittentibus* (Mainz: Alef, 1787), 26.

[117] Schaefer, *De Christo et Apostolis*, 43.

Socinian accommodation.[118] As we have discussed, Semler's historical-critical hermeneutic coupled with Socinian accommodation deemed the Bible full of error and erroneous doctrine. As far as what to make of the errors identified through Socinian accommodation, Semler advanced a hermeneutic that would exclude such matters from divine revelation. For Schaefer, Semler's repetition of Bekker's stance on demonology was a clear violation not only of the doctrine of accommodation but also of the Bible's authority.[119]

Schaefer addressed nothing new to our previous discussion of Teller and his *Wörterbuch*. He objected to Teller's notion that many ceremonial practices were the result of an accommodation to ancient Israel and that they thus held no real meaning for Christians today.[120] He also discussed topics such as the earthly kingdom of God as an accommodation to worldly expectations. And he briefly treated the ramifications of Teller's use of accommodation to doctrines of faith and salvation.

Of the four individuals Schaefer grouped together as holding to heterodox accommodation, Johann Bernhard Basedow stood apart from the others because his vocation was outside theology. Known for his educational reform in Dessau, the former student of theology turned to philosophy at Leipzig, developing a career in pedagogical matters. While his educational work showed great similarity to Jean-Jacques Rousseau (1712–1778), his understanding of the Bible was more in line with Lessing or Reimarus, and as Schaefer argued, he held an understanding of accommodation on par with Socinus and Semler.[121]

For Basedow, the Bible contained numerous elements of accommodation to erroneous thinking. Especially in the Old Testament, these accommodations made reading and understanding difficult for

---

[118] Schaefer, *De Christo et Apostolis*, 5.

[119] Schaefer, *De Christo et Apostolis*, 7.

[120] Schaefer, *De Christo et Apostolis*, 9.

[121] Lessing's pedagogical understanding of the Bible was even more extreme than Basedow. Lessing understood the accommodated nature of the Bible to mean that it was written only for a specific people and at a "certain age." The circumstantial and accommodated text resulted in a Bible that could be described only as an "elementary book" written for "childish people." What separated Basedow from Lessing was that Basedow was unwilling to forgo the text entirely for the good of rational religion. Jonathan Sheehan, *The Enlightenment Bible: Translation, Scholarship, Culture* (Princeton, NJ: Princeton University Press, 2005), 135; Gotthold Ephraim Lessing, *Die Erziehung des Menschengeschlechts* (Berlin: Christian Friedrich Voss and Son, 1780), 51–53.

children. This being so, it was improper for a child, or one with little understanding, to read the Bible without instruction. Before a child was to read the Bible, he or she had to first gain a certain amount of rationality and morality to make sense of difficult passages of the Bible, including accommodated texts. Coupled to this pedagogical approach to the Bible was Basedow's rejection of many orthodox doctrines, including the doctrine of the Trinity.[122]

Schaefer's last target was neologian Gotthelf Samuel Steinbart. Born in Züllichau from a pietistic family, Steinbart went on to study under Baumgarten and Johann Gottlieb Töllner (1724–1774). After a time in Berlin and then in Züllichau to take over his father's position as head of an orphanage, he eventually succeeded his teacher Töllner. Similar to Basedow, Steinbart wrote on educational reform issues. Also in agreement with Basedow, Steinbart argued somewhat more forcibly that happiness was the true end of philosophy and religion. Steinbart expressed his naturalism in starker terms than Basedow, though this may have been due to greater opportunity rather than an actual difference between their theologies.

Steinbart argued in his popular work *System der reinen Philosophie oder Glückseligkeitslehre des Christenthums* (1778), which would go on to four editions, that true Christianity must be void of accommodated human elements. In order to decipher God's universal message, the modern interpreter had to rid the Bible of accommodated elements intended only for ancient Israel. Proper interpretation needed to recognize and disregard accommodated matters of "local circumstances, and prevailing customs and prejudices."[123] These accommodations were necessary due to the sensual thought patterns of ancient Israel but were superfluous for modern readers.[124] Thus the interpreter had

---

[122] Evidence of Basedow's naturalism can be found in his *Philalethie: Neue Aussichten in die Wahrheiten und Religion der Vernunft bis in die Gränzen der glaubwürdigen Offenbarung* (Altona: Iverson, 1764) but even more so in his *Methodischer Unterricht in der überzeugenden Erkenntniss der biblischen Religion* (Altona: Iverson, 1764). For a review of *Philalethie* see Johann August Ernesti, *Neue theologische Bibliothek: darinnen von den neuesten theologischen Büchern und Schriften Nachricht gegeben wird* (Leipzig: Bernard Christoph Breitkopf, 1760–1771), vol. 5, 56–87.

[123] Gotthelf Samuel Steinbart, *System der reinen Philosophie; oder, Glückseligkeitslehre des Christenthums* (Züllichau: Waysenhaus and Frommann, 1778), 216.

[124] Steinbart, *System der reinen Philosophie*, 216.

to distinguish what was of Jewish "historical garb" from what was "still useful for our people."[125]

The last work we will address in this chapter is a little known disputation from an equally unknown author, Ernst Wilhelm Opitz(?). What is known of Opitz is merely from what can be inferred from his work. The disputation, *De accommodationis Christi et apostolorum didacticae natura* (1789), was presided over by Michael Weber (1754–1833), a professor of theology at Wittenberg. Opitz saw his work as a progression of Reinhard's *Utrum et quando possint oratores divini*. He repeated Reinhard's argument that the Messianic kingdom was an accommodation to Jewish expectation.[126] Though the Israelites misunderstood Jesus's role, Jesus took upon himself this error and taught that he would establish an earthly kingdom. However, what Reinhard expressed implicitly about human error within divine accommodation, Opitz made explicit.

Opitz offered six categories of accommodation in Christ's and the apostles' teaching, many of which could be in agreement with orthodoxy in principle. The overarching concept was that the teaching ministry of Christ and the apostles used accommodation in deciding such matters as what, when, and how specific doctrines and teachings should be communicated. Opitz also stipulated that their teaching ministry included the errors of their audience but did not introduce any new error or deception.[127] While at first glance it would appear that Opitz's use of accommodation aligned with orthodox accommodation in the first five categories of accommodation and only diverged in the last one, a closer look clearly shows that Socinian accommodation permeated all uses of accommodation for Opitz. The manner in which the disciples taught using various methods or the way Paul distinguished between milk and solids were admirable expressions of accommodation.[128] However, for Opitz, such measures inherently included error within their very teachings. His definition of accommodation assumed that the inclusion of error would be a necessary element of

---

[125] Steinbart, *System der reinen Philosophie*, 216.

[126] Ernst Opitz, *De accommodationis Christi et apostolorum didacticae natura* (Wittenberg: Tzschiedrichius, 1789), 16.

[127] Opitz, *De accommodationis*, 11.

[128] Opitz, *De accommodationis*, 12–13.

accommodation.[129] The erroneous thinking of ancient Israel was essentially woven into every aspect of Christ's and the apostles' teaching.

Though Opitz referenced scholars who used an orthodox accommodation such as Unselt, Opitz's actual practice reflected a heterodox definition. He argued that Christ by necessity allowed erroneous thinking not only to enter into the text of the Bible but also to dictate matters of doctrine.[130] As with Reinhard, Opitz attempted to use the language of orthodox accommodation to disguise his Socinian definition.

Conclusion

The first stage of the accommodation debate takes us from 1761 to 1789. We saw how the doctrine was critical to understanding Ernesti's hermeneutics and Zahcariae's theology. Accommodationists did not consider the doctrine as a peripheral matter, but integral to much larger issues. For instance, throughout the debate, accommodation was closely tied to a historical approach to exegesis. Scholars such as Semler, Storr, and Eifert may have differed on their understanding of accommodation, but for all, the doctrine was foundational in their historical approach to biblical interpretation. For the former, historical criticism was unthinkable without Socinian accommodation, thus forming a formidable partnership that provided justification for the other.

A hotly debated point during this period was the exact extent to which Jesus and the apostles used accommodation within their teaching ministry. While it was commonly understood that New Testament teaching had to condescend to the level of the common man, it was debated whether this adaptation was limited to the manner of teaching or whether it also included the matter of the teaching—a knotty nuance that became the epicenter of the accommodation debate. These matters pitted Reinhard and Lüderwald against Unselt, Pisanski, and Schaefer. The accommodation debate was not a matter of semantics or confusion over terms. Both sides acknowledged the difference between the two uses of accommodation, resulting in two mutually exclusive positions. As we will see in the coming chapters, these opposing views on accommodation would continue to be heavily debated through the end of the eighteenth century and into the nineteenth century.

---

[129] Opitz, *De accommodationis*, 16.
[130] Opitz, *De accommodationis*, 22.

Bibliography

Bahrdt, Karl Friedrich. *Briefe über die Bibel im Volkston*. Halle: Johann Friedrich Dost, 1782.

Bang, Johann Christian. *Verhandeling, waarin ondersogt wordt, in hoe verre Jesus en zyne Apostelen zich geschikt hebben naar de vatbaarheid der Jooden in het vorstellen der Christelijke leere*. Amsterdam: Allart, 1789.

Basedow, Johann Bernhard. *Methodischer Unterricht in der überzeugenden Erkenntniss der biblischen Religion*. Altona: Iverson, 1764.

———. *Philalethie: Neue Aussichten in die Wahrheiten und Religion der Vernunft bis in die Gränzen der glaubwürdigen Offenbarung*. Altona: Iverson, 1764.

Bauer, Karl Ludwig. *Logica Paullina, vel notatio rationis, qua utatur Paullus Apostolus in verbis adhibendis, interpretando, definiendo, enuntiando, argumentando, et methodo univers*. Halae Magdeburg: Orphanotrophei, 1774.

Bock, Friedrich Samuel. *Lehrbuch für die neueste Polemik*. Halle: Johann Jacob Gebauer, 1782.

Bollacher, Martin. "Wilhelm Abraham Teller: Ein Aufklärer der Theologie." In *Über den Prozess der Aufklärung in Deutschland im 18. Jahrhundert*, edited by Hans Erich Bödeker and Ulrich Hermann, 39–52. Göttingen: Vandenhoeck & Ruprecht, 1987.

Brecht, Martin, ed. *Geschichte des Pietismus*. 4 vols. Göttingen: Vandenhoeck & Ruprecht, 1993–2004.

Danneberg, Lutz. "Schleiermacher und das Ende des Akkommodationsgedankens in der *hermeneutica sacra* des 17. und 18. Jahrhunderts." In *200 Jahre "Reden über die Religion*,*"* edited by Ulrich Barth and Claus-Dieter Osthövener, 194–246. Berlin: de Gruyter, 2000.

Detharding, Georg. *Commentatio theologica de accommodatione verbi divini ministri ad captum vulgi*. Göttingen: Dieterich, 1782.

Dorrien, Gary J. *Kantian Reason and Hegelian Spirit: The Idealistic Logic of Modern Theology*. Malden, MA: Wiley-Blackwell, 2012.

Eichhorn, Johann Gottfried. *Allgemeine Bibliothek der biblischen Litteratur* 1–14 (1787–1801).

Eifert, Carl Traugott. *Untersuchung der Frage: Könnte nicht die mosaische Erzählung vom Sündenfalle buchstäblich wahr, und durch den Fall ein erbliches Verderben auf die Menschen gekommen seyn?* Halle: Hemmerde, 1781.

Ernesti, Johann August. *Institvtio Interpretis Novi Testamenti*. Leipzig: Weidmanni, 1761.

———. *Neue theologische Bibliothek: darinnen von den neuesten theologischen Büchern und Schriften Nachricht gegeben wird*. Leipzig: Bernard Christoph Breitkopf, 1760–1771.

Frei, Hans W. *The Eclipse of Biblical Narrative: A Study in Eighteenth and Nineteenth Century Hermeneutics.* New Haven, CT: Yale University Press, 1974.

Hauff, Karl Viktor. *Bemerkungen über die Lehrart Jesu mit Rücksicht auf jüdische Sprache- und Denkungsart.* Offenbach: C. L. Brede, 1788.

Hayden-Roy, Priscilla. "Sensate Language and the Hermetic Tradition in Friedrich Christoph Oetinger's *Biblisches und Emblematisches Wörterbuch.*" In *Subversive Sublimities: Undercurrents of the German Enlightenment,* edited by Eitel Timm, 58–69. Columbia, SC: Camden House, 1992.

Hemert, Paulus van. *Oratio de prudenti christi, apostolorum, atque evangelistarum consilio, sermones suos et scripta, ad captum atque intellectum vulgi, quantum illud fieri potuit, accommodantium.* Amsterdam: M. Schalekamp, 1791.

Heringa, Jodocus Ezn. *Über die Lehrart Jesu und seiner Apostel mit Hinsicht auf die Religionsbegriffe ihrer Zeitgenossen.* Offenbach: Weiss & Brede, 1792.

Hess, Johann Jakob, *Geschichte der drey letzten Lebensjahre Jesu.* Zurich: Orell, Geßner, Füeßlin, 1768.

Hirsch, Emanuel. *Geschichte der neuern evangelischen Theologie: im Zusammenhang mit den allgemeinen Bewegungen des europäischen Denkens.* Gütersloh: Mohn, 1952.

Hornig, Gottfried. *Die Anfänge der historisch-kritischen Theologie.* Göttingen: Vandenhoeck & Ruprecht, 1961.

———. "Wilhelm Abraham Tellers *Wörterbuch* des Neuen Testaments und Friedrich Christoph Oetingers *Emblematik.*" *Das achtzehnte Jahrhundert* (1998): 76–88.

Israel, Jonathan. *Radical Enlightenment: Philosophy and the Making of Modernity 1650–1750.* New York: Oxford University Press, 2001.

Lang, Georg Heinrich. *Zur Beförderung des nützlichen Gebrauches des Wilhelm Abraham Tellerischen Wörterbuchs des neuen Testaments.* 4 vols. Anspach: Benedict Friederich Haueisen, 1778–1785.

Lessing, Gotthold Ephraim. *Die Erziehung des Menschengeschlechts.* Berlin: Christian Friedrich Voss and Son, 1780.

Lüderwald, Johann Balthasar. *Die allegorische Erklärung der drey ersten Capitel Mosis.* Helmstädt: Johann Heinrich Kühnlin, 1781.

———. *Die Wahrheit Gewißheit der Auferstehung Jesu Christi.* Helmstädt: Kühnlin, 1778.

———. *Gedanken von dem Unterscheid der Lehre und des Lehrvortrags im Christenthum in Absicht auf seine nationellen Vorzüge.* Helmstädt: Kühnlin, 1781.

Michaelis, Johann David. *Einleitung in die göttlichen Schriften des Neuen Bundes.* 2 vols. Göttingen: Vandenhoeck, 1765–66.

Oetinger, Friedrich Christoph. *Biblisches und emblematisches Wörterbuch, dem Tellerischen Wörterbuch und Anderer falschen Schrifterklärungen entgegen gesetzt.* Hildesheim: Georg Olms, 1776.

Opitz, Ernst. *De accommodationis Christi et apostolorum didacticae natura.* Wittenberg: Tzschiedrichius, 1789.

Pappelbaum, Georg Theophil. *De Christo sapienter ac licite simulante et dissimulante.* Stargard: Joannis Ludouici Kunstii, 1763.

Pisanski, Georg Christoph. *Adversaria de Accommodationibus Veteris Testamenti in Novo Obviis.* Göttingen: Wedeliane, 1781.

Reinhard, Franz Volkmar. *System der christlichen Moral.* 5 vols. Wittenberg: Zimmermann, 1791–1792.

———. *Utrum et quando possint oratores divini in administrando munere suo demittere se ad vanas hominum opiniones.* Wittenberg: Adamus Christianus Charisius, 1782.

———. *Versuch über den Plan, welchen der Stifter der christlichen Religion zum Besten der Menschheit entwarf.* Wittemberg: Samuel Gottfried Zimmermann, 1784.

Reuss, Jeremias Friedrich. **Disquisitio theologico-hermeneutica de Oeconomia, qua in docendo ipse etiam Dominus usus esse dicitur.** Tübingen: Fues, 1773.

Sailhamer, John H. "Johann August Ernesti: The Role of History in Biblical Interpretation." *Journal of the Evangelical Theological Society* 44, no. 2 (June 2001): 193–206.

———. *The Meaning of the Pentateuch: Revelation, Composition, and Interpretation.* Downers Grove, IL: IVP Academic, 2009.

Sandys-Wunsch, John. "Early Old Testament Critics on the Continent." In *Hebrew Bible / Old Testament: The History of its Interpretation.* Vol. 2, *From the Renaissance to the Enlightenment,* edited by Magne Saebø, 971–984. Göttingen: Vandenhoeck & Ruprecht, 2008.

Schaefer, Franz Peter. *De Christo et Apostolis in tradenda religione ad hominum captum sese demittentibus.* Mainz: Alef, 1787.

Schmidt, Christian Friedrich. *Iudaeorum qui Christi tempore vixerunt de eodem varias opiniones accommodata ad Loca N. T. enarrar et ad Solemnem Doctoris Theologi Inaugurationem.* Wittenberg: Litteris Caroli Christiani Dürrii, 1775.

Schweitzer, Albert. *The Quest of the Historical Jesus: A Critical Study of Its Progress from Reimarus to Wrede.* Translated by W. Montgomery. London: Adam and Charles Black, 1910.

Semler, Johann Salomo. *Vorbereitung zur Theologie Hermeneutik.* 8 vols. Halle: Hemerde, 1761–1769.

Sheehan, Jonathan. *The Enlightenment Bible: Translation, Scholarship, Culture.* Princeton, NJ: Princeton University Press, 2005.

Spindler, Guntram, ed. *Glauben und Erkennen: Die Heilige Philosophie von Friedrich Christoph Oetinger.* Metzingen: Franz, 2002.

Steinbart, Gotthelf Samuel. *System der reinen Philosophie; oder, Glückseligkeitslehre des Christenthums.* Züllichau: Waysenhaus and Frommann, 1778.

Storr, Gottlob Christian. *De sensu historico.* In *Opuscula Academica ad Interpretationem Librorum Sacrorum Pertinentia*, 1:1–88. Tubingen: Joannis Georgii Cottae, 1796. Originally published in Tübingen: Fuesianis, 1778.

Teller, Wilhelm Abraham. *Wörterbuch des Neuen Testaments zur Erklärung der christlichen Lehre.* Berlin: Mylius, 1772.

Tholuck, August. *A Commentary on the Epistle to the Hebrews.* 2 vols. Translated by James Hamilton. Edinburgh: Thomas Clark, 1842.

Töllner, Johann Gottlieb. *Grundriß einer erwiesenen Hermeneutik der heiligen Schrift.* Züllichau: Waisenhaus, 1765.

Unselt, Samuel Fridericus. *Dissertatio philologica de locorum Veteris Testamenti in Novo accommodatione orthodoxa.* Leipzig: Breitkopf, 1766.

Zachariae, Gotthilf Traugott. *Theologische Erklärung der Herablassung Gottes zu den Menschen.* In Gotthilf Traugott Zachariae, *Philosophisch-Theologische Abhandlungen als Beilagen zur Biblischen Theologie*, ed. Christian Gottlieb Perschke, 541–800. Lemgo: Meyer, 1776. Originally published in Bützow: Wismar, 1762.

CHAPTER 5

The Middle Years of the Accommodation Debate, 1790–1799

As we come to the end of the eighteenth century, it may seem peculiar that Immanuel Kant has failed to enter into our discussion. Due to his great influence in modern scholarship, Kantian philosophy has become synonymous with the Aufklärung. However, this assessment is an unbalanced depiction.[1] While Kant's influence during the Aufklärung cannot be minimized, it should be remembered that his *Critique of Pure Reason* was not published until 1781. Arriving late to the Aufklärung, which itself was a comparatively late movement compared to the Enlightenment in England and France, Kant's influence was most present during the latter years of the century.

Even before the turn of the century, a challenge to Kant's critical system was mounting. Not long after the publication of *Critique of Pure Reason*, romanticism and idealism would bring their objections to rationalism. Though Kant's call for reason and autonomy was received by many, it also created a sense of disillusionment with the prowess of rationalism. A creeping fear steadily grew over the consequences of an unrestrained reason. On the current path of rationalism, the gains would

---

[1] For instance, while Kant's "Was ist Aufklärung?" (1784) receives the most attention today, Moses Mendelssohn's "Beantwortung der Frage: Was ist Aufklärung?" (1784) provided a more moderate position. Hamann's letter to Christian Jakob Kraus should also be consulted for further demonstration of the varying understandings of the Enlightenment. Johann Georg Hamann, *Briefwechsel*, ed. Walther Ziesemer and Arthur Henkel (Wiesbaden: Insel, 1955–1975), 5:289–292.

become overshadowed by the counterproductive dismantling project of critical reason. Even supporters of Kant soon tired of upholding the phantom thing-in-itself, giving credence to his critics' accusation of solipsism.[2] Hamann's prophetic metacritique gained resurgence through movements such as the Sturm und Drang and German romanticism.

Amid this turmoil, the accommodation debate continued to shape and be shaped by eighteenth-century hermeneutics and historical criticism. Though the last decade of the century would witness the end of the Enlightenment, the accommodation debate had only reached its halfway point. The debate would continue into the nineteenth century, wrestling with the rationalistic exegesis, the progression of modern interpretation, and the quest for the historical Jesus. But before we get ahead of ourselves, we should note three changes in the 1790s. First, those within the Socinian camp made a greater association between the modern age, the bygone need for accommodation, and a duty to dispel the accommodations found in the Bible. This sentiment had been evident in past decades, but it became a prominent characteristic of Socinian accommodation in the 1790s. Second, Kantian thought did not become a significant component of the debate until the 1790s. Though Kant developed his critical philosophy in the previous decade, his own treatment of accommodation appeared in his 1793 work *Die Religion innerhalb der Grenzen der bloßen Vernunft*. Third, this period of the debate was characterized by a drastic swing toward the Socinian party. While numerical quantification alone is not indicative of the impact of the debate, it is of some significance that the vast majority of works during the 1790s advanced the Socinian definition. We will explore these issues in reverse order.

The Shift Toward Socinian Accommodation

The decade began with a series of works addressing familiar issues, such as demonology, but they also introduced new applications of the doctrine, particularly in the concept of fear and God. These works varied from lengthier treatments of accommodation to a short exploration of a specific historical dimension of the doctrine. The authors also

---

[2] Frederick C. Beiser, *Fate of Reason: German Philosophy from Kant to Fichte* (Cambridge, MA: Harvard University Press, 1987), 5.

differed as much as the works they wrote, writing from a wide stretch of geographical locations and various positions.[3] However, all of these four early works shared a common objective: to sway the balance of the debate over to a Socinian definition.

Though the number of works favoring a Socinian definition during the debate decades had usually outnumbered those adhering to the historical definition, this disproportion became further exaggerated during the century's last decade. The vast majority of treatments of the doctrine argued for the understanding that when God or the biblical authors made adaptations for their audience, they inevitably introduced erroneous matters into the text of the Bible. These misunderstandings were not limited to the accuracy of science but often shaped the core doctrines of what had become known as historical Christianity. However, these accommodations were not an end unto themselves. They served a critical purpose during a time when God and the biblical authors were restricted by the limited capacity of their audience. Whether it was for the promotion of rational, moral, or universal truth, the use of false understanding facilitated this higher purpose.

Hermann Friedrich Behn

Bridging the Socinian use in the previous decade to the 1790s, Hermann Friedrich Behn (1767–1846) wrote the decade's first work on accommodation.[4] Born in Lübeck, Behn went on to conduct his studies at Jena. He returned to Lübeck as a minister, serving at the city's St. Peter's. After almost thirty years, he was promoted to the head position at St. Peter's and then several years later to a position overseeing all

---

[3] The debate made its way up to Denmark. Petrus Christianus Cramer, *Dissertatio de sapientissima Jesu Christi in vero se Messia declarando oikonomia* (Copenhagen: P. M. Höpffneri, 1792).

[4] That same year Hauff published an essay expounding on an Augustinian position. The essay is a reworking of his previous publication, *Bemerkungen über die Lehrart Jesu mit Rücksicht auf jüdische Sprache- und Denkungsart* (Offenbach: Brede, 1798). The later work is titled "Gedanken über die Frage: ob und inwiefern sich Jesus und die Apostel zu einigen jüdischen Ideen herabgelassen haben?," in *Beyträge zur Beförderung des vernünftigen Denkens in der Religion*, 15 (1791): 1–25. Also see Friedrich Wilhelm Dresde, *De suluhi Fausti Socini libros Sacros interpretandi ratione* (Wittenberg, Charisius, 1790), for a study of how Socinian exegesis was understood in the 1790s.

of Lübeck. Though the debate did not often travel so far north, Behn's work does indicate the range of its impact.

As the title states, Behn returned to the issue of the teaching ministry of Jesus and the apostles in *Ueber die Lehrart Jesu und seiner Apostel: in wie fern dieselben sich nach den damals herrschenden Volksmeinungen bequemt haben* (1791).[5] This time Behn had the added advantage of writing with hindsight. Having witnessed the debate during the 1780s, Behn recognized the polarizing parties of the debate. With the benefit of this history, Behn used the work to provide an assessment of the accommodation debate thus far, discuss the major areas of contention over New Testament teaching and demonology, and align himself with the Socinian party, particularly with Teller and Lüderwald.

The crux of the work examined the extent to which accommodation was used in New Testament teaching. After a brief overview of how the doctrine of *oikonomia* was understood by the early church fathers, Behn argued his case for the necessity of accommodation to error. As a good teacher would adapt lessons according to his students' ability, Jesus and the apostles developed a successful teaching ministry on their method of condescending through preexisting concepts, which were at times accurate and at times not.[6]

The appropriation of preexisting ancient religion and philosophy was a necessary measure to ensure proper instruction with limited resources.[7] Jesus's audience was not equipped to handle solid food, thus he had to provide his teaching in the form of milk.[8] Jesus was hindered not only by the limited capacity of his audience but also by the time constraints of a mere three years. Thus, accommodation became a necessity for Jesus,

---

[5] For a review of the work, see Johann Gottfried Eichhorn, *Allgemeine Bibliothek der biblischen Litteratur* 3 (1787–1801): 920–935.

[6] Hermann Friedrich Behn, *Ueber die Lehrart Jesu und seiner Apostel: in wie fern dieselben sich nach den damals herrschenden Volksmeinungen bequemt haben* (Lübeck: Christian Gittfried Donatius, 1791), 7. Also see Hermann Friedrich Behn, *Ein kleiner Beytrag zu Untersuchung der Frage: Ob und wie weit es einem weisen Manne überhaupt, und besonders einem göttlichen Lehrer anständig und erlabut sey, sich zu den Meynungen und Irrthümern anderer herabzulassen?* (Breslau: Meyer, 1791).

[7] Behn, *Ueber die Lehrart Jesu und seiner Apostel*, 43, 46. At times Behn used a polemical tone of condemnation that revealed his anti-Semitism. Behn, *Ueber die Lehrart Jesu und seiner Apostel*, 136.

[8] Behn, *Ueber die Lehrart Jesu und seiner Apostel*, 50.

who could only correct the gravest errors in their thinking and who was forced to let less harmful errors stand unaddressed.[9]

According to Behn, much of the accommodation found in the New Testament was a passive form that allowed the New Testament figures to continue teaching without challenging preexisting notions.[10] Jesus and the apostles could choose to remain silent when faced with an erroneous concept. This method of accommodation freed the teacher from having to address a matter that would otherwise distract listeners from his teaching ministry. For instance, rather than correcting Israel's understanding of Christ's kingdom in John 12:34, Jesus and the apostles chose to let the expectation of an earthly kingdom stand. The misunderstanding of an earthly kingdom would come to light as people gained a better understanding of Christ's universal kingdom.[11] Paul's use of the rock in 1 Corinthians 10:4 was another example of this passive accommodation.[12]

In addition to passive accommodation, the active form of accommodation borrowed erroneous ideas and doctrines for the proclamation of truth. This method of accommodation extended beyond the passive form not only by the teachers remaining silent when faced with erroneous thinking but also by them implementing these false concepts into their teaching. These two uses of accommodation did not contradict each other but in complementary fashion addressed different facets of New Testament teaching. Much of Behn's work is a discussion of active accommodation, primarily concerning but not limited to New Testament demonology.

Responding to the common objection to Socinian accommodation that any aspect of the Bible could be claimed as an accommodation to erroneous thinking, Behn qualified the doctrine with the disclaimer that accommodation could not be applied to the New Testament without a guiding principle. Behn's criterion was based on the subject matter rather than on specific rules for how accommodation was used. For Behn, accommodation was both an adaptation of manner and matter—there was no difference between the two. What identified valid accommodation was not how accommodation was applied but to

---

[9] Behn, *Ueber die Lehrart Jesu und seiner Apostel*, 50.
[10] Behn, *Ueber die Lehrart Jesu und seiner Apostel*, 12.
[11] Behn, *Ueber die Lehrart Jesu und seiner Apostel*, 12, 34.
[12] Behn, *Ueber die Lehrart Jesu und seiner Apostel*, 41.

what it was applied. For instance, when the biblical text addressed core doctrinal matters such as issues of morality, peace, and the happiness of mankind, one was safe to assume that that the authors did not use accommodation.[13] Jesus sought to establish such ideas, and hence they were not a result of the notions of common man but were directly from God. On the other hand, when the Bible described matters of scientific or doctrinal error, such as demon possession, there was a clear reason to expect an act of accommodation.

The second portion of the work addressed demonology within the New Testament. As stated, Behn situated his book squarely within the Socinian camp. Though Behn briefly indicated that Semler extended the doctrine of accommodation to matters that Behn would not, his general impression was that Semler was right to apply the doctrine to New Testament teaching, especially in the area of demonology. In addition to an affirmation of Semler's use of the doctrine, Behn also gave approval to Teller and Lüderwald.[14]

Though Behn could not identify the exact origin of the belief in demons, it sufficed to recognize the Chaldean and Persian influence on ancient Israelite demonology.[15] Since the Chaldeans and Persians were known as predecessors to the Israelites, it could safely be assumed that their concept of fallen angels continued into early Israelite thinking. Also, while the main source for Israelite demonology was derived from these ancient sources, New Testament demonology could also be attributed to Platonic thought and ancient Greek philosophy.[16]

In agreement with Semler, Behn contended that cases of New Testament demonology were in fact occurrences of mental illness. They were not narratives of imagination or falsified accounts of deception. Rather, they were mistaken diagnoses of mental illness related to epilepsy, schizophrenia, and bipolar disorder.[17] The idea that the "insane" were possessed by demons was a common misunderstanding, to the extent

---

[13] Behn, *Ueber die Lehrart Jesu und seiner Apostel*, 67, 77. Behn listed six cases where there is no accommodation. Behn, *Ueber die Lehrart Jesu und seiner Apostel*, 77–78.

[14] Behn, *Ueber die Lehrart Jesu und seiner Apostel*, 65.

[15] Behn, *Ueber die Lehrart Jesu und seiner Apostel*, 93.

[16] Behn, *Ueber die Lehrart Jesu und seiner Apostel*, 103.

[17] Behn, *Ueber die Lehrart Jesu und seiner Apostel*, 108.

that "it was widely prevalent in the time of Christ that one supposed demonic and lunatic to be synonymous."[18]

Jesus and the apostles were aware that demon possession was a misunderstanding of mental disorders. The exorcizing of demons was not a mystical power or even of divine authority. Rather, the knowledge of science and medicine equipped them to heal the mentally stricken. This understanding of medicine was well advanced compared to their audience, but it was not entirely unknown during their time. For instance, the Gospel of John did not contain accounts of demon possession due to his audience in Ephesus and Asia Minor, who correctly diagnosed mental illness.[19]

Accommodation was a suitable way to gradually bring their audience to truth without being hindered by insignificant matters. Such an approach to mental illness was the "best way" to lead their audience to "gradual enlightenment."[20] The limited knowledge of medicine and science forced the New Testament teachers to adapt their teaching to primitive ideology. In relaying this conviction, Behn examined two passages, the first being the narrative of the demon-possessed man and the herd of swine. Following Semler, Behn argued that Jesus's wisest method of treatment was to act as if the person was in fact demon possessed. Though it was really a case of delusion and mental illness, Jesus's best course of action was to work within the delusion rather than disprove it.[21] The alternative would have further complicated matters.

It should be noted that Behn gave several qualifiers to Jesus's supposed sending of the demons into the herd of swine. First, he never actively taught a doctrine of demon possession.[22] His actions were a response to the preexisting errors of his audience. It was a passive form of accommodation rather than an active promotion of error. Second, Jesus's accommodation fits within his overall ministry. He came to correct not all errors but only the critical errors related to moral religion.[23] Correcting medical understanding and properly diagnosing mental illness was not necessary to accomplishing his larger goal.

---

[18] Behn, *Ueber die Lehrart Jesu und seiner Apostel*, 102.
[19] Behn, *Ueber die Lehrart Jesu und seiner Apostel*, 126.
[20] Behn, *Ueber die Lehrart Jesu und seiner Apostel*, 112.
[21] Behn, *Ueber die Lehrart Jesu und seiner Apostel*, 122.
[22] Behn, *Ueber die Lehrart Jesu und seiner Apostel*, 125.
[23] Behn, *Ueber die Lehrart Jesu und seiner Apostel*, 125.

The second case study was of the demon-possessed man in Luke 4:33–36. Behn continued his line of reasoning by contending that modern medicine best explained the bizarre actions of the man in the synagogue. With a proper diagnosis, what appeared to be a case of demon possession had a more "natural" explanation.[24] But Jesus's accommodation to his audience involved using the "ordinary vernacular" of his day.[25] In identifying an unclean demon within the person, Jesus was referring to the "spirit" of such a demon *if* it were to exist.[26] It should not be assumed that if Jesus used the language of demonology, then demons actually existed. The doctrine of accommodation and the use of vernacular language explained such use of these terms. Just as it would be faulty logic to argue that since Jesus addressed the sea and winds, these elements existed as actual entities, so too the language of demonology did not prove that demons actually existed. Jesus's treatment was a cure for the illness but not for the cultural misunderstanding.[27] Their request was strictly for a cure and not for deeper insight into the cause and true nature of their affliction.[28] Hence, Jesus did not encourage or promote this error with a confirmation. Instead, he worked with the error while neither affirming nor denying their thought.[29]

Wilhelm Traugott Krug

While Behn's work was a nod to the debate of the 1780s, Wilhelm Traugott Krug's (1770–1842) study embarked on new territory. Born in Radis, Krug came from a rural setting and went on to study at Wittenberg, Jena, and Göttingen. Upon completion of his studies at Göttingen in 1794, he returned to Wittenberg to lecture on philosophy in an auxiliary manner. He gained his first position in 1801 at Frankfurt. In 1805, Krug left Frankfurt for Königsberg as Kant's successor. However, in 1809, Krug relocated once again to his final destination. In

---

[24] Behn, *Ueber die Lehrart Jesu und seiner Apostel*, 127.

[25] Behn, *Ueber die Lehrart Jesu und seiner Apostel*, 128. This also included anthropomorphic expressions. Behn, *Ueber die Lehrart Jesu und seiner Apostel*, 70.

[26] Also see Behn, *Ueber die Lehrart Jesu und seiner Apostel*, 140, where he applied the same thinking to Peter's condemnation in Matt. 16:23.

[27] Behn, *Ueber die Lehrart Jesu und seiner Apostel*, 129.

[28] Behn, *Ueber die Lehrart Jesu und seiner Apostel*, 131.

[29] This is also true of demonic servant girl in Acts 16:16–18.

Leipzig he taught as professor of philosophy, served as a captain in the War of Liberation (1813–1814), and integrated himself within the city's Masonic order. His service to the city earned him an honorary citizenship in 1841.

Krug is known best for his philosophical work, in which he attempted to bridge realism and idealism in transcendental synthesis.[30] Though Krug's reworking of Kant's philosophy with the *Ego* and the first principle of knowledge is an area worth discussing elsewhere, for our purposes we are concerned with one of Krug's early writings. In 1792, Krug penned a short piece titled *Principium, cui religionis christianae auctor doctrinam de moribus superstruxit, ad tempora eius atque consilia aptissime et accommodatissime constitutum*, in which he worked out his understanding of the doctrine of accommodation. While Reinhard and Krug applied the doctrine to different subjects, Reinhard's influence was clearly visible in Krug's frequent mention of his Wittenberg teacher. Whereas God's kingdom was the primary subject of Reinhard's application of the doctrine, Krug turned his attention to the motif of *the fear of the Lord*.

Though Krug was specifically addressing the fear of God, he stated that his understanding of accommodation was applicable to other areas of the Bible. Accommodation served as an interpretive tool for the entirety of the Bible, which aided in deciphering the meaning of many difficult passages.[31] Having established this disclaimer, Krug proceeded with his study of the fear of the Lord. He explained the problematic nature of the motif when referring to passages of the Bible such as Job 1:1, which identified the fear of the Lord as a quality of a man of God. Krug contended that such descriptors, along with the larger motif of fearing God and all related doctrinal elements, were an accommodation to the misunderstanding of ancient Israel.

The concept of fearing God was not original to the Old Testament but rather held a historical pedigree reaching back prior to Israel. It was a common trait of pagan religions preceding and during the time of

---

[30] Wilhelm Traugott Krug, *Fundamentalphilosophie* (Züllichau, Darnmannsch, 1803).

[31] Wilhelm Traugott Krug, *Principium, cui religionis christianae auctor doctrinam de moribus superstruxit, ad tempora eius atque consilia aptissime et accommodatissime constitutum* (Wittenberg: Dürr, 1792). I am working from the second volume of the 1828 edition of Wilhelm Traugott Krug, *System der praktischen Philosophie* (Königsberg: August Wilhelm Unzer, 1828).

ancient Israel. Israel incorporated the motif as a remnant of the paganism from which the nation developed. The biblical authors promoted the idea that one was to fear God in order to direct the attention of the Israelites to God. By maintaining this fear, simpleminded folk would be kept in check. For instance, in a time when ancient Israelites lacked a devout worship of God, Moses developed a system of fear and respect to move his people toward godliness.[32] Moses was not alone in promoting the belief that God was to be feared. Ancient Greek philosophers also upheld this erroneous belief for the betterment and order of the people.[33] In the East, Confucius too allowed his countrymen to remain in this error since fearing God was better than the alternative ungodliness that would ensue if the belief was corrected too abruptly.[34]

As for Moses, his efforts involved an intricate system of customs and laws, which expanded beyond the center of fear. This included the numerous customs, dietary restrictions, laws, rituals, and other regulations found in the Old Testament.[35] The entirety of the Mosaic Law stemmed from this false accommodation to the culture of ancient Israel. But this mistaken accommodation also had far-reaching influence, including other doctrinal matters such as the belief in angels and demons.[36] As a byproduct of the fear motif, the system of angels and demons was intended to foster a sense of awe for the divine.

Since the fear motif rested on an accommodation to erroneous thinking, the natural consequence for the modern Christian was that it no longer held any authority, salvific or otherwise. Krug contended that with the modern use of reason, readers of the Bible recognized that God desired love and devotion, not to be feared as a dictator. The fear motif was only a temporary measure, which passed once humanity gained greater understanding and reason. Additionally, since the fear motif relied on what was essentially an antiquated and completely inaccurate understanding of God, the subsequent doctrines based on this original error also lacked truth and authority for the modern Christian.

---

[32] Krug, *Principium*, 29.
[33] Krug, *Principium*, 45.
[34] Krug, *Principium*, 34.
[35] Krug, *Principium*, 13.
[36] Krug, *Principium*, 60.

Perhaps the most controversial aspect of Krug's work was the conclusion that Jesus's sacrifice held no atonement value. The Old Testament practice of animal sacrifice was clearly both an attempt to appease the anger of God and a negative outcome of the fear motif.[37] Both animal and human sacrifices were prevalent in the cultures surrounding ancient Israel. This practice was continued by the Israelites as an essential component of the fear motif. The New Testament discontinued sacrifices not because of the Israelites' progress in understanding but rather because the Romans forbade the practice, putting an end to sacrifices but not to the fear motif. Fearing God remained in the hearts of the Israelites, ultimately portrayed in Jesus's death on the cross. The belief that God required appeasement, which Jesus paid for all mankind by dying on the cross, resulted from generations of continuing an erroneous accommodation, originating from the fear motif.[38]

Jesus's message in the New Testament departed from this erroneous accommodation of fear and instructed his followers to attain happiness. Krug argued that when reading the parable of the Good Samaritan, readers came to see all that was required to attain true happiness.[39] Sacrifice or fearing God was not the answer; rather, an altruistic love for mankind was the key to happiness. This is not to say that Jesus did not employ the doctrine of accommodation. In fact, Jesus made extensive use of the doctrine—yet always to advance a love of God, not a fear of God.[40] Though both the fear motif and the message of God's love relied on accommodation, the former was an accommodation to superstition, while the latter never required laws, rituals, or the concept of sacrifice.[41]

Carl Friedrich Senff

In the decade's longest work on accommodation, Carl Friedrich Senff (1739–1814) advanced the Socinian cause with a treatment of many aspects of the debate thus far discussed. More importantly, his work also provided an extensive development of the doctrine in conjunction with

---

[37] Krug, *Principium*, 15.
[38] Krug, *Principium*, 45.
[39] Krug, *Principium*, 64.
[40] Krug, *Principium*, 65.
[41] Krug, *Principium*, 67.

the idea of God as Father and Jesus as a propitiatory sacrifice. After his theological and philosophical studies at Leipzig, Senff gained a reputation as a preacher. Through his natural eloquence and use of popular language, Senff's skills as a preacher gained him a rectorship in Halle. He would remain in the city until his death, rising within the city's hierarchy and eventually earning a doctorate from the university.

Though known mostly for his hymns, sermons, and texts on homiletics, Senff's *Versuch über die Herablassung Gottes in der christlichen Religion zu der Schwachheit der Menschen* (1792) should not be overlooked, constituting one of the most important texts for the accommodation debate during the 1790s. In *Versuch über die Herablassung Gottes*, Senff extensively covered the various elements of the accommodation debate, while applying a Socinian definition to most of the matters thus far discussed.

Biblical accommodation included the use of inaccurate terminology such as describing the sun's rising and setting. Though the authors knew better, they used such terms not only as a phenomenological language but also because their audience lacked accurate scientific knowledge.[42] In addition to matters of natural science, the biblical authors had to adopt erroneous anthropomorphic descriptions of God since ancient Israel was captive to these pagan beliefs. In agreement with Krug, Senff deemed the fear motif an erroneous accommodation for the benefit of ancient Israel. Senff also connected the accommodation of the Mosaic Law to the fear motif.[43] And he addressed the common topic of demon possession with the typical Socinian interpretation.[44] While his belief in angels was somewhat ambiguous, Senff argued that it was highly feasible that angels existed only as accommodations to a simplistic ideology of

---

[42] Carl Friedrich Senff, *Versuch über die Herablassung Gottes in der christlichen Religion zu der Schwachheit der Menschen* (Leipzig: Barth, 1792), 162–163.

[43] Senff, *Versuch über die Herablassung Gottes*, 15, 279. However, Senff broke with Krug in his understanding of New Testament accommodation. While Krug argued that New Testament accommodation differed from the Old Testament use of the fear motif, Senff did not make such a distinction. For Senff, New Testament accommodation was a natural continuation from that of the Old Testament. Senff, *Versuch über die Herablassung Gottes*, 292.

[44] Senff, *Versuch über die Herablassung Gottes*, 132–133.

[45] Senff, *Versuch über die Herablassung Gottes*, 195.

celestial beings.⁴⁵ Finally, Senff reiterated Reinhard's application of the doctrine to the mistaken expectation of an earthly kingdom.⁴⁶

Senff extended the doctrine to a wide range of issues, including doctrines related to eschatology, hamartiology, miracles, and the atonement. Most accommodations were rooted in the pagan and antiquated understanding of Old Testament Israel. Their limited capacities required the use of sensual learning patterns, which inevitably resulted in misunderstanding and inaccuracy.⁴⁷ However, Senff made little distinction between the Old Testament and New Testament use of the doctrine, since the New Testament was dependent on Old Testament times. For example, he viewed nearly the entire book of Hebrews as a web of accommodations, given its affinity to the Old Testament.⁴⁸ Due to the historically situated nature of the Bible, it was vital that the context was the primary hermeneutical key. The modern interpreter had to decipher between what was an adoption of Israel's customs, ideologies, and language and what was divine truth.⁴⁹

Senff's most significant contributions were the two objectives central to the work. First, Senff desired to show how accommodation to error was a testament to God's role as a Father. While some may have thought such condescension was unbecoming of God, Senff argued that accommodation was "worthy" of his divinity and should result in reverence and worship.⁵⁰ Senff repeatedly stated that God's desire was for the salvation of humankind. However, his saving message of "peace and joy" was only made known by condescending and adopting the profane.⁵¹ God as Father took upon himself the act of condescension to the limited capacity of mankind in general and of ancient Israel specifically.

Using the same term found in Kant's "What is Enlightenment?" Senff argued that "minor children" required a father who understood their

---

⁴⁶ Senff, *Versuch über die Herablassung Gottes*, 165.

⁴⁷ Senff, *Versuch über die Herablassung Gottes*, 23.

⁴⁸ Senff, *Versuch über die Herablassung Gottes*, 170. This understanding of accommodation was universally applied to all New Testament citations of the Old Testament by Jakob Christoph Rudolf Eckermann (1754–1837) in *Handbuch für das systematische Studium der christlichen Glaubenslehre* (Altona: Johann Friedrich Hammerich, 1801–1803), and *Theologische Beyträge* (Altona: Johann Friedrich Hammerich, 1792–1799).

⁴⁹ Senff, *Versuch über die Herablassung Gottes*, 19.

⁵⁰ Senff, *Versuch über die Herablassung Gottes*, 249.

⁵¹ Senff, *Versuch über die Herablassung Gottes*, 153, 296.

predicament.⁵² It could not be expected of children to comprehend at a level of an adult. Nor could children be faulted for their pedagogical needs. By using preexisting beliefs, the father was able to teach new ideas through a gradual and mutually benefiting approach. In his act of "condescension to the weakness of men," God revealed himself as a loving and thoughtful Father, aware of the limitations of his children.⁵³

God was not only like the father who accommodated but was also portrayed as a father in the Bible, and thus Senff applied the doctrine to the way Israel understood his being. The parables of the lost sheep, lost coin, and prodigal son aptly illustrated this principle. According to Senff, Jesus's use of the parables taught his audience to think of God as a Father. However, this was only possible through the accommodation of the erroneous idea that God could be surprised or unaware of what was lost.⁵⁴ The Jewish understanding of fatherhood and the characteristics of a father were applied to God, regardless of whether these descriptions were fitting of the divine.

The appropriation of the father image involved more than an accommodation of anthropomorphic characteristics. One of the consequences of the father model was the development of petitionary prayer. Despite the Bible and even Jesus's own instructions and illustrations of prayer, Senff argued that the use of petitionary prayer was an accommodation to a simplistic grasp of divine fatherhood. Petitionary prayer reflected Jewish theology, not the manner in which God operated. The Old Testament practice of petition continued in the New Testament with the introduction of Jesus as the intercessor and the sending of the Holy Spirit after Jesus's ascension.⁵⁵

Second, within this accommodation was the misperception of Jesus as the "Versöhnopfer" or propitiatory sacrifice. Similar to Krug, Senff argued that once we perceived God as Father and not as one whom we should fear, then Jesus's role as a propitiatory sacrifice could be correctly understood as a temporary accommodation to the misunderstanding of ancient Israel. Senff contended that Jesus's supposed atonement was an accommodation to Israel's desire for pagan sacrifice. A positive outcome

---

[52] Senff, *Versuch über die Herablassung Gottes*, 22.
[53] Senff, *Versuch über die Herablassung Gottes*, 22.
[54] Senff, *Versuch über die Herablassung Gottes*, 178.
[55] Senff, *Versuch über die Herablassung Gottes*, 184–191.

of an understanding of God as father, then, was the annulment of the system of substitutionary atonement, which ancient Israel had completely missed.

In agreement with Krug, Senff argued that the concept of a blood sacrifice stemmed from Mosaic Law. Prior to Moses the Bible had little discussion of blood sacrifice. Through his introduction, the concept of sacrifice became an integral component of Jewish spirituality. Jesus's act of sacrifice, along with much of his earthly ministry, served as the temporary but "wisest condescension" to the nation of Israel.[56] Jesus's death was not a "reconciliation of divine wrath" but only a "condescension to the weakness of the people for a sacrifice."[57] While God as Father did not require such reconciliation, he allowed this accommodation to stand, since to dispel the error would have done more harm than good.[58] For Senff, it was only in his modern age that readers of the Bible could correct the notion that Jesus was the Versöhnopfer.

Friedrich August Carus

The last of the early 1790s series of Socinian publications was Friedrich August Carus's (1770–1807) *Historia antiquior sententiarum ecclesiae graecae de accommodatione Christo inprimis et Apostolis tributa*. Born in Budissin, Carus conducted his studies in Leipzig, and after a short period in Göttingen, he returned to Leipzig as professor of philosophy. As with fellow Leipzig resident Krug, Carus's philosophy was greatly influenced by Kant. Also like Krug, Carus penned a work on accommodation in his early years. In *Historia antiquior sententiarum ecclesiae graecae*, Carus presented a history of the doctrine, especially during the period of the early church fathers and ancient Greek philosophers.

While Carus identified participants of the accommodation debate, such as Semler and Storr, Carus's objective was not to address the accommodation debate directly but rather to provide a history of the doctrine. Carus attempted to bridge the principles of the doctrine found in ancient Greek poetry and philosophy to the early church fathers and ultimately to the Socinian accommodation found in the eighteenth

---

[56] Senff, *Versuch über die Herablassung Gottes*, 124.
[57] Senff, *Versuch über die Herablassung Gottes*, 128.
[58] Senff, *Versuch über die Herablassung Gottes*, 131.

century. After providing a brief account of the accommodation debate, he introduced the basis of accommodation found within ancient Greek philosophy and poetry.[59] By discussing the principle of adapting to the capacity of the common man in the poetry of Cicero and Homer and the philosophy of Socrates, Plato, and Aristotle, Carus argued that the doctrine of accommodation was based on a rhetorical and pedagogical concept. It was Carus's understanding that the Platonic thought found in the early church fathers was the main avenue by which this Greek understanding of accommodation came to the early church fathers. Hence, when Clement of Rome discussed the anthropomorphism of the Bible, the issue of demon possession, and the accounts of prophecy, Carus applied what he identified as Greek accommodation to Clement's use of the doctrine.[60]

Kant and Accommodation

One of the changes in the latter years of the Aufklärung was the displacement of the Leibnizian-Wolffian system by Kantian critical philosophy. Beginning with *Critique of Pure Reason* (1781), Immanuel Kant went on to work out his case for human autonomy and its foundational role in science, philosophy, morality, and religion in *Critique of Practical Reason* (1788) and *Critique of the Power of Judgment* (1790). The influence of Kantian philosophy on modern theology has been argued unwaveringly by Gary Dorrien. Dorrien contends that "every major option from Schleiermacher and Hegel, to Kierkegaard and David Friedrich Strauss, to Ritschl and Troeltsch, to Rashdall and Temple, to Tillich and Barth got its bearings by figuring its relationship to Kantian and post-Kantian ideas."[61] Liberal theology, which Dorrien views as synonymous with modern theology, is described as containing three parts:

> Firstly, it is the idea that all claims to truth, in theology and other disciplines, must be made on the basis of reason and experience, not by appeal to external authority. ... Secondly, liberal theology argues for the viability and

---

[59] Friedrich August Carus, *Historia antiquior sententiarum ecclesiae graecae de accommodatione Christo inprimis et Apostolis tributa* (Leipzig: Schulze, 1793), 3, 4.

[60] Carus, *Historia antiquior sententiarum ecclesiae graecae*, 22.

[61] Gary Dorrien, *Kantian Reason and Hegelian Spirit: The Idealistic Logic of Modern Theology* (Chichester: Wiley-Blackwell, 2012), 11.

necessity of an alternative to orthodox over-belief and secular disbelief. ... [Thirdly,] the liberal tradition reconceptualizes the meaning of Christianity in the light of modern knowledge and values.[62]

Kant's Approach and Philosophical Foundation

While it would be inaccurate to argue that the doctrine of accommodation was as formative to Kant's theology as some of the other scholars we have discussed thus far, it would be safe to say that Kant was well-informed of the doctrine, which he employed in his *Die Religion innerhalb der Grenzen der bloßen Vernunft* (1793), and that his use of the doctrine served his critical philosophy well. Kant's first written encounter with the doctrine was perhaps the unsolicited admonishment from fellow Königsberg resident Hamann. In a series of awkward events, Kant served as an ambassador for rationalistic thought as he attempted to change the mind of Hamann, recently converted to Christianity. In one of these episodes, Kant, as a favor to a mutual friend, invited Hamann to cowrite a physics text for children. In scolding fashion, Hamann expounded on the futility of Kant's project due to the philosopher's failure to understand God's triune condescension to man. Hamann wrote, "Creation is not a work of vanity, but of humility, of condescension."[63] All such endeavors were abandoned, yet the two would remain lifelong friends. Later, Kant would even provide financial support by securing a position for Hamann and waiving the instruction fees for his son. Hamann reciprocated by arranging for the publication of Kant's first *Critique*, upon which Hamann withheld publishing his damning response due to their friendship.

Though Kant never responded to Hamann's rebuke, we do find Kant's use of the doctrine in his *Religion*. The work was originally intended as a four-part series in the *Berlinische Monatsschrift*.[64] The first installment went according to plan, being published in the April 1792 issue as "Of Radical Evil in Human Nature." However, Kant's plans for the subsequent sections were halted when the second portion

---

[62] Dorrien, *Kantian Reason and Hegelian Spirit*, 4–5.

[63] Johann Georg Hamann, *Briefwechsel*, ed. Walther Ziesemer and Arthur Henkel (Wiesbaden: Insel, 1955–1975), 1:452.

[64] For a more detailed account of the series of events relating to *Religion*, see Manfred Kuehn, *Kant: A Biography* (Cambridge: Cambridge University Press, 2001), 361–372.

was rejected on grounds of the 1788 Edict on Religion.[65] As a result of Johann Christoph Wöllner's (1732–1800) influence on Frederick William II (1744–1797), the edict heavily censured theological works antagonistic to the conservative theology of the king. The edict was resisted by many, including Kant, who yearned for the academic freedom characteristic of Frederick the Great's reign. Kant bypassed the censorship by submitting the completed work for publication under the guise of a philosophical rather than a religious writing. Though Kant's efforts were successful, he did not escape the king's reprimand. For Kant's deception, which included the publication of the portion already banned, Kant was forced to refrain from further publication in the realm of religion. Kant upheld this interdict until the death of Frederick William II.

The overarching intention of the work was an attempt to provide legitimate grounds for rational and moral faith.[66] To do so, Kant rejected the traditional faith found in a theoretical sphere and established a rational faith firmly within practical reason. Only by practical reason could rational faith be permitted to speak of spiritual and moral matters. While traditional faith was held captive by forces such as the church, rational faith affirmed by practical reason allowed people to respond and interact with moral law. Dorrien states that *Religion* "distinguished between the parts of Christianity that reflected its basis in 'pure rational faith' and the parts that degenerated, however inevitably, into sectarian dogmas that distracted from pure moral faith."[67] As Kant argued in *What is Enlightenment?* the general public was trapped in a "self-incurred immaturity." Content to forgo one's autonomy, mankind remained under the authority of the dogmas of the church.

---

[65] See Michael J. Sauter, *Visions of the Enlightenment: The Edict on Religion of 1788 and the Politics of the Public Sphere in Eighteenth-Century Prussia* (Leiden: Brill, 2009).

[66] See Georg Samuel Francke, *De ratione qua est critica philosophia ad interpretationem librorum, inprimis sacrorum* (Schleswig: Serringhaus, 1794); Johann Evangelist Hofer, *De Kantiana S. Scripturae interpretatione programma* (Salisburg: Salisburg, 1800); Karl Heinrich Pölitz, *Beytrag zur Kritik der Religionsphilosophie und Exegese unseres Zeitalters* (Leipzig: Breitkopf, 1795); August Christian Stauss, *Utrum philosophica Scripturae interpretatio, quam commendavit Kantius, admitti possit in explicando N. T.* (Wittenberg: Tzschiedrich, 1795); Gottlob Christian Storr, *Bemerkungen über Kants philosophische Religionslehre* (Tübingen: Cotta, 1794); Jakob Gottlieb Wurm, *Observationes ad philosophicum Kantii de hermeneutica sacra decretum* (Tübingen: Fues, 1799).

[67] Dorrien, *Kantian Reason and Hegelian Spirit*, 51.

Kant's understanding of pure religious faith was not simply juxtaposed against historical faith as polar opposites. Admittedly, there were limitations to historical faith, which, when "based on facts, can extend its influence no further than the tidings relevant to a judgment on its credibility can reach."[68] The historical faith of Christianity was bound by the constraints of ancient Near Eastern times, which included not only the historical setting but also preexisting thought patterns and the people's limited capacity to comprehend higher levels of truth. Hence, difficult matters needed to be accommodated to the lower levels of comprehension of the ancient Near East.[69] Due to the accommodated nature of historical faith, this inferior form of religion became much easier to disseminate among the masses.

These remarks are further explained when compared to Kant's distinction between a pure religious faith and an ecclesiastical faith:

> Yet, due to a peculiar weakness of human nature, pure faith can never be relied on as much as it deserves, that is [enough] to found a Church on it alone. ... [Y]et, because of the natural need of all human beings to demand for even the highest concepts and grounds of reason something that *the senses can hold on to*, some confirmation from experience or the like, (a need which must also be seriously taken into account when the intention is *to introduce* a faith universally) some historical ecclesiastical faith or other, usually already at hand, must be used.[70]

---

[68] Immanuel Kant, *Religion within the Boundaries of Mere Reason and Other Writings*, trans. and ed. Allen Wood and George Di Giovanni, Cambridge Texts in the History of Philosophy (Cambridge: Cambridge University Press, 1998), 113.

[69] Johann Ernst Christian Schmidt (1772–1831) affirmed Kant's moral and historical interpretation of the Bible. Schmidt adhered to Eckermann's use of accommodation, finding accommodations throughout the New Testament in matters such as miracles and prophecies. Johann Ernst Christian Schmidt, *Ueber den Einfluss der Kantischen unterscheidung der Geschaefte des historishen und moralischen Auslegers auf die Schrifterklarung*, in *Bibliothek für Kritik und Exegese des Neuen Testaments und älteste Christengeschichte* 1: 588–601. On the other hand, the Halle theologian Johann August Nösselt (1734–1807) was not too keen on Kant's moral exegesis. Under Baumgarten and Johann Georg Knapp (1705–1771), Nösselt learned to favor a grammatical approach to hermeneutics, similar to Ernesti. In his *Animadversiones in sensum librorum sacrorum moralem* (1795), Nösselt compared the two methods and found Kant's moral exegesis to lack the textual and historical foundation of a grammatical approach. However, he did not fault Kant for his understanding of accommodation. In fact, Nösselt used a similar definition throughout the work.

[70] Kant, *Religion*, 113, 118.

Due to the limited capacity of the masses—or, in Kant's estimation, those who were unenlightened—the church had to be established in order to accommodate to their lower level of comprehension. This included all aspects of traditional faith, such as dogma and the Bible.

Kant expounded on the difference between an accommodated idea and the truth that lies behind the accommodation in a footnote addressing the atonement. Here he was speaking of God's love for humankind. According to Kant, the depth of this truth was profound yet overlooked because of its incomprehensibility. Due to the difficulty of grasping God's love, mankind would soon ignore or bypass what they could not understand. Thus, the image of self-sacrifice on a cross was given to those who required an image to bridge the gap between the common understanding of man and the unfathomable divine. Christ on the cross was a "*schematism of analogy*, with which (as a means of explanation) we cannot dispense. But to transform it into a *schematism of objective determination* (for the extension of our knowledge) is *anthropomorphism*, which has, from the moral point of view (in religion), most injurious consequences."[71] In Kant's view, it was critical not to confuse the two (the accommodated idea and the truth behind it), but it was equally critical not to contend that such use of accommodation was unnecessary.

Giving credence to a central objective of the *Religion*, the doctrine of accommodation supported Kant's reconceptualization of traditional theological terms. Kant was not as interested as others such as Semler in using accommodation to justify his redefinitions. For Kant, the need to reformulate the dogmatic understanding of theology was a given within his critical philosophy and a necessary measure for asserting both autonomy and rational faith according to practical reason. Accommodation provided a convenient way to make these changes through a theological and exegetical method rather than a purely philosophical one.

Kant applied the same principle in dispelling traditional doctrines as he did in reconceptualizing theological terms. He argued that the belief in miracles was a bygone of dogmatic faith. In establishing rational and moral religion, "eventually all the miracles which history connects with its inception must themselves render faith in miracles in general

---

[71] Kant, *Religion*, 83. Kant also applied this line of thinking to the virgin birth of Jesus. Kant, *Religion*, 95.

dispensable."[72] Working within the "ordinary human way of thinking," a "religion of mere cult" greatly benefited from the genre of miracles, but rational religion had no need for such accommodation. According to Kant, due to the limited capacity of unenlightened mankind, without accommodations to the belief in miracles, such a religion would not have been possible.[73] Though modern religion had to deny the existence of miracles on rational grounds, rational religion at the same time initially "needed introduction" through the accommodation of miracles. Thus, Kant appreciatively acknowledged past accommodations; however, the mistaken belief in miracles was ultimately a mere pedagogical tool that was no longer needed or profitable.[74]

Though Kant did not address demon possession as extensively as Semler or those who responded to the Halle theologian, Kant did lend his voice to the conversation. Kant was uninterested in denying the existence of evil. Rather, he sought only to clarify Scripture's delineations concerning evil. How does one relate an intangible and difficult concept such as evil to an audience prone to superstition and myths? Fault lay not with the biblical authors—they merely used the doctrine of accommodation in a less than optimal situation. As Kant stated, "We should not, therefore, be disconcerted if an apostle represents this invisible enemy—this corrupter of basic principles recognizable only through his effects upon us—as being outside us, indeed as an evil spirit."[75] By using a tool, such as the belief in demons, they used a simpler idea to address a more difficult concept.

Kant proposed not that evil existed outside man but that by appropriating demonology, Jesus and the apostles were able to instruct their audience about the evil that existed within man. He explained, "This expression does not appear to be intended to extend our cognition beyond the world of the senses but only to make intuitive, for practical use, the concept of something to us unfathomable."[76] The critical nature of Kant's statement is not lost on James DiCenso, who writes, "One must pay careful attention to the precise language used here, because it

---

[72] Kant, *Religion*, 98.
[73] Kant, *Religion*, 98.
[74] Kant, *Religion*, 99.
[75] Kant, *Religion*, 79.
[76] Kant, *Religion*, 79.

consolidates and clarifies the interpretive approach governing the entirety of Kant's analyses of religious doctrines and images."[77] Kant's use of accommodation with regard to evil can be applied to a vast number of traditional doctrines. The Bible's proliferation of such doctrines is not an endorsement of these doctrines but a savvy method of communicating intricate principles through the means of primitive ideas.

Johann Wilhelm Schmid's Development of Kantianism

As part of the cadre of theologians who developed Kantian philosophy in their theology, Johann Wilhelm Schmid (1744–1798) would become known for his development of Kantian moralism.[78] Joining the ranks of fellow Kantian theologians Christoph Friedrich Ammon (1766–1850) and Carl Friedrich Stäudlin (1761–1826), Schmid's efforts gained him the moniker "Moralschmid." Ammon and Stäudlin established themselves in Göttingen, but Schmid spent most of his life in Jena. After completing his studies at Jena, Schmid tutored and traveled for several years before eventually returning to Jena, taking an adjunct position in 1769 and earning a professorship in theology in 1784.

Schmid, as so many in his time, was educated under Wolffian philosophy. Though benefiting from a mixture of Wolffianism and Pietism, Schmid rejected both in favor of a more rationalist position. He developed his understanding of the moral system of critical philosophy while a professor of theology at Jena. This combination of rationalism, moral religion, and Kantian philosophy first found expression in *De consensu principii moralis Kantiani cum ethica christiana* (1788/1789). Schmid would go on to further develop his ideas in *Ueber den Geist der Sittenlehre Jesu und seiner Apostel* (1790) and *De populari usu praeceptorum rationis practicae* (1792). However, Schmid's full position did not come out until his *Theologischen Moral* (1793/1794), and even this he

---

[77] James DiCenso, *Kant's Religion within the Boundaries of Mere Reason: A Commentary* (Cambridge: Cambridge University Press, 2012), 93.

[78] For an example of Kantian accommodation, see Karl Ludwig Nitzsch's eleven-part series *De Iudicandis Morum Praeceptis In Novo Testamento A Communi Omnium Hominum Ac Temporum Usu Alienis* (Wittenberg: Dürr, 1791–1802). Also see Paul Joachim Siegmund Vogel, *Aufsätze theologischen Inhalts* (Nürnberg and Altdorf: Monath and Kußler, 1796–1799), 53–75.

expanded in his *Christliche Moral* (1797–1804), a three-volume work edited by Karl Christian Erhard Schmid (1761–1812).

In a work similar to Kant's *Religion*, Schmid's *Ueber christliche Religion* (1797) attempted to come to grips with how Christianity was to be understood in his age. Defining Christianity in Kantian moral and universal categories, Schmid argued for a "natural" and "positive" religion.[79] However, in establishing Christianity as a universal and moral religion, Schmid still recognized that one had to make sense of the historical nature of the biblical text. Even though the Bible contained matters that were inaccurate, antiquated, or of little value to the modern reader, Schmid, as with Kant, did not want to completely jettison the biblical text. Schmid proposed that a proper understanding of such historical matters resulted from acknowledging that God accommodated to the times of the biblical audience. With this understanding, the modern interpreter was free to uphold the Christian faith along with the Bible upon which it rested.

Again echoing Kant, Schmid held that while accommodation was necessary in the past, in his day such measures were no longer needed.[80] He juxtaposed "sensual inclinations" with reason and morality. Through reason, modern readers were able to truly understand moral and universal Christianity. Those of biblical times were trapped by their limited capacity. Held captive to the "prejudices and misconceptions" that misled people away from reason and universal truth, ancient Israel could only learn through sensual means.[81]

Accommodation was necessary due to the age in which the Bible was given. By using the common thinking of the people, God could teach universal truths in a way that they could comprehend them. God would not rashly undo centuries of misunderstanding and error. Rather, by providing the "truths of reason" through "prevailing prejudices and sensuous representations," universal religion was given to ancient Israel

---

[79] Johann Wilhelm Schmid, *Ueber christliche Religion: deren Beschaffenheit und zweckmäßige Behandlung als Volkslehre und Wissenschaft für das gegenwärtige Zeitalter* (Jena: Wolfgang Stahl, 1797), 83–100.

[80] Schmid, *Ueber christliche Religion*, 106. In addition to Kant, Schmid referred to the discussion of accommodation by Behn, Heringa, Eichhorn, and Eckermann. *Ueber christliche Religion*, 114–115.

[81] Schmid, *Ueber christliche Religion*, 102.

through historical religion.[82] That is, God needed to adapt revelation to the specific time and place of the original recipients of the revelation. If the Bible had been received by the rational people of Schmid's day, revelation would have been sent in its pure form. However, since it was given to ancient Israel, the Bible was provided "according to the skills of comprehension" of the Israelites and not in universal form.[83] This entailed leaving some things as misconceptions, clothing truths in a "sensual envelope," and speaking in local, temporal concepts. Thus, there was a major difference between the revealed text and the universal and moral truth to which it referred.

According to Schmid, this condescension did not entail any wrongdoing on the part of God. By using only preexisting ideas, he did not introduce any new errors.[84] Nor did God intend for his readers to continue living in error. God was working from preexisting concepts to guide mankind toward a moral and universal religion. These accommodations were a temporary stage that would become obsolete in due time and that paled in comparison to the universal truth it reflected. God was merely working within the boundaries of the ancient Near East.[85] This form of gradual instruction used existing error to teach truth, which with time would overcome these past errors.

The End of the Century and the Continuation of the Accommodation Debate

Though those who held to Socinian accommodation dominated the debate in the 1790s, the exegetical use of the doctrine continued to be applied inconsistently by some who wished to maintain a Socinian definition and yet uphold the authority of divine revelation. This conflicting position was seen in earlier figures such as Baumgarten, whose model Semler carried to its logical exegetical conclusion. While most Socinian accommodationists would favor Semler's approach, there remained some rational supernaturalists, such as Gottlieb Jakob Planck (1751–1833), who wavered in their allegiance to the implications of Socinian accommodation.

---

[82] Schmid, *Ueber christliche Religion*, 109.
[83] Schmid, *Ueber christliche Religion*, 103.
[84] Schmid, *Ueber christliche Religion*, 104.
[85] Schmid, *Ueber christliche Religion*, 106.

Gottlieb Jakob Planck

Born in Würtemberg, Planck went on to work as a minister first in Tübingen and then in Stuttgart. When he left Stuttgart in 1784, Planck began a new career as a professor of theology at Göttingen. Over the years, he gained a reputation as a first-rate church historian. He remained in Göttingen until his death. In addition to his work as a church historian, Planck's career was marked by his unique position as neither a strict rationalist nor a strict supernaturalist. Convinced of critical reason, he adhered to the theology and exegesis of his rationalist peers. However, as a supernaturalist, Planck wanted to uphold the authority of the Bible as divine revelation, including the supernatural elements of the Bible that his colleagues rejected. Planck's attempt to balance rationalism and supernaturalism is most poignantly found in his *Einleitung in die Theologische Wissenschaften* (1794–1795).

Planck's rational supernaturalism stipulated three principles of exegesis.[86] The first rule of hermeneutics was that the interpreter had to seek the literal meaning of the text. Opposed to Kant's moral exegesis, Planck favored the more grammatical approach of Ernesti. Second, when interpreting a text, the interpreter had to be aware of the "spirit and mode of thinking of the age" for which the Bible was intended.[87] Third, the author was just as important as the audience. Included within the word *author* were both the human and the divine sources of the Bible.

It was in the second law of hermeneutics that Planck set his understanding of accommodation. The original audience of ancient Israelites required God to adapt revelation according to their limited capacity.[88] As a wise teacher tailored his instruction to the student's level of comprehension, so too did God adapt his revelation to Israel. For Planck, this necessitated the use of misunderstanding and preexisting error.[89] Planck argued that without this use of error, Israel would not have understood God's message of salvation and truth. While the biblical authors participated in accommodating to Israel, they at times also shared the same errors as their countrymen, and thus God had to accommodate to them as well.

---

[86] Gottlieb Jakob Planck, *Einleitung in die Theologische Wissenschaften* (Leipzig: Siegfried Lebrecht Crusius, 1795), 2:101–110.

[87] Planck, *Einleitung in die Theologische Wissenschaften*, 141.

[88] Planck, *Einleitung in die Theologische Wissenschaften*, 111–112.

[89] Planck, *Einleitung in die Theologische Wissenschaften*, 114.

These accommodations included nondogmatic matters such as natural phenomena. It is safe to say that ancient Israel did not possess the same knowledge to which the modern age was privy. While some interpreters might have attributed these descriptions to phenomenological language, Planck argued that these texts were accommodations to erroneous natural science. However, not limited to matters of science, Planck's use of accommodation also extended to doctrines such as demon possession. In addition to adhering to Semler's case for identifying demonology as misunderstood mental illness, Planck also revisited Reinhard's argument for God's earthly kingdom as an accommodation to Jewish expectation.[90]

While the merits of accommodation allowed the modern interpreter to make sense of the historical elements within the Bible, the abuse of the doctrine permitted the interpreter to claim any passage as an accommodation to erroneous thinking.[91] This point was refuted by Augustinian accommodationists who contended that such accommodation violated the holiness of God and went against divine morality.[92] Nonetheless, in Planck's view, when a passage was correctly identified as containing an accommodation, it implied that "nothing really true is contained in it."[93] All told, there was little to stop the reader from interpreting a passage with which he disagreed as a product of Israel's error and as possessing no authority for the modern reader.

If Planck's second law of hermeneutics justified Socinian accommodation, the third law complicated the nature of accommodation. By keeping in mind the author(s), both the human author and the Holy Spirit, it was up to the interpreter to decide whether it was becoming of the author to accommodate to error. Planck raised the issue of whether God—and to a lesser extent the human authors—could accommodate to error.[94] However, Planck did not come to any conclusions on the matter. In his rational supernaturalism, he merely recognized the dilemma, though in practice he ultimately sided with rational accommodation without addressing his inconsistencies.

---

[90] Planck, *Einleitung in die Theologische Wissenschaften*, 118.

[91] Planck, *Einleitung in die Theologische Wissenschaften*, 119–120.

[92] Gottlob August Baumgarten-Crusius, *Schrift und Vernunft für denkende Christen* (Berlin: Joachim Pauli, 1796), 204–212.

[93] Planck, *Einleitung in die Theologische Wissenschaften*, 119.

[94] Planck, *Einleitung in die Theologische Wissenschaften*, 125–126.

Magazin für Religionsphilosophie, Exegese und Kirchengeschichte

As we have seen, rationalists versed in the accommodation debate mostly upheld a Socinian definition. This was true for Heinrich Philipp Konrad Henke (1752–1809), editor of the *Magazin für Religionsphilosophie, Exegese und Kirchengeschichte*. Henke received his education at Helmstedt under Johann Benedict Carpzov IV (1720–1803), whose daughter he would eventually marry in 1780. After a brief period away, Henke returned to Helmstedt where he was made professor of philosophy in 1777, professor of theology in 1778, and full professor in 1780. Though Henke's tenure at Helmstedt began after that of Teller, both shared a similar rationalistic theology and Socinian approach to accommodation.

Gaining a reputation as a theologian, Henke also wrote extensively on church history. Henke's multivolume church history *Allgemeine Geschichte der christlichen Kirche nach der Zeitfolge* (1788–1791) was praised by Ferdinand Christian Baur (1792–1860). The family trait was continued by his son Ernst Ludwig Theodor Henke (1804–1872), who was a distinguished church historian. In addition to his scholarship as a historical theologian, Henke edited the journal *Magazin für Religionsphilosophie, Exegese und Kirchengeschichte* between the years 1793 and 1804. As editor, he used the magazine as a platform to further his rationalistic theology. Addressing all matters related to theology, philosophy, biblical studies, and history, Henke was able to promote his theology through the publications of similar-minded scholars.

In the *Magazin*, the image of a mourning mother became a repeated illustration for the discussion of accommodation. The first story was of an inconsolable mother whose spirits could not be lifted because her son had died.[95] The husband attempted any measure to bring a sense of peace to his mourning wife but to no avail. It was not until the mourning mother became overwhelmed by the thought of the wellness and happiness of her son that the husband understood what he had to do. Reminiscent of Senff's depiction of God as Father, the father in this story convinced his wife that for their child to be happy in the afterlife, the mother had to be happy as well. As long as she remained in a state

---

[95] Anonymous, "Bruchstück einer Vorlesung: Ueber die Accommodationen im Neuen Testament," *Magazin für die Religionsphilosophie, Exegese und Kirchengeschichte* 2, part 2 (1798): 249–253.

of mourning, their child could not be happy. For the well-being of their child, the mother had to overcome her loss and be happy for her son.

The actions of the father were justified by the anguish of his wife. No matter what he did, nothing alleviated her pain. The father knew that what he said concerning their son in the afterlife was not accurate, but he had no choice in the matter if he wanted to help his wife. It was not a harmful lie but in fact, one that would bring much peace and comfort. Hence, the father was free from any guilt for his actions, and his wife was freed from her pain.

It is easy to see what the author intended with his illustration. The mourning mother represented ancient Israel, while the father portrayed the actions of God, Jesus, or any of the biblical authors. Accommodation was a necessity for ancient Israel.[96] To this "less prepared people," accommodation allowed for the communication of truth that was otherwise impossible.[97] Not only was accommodation needed, it required the use of error to convince ancient Israel of the truths possessed by the various figures represented by the father.

As with the father, the ones who accommodated committed no wrong. Through the use of such false concepts, Jesus and the biblical authors were able to use these misunderstandings temporarily until "better instruction" could be given.[98] According to the author of the journal article, in his day of better understanding, such instructions could be understood without further recourse to these accommodations.

Johann Carl Christoph Nachtigal (1753–1819) repeated a similar story several years later in the *Magazin*. In Nachtigal's story, the mourning mother grieved for her child but only for a period. This time the mother came to terms with her child's death, but she was only able to do so by holding on to a misconstrual of God's promises regarding death. The husband saw the comfort that this misperception brought to his wife, but rather than correcting his wife, he allowed her misunderstanding to stand, for her well-being was more important than precise theology.

---

[96] Also see within the same volume "Ist die Lehre von den Akkommodationen im N. T. Neologie?"

[97] Anonymous, "Bruchstück einer Vorlesung," 252.

[98] Anonymous, "Bruchstück einer Vorlesung," 253.

While the story may have been slightly different, the lesson to be learned remained the same. The sensual learning patterns of ancient Israel failed to lead them to a fulsome morality and reason.[99] Rather, they were victim to erroneous thinking such as the Mosaic Law. However, the principle of accommodation provided a better way of communication. By adapting to their thinking, God enabled ancient Israel to understand his truth while at the same time not shocking them by correcting their longstanding ideology.

Jesus perfected the pedagogical tool of accommodation in his earthly ministry.[100] He never swayed from his purpose of teaching eternal truth, but at the same time, he was able to introduce these truths gently. By using metaphors Jesus appropriated preexisting ideas, accurate or not, for the greater good. This included the belief in demons, such as is found in Matthew 12:38–45. Though Jesus was speaking as if demon possession existed, he was merely using this erroneous thought in order to teach about the evil of man.[101] While Jesus could have corrected this thinking, it would have been possible with only a small number of people—and given his short time on earthly, highly unlikely.[102] The principle of accommodation continued in Paul's ministry. As stated in 1 Corinthians 9:19, to the Jews he became a Jew, and to the Gentiles he became a Gentile. Seen in Paul's ministry to the Athenians in Acts 17, accommodation was a core principle in his ministry.[103] By adapting the revelation he had received to the thoughts of his audience, Paul was able to successfully instruct all people in the way of universal truth.

Lastly, Nachtigal repeated the understanding that with the coming age of reason Christians should be able to perceive these accommodations in the Bible as superfluous for rational, moral, and universal

---

[99] Johann Carl Christoph Nachtigal, "Bruckstücke einer Vorlesung: Ueber die Akkommadationen, besonders im N. T.," *Magazin für die Religionsphilosophie, Exegese und Kirchengeschichte* 5, part 1 (1801): 114. Nachtigal may very well have been the author of the 1798 article.

[100] For a treatment of Jesus's teaching and the role of accommodation in theological teaching, see Ernst Gottlob Winkler, *Versuch über Jesus Lehrfähigkeiten und Lehrart: in sofern sich diese zur Fassungskraft der Zuhörer herabläßt, und für die Religionslehrer Muster ist* (Leipzig: Barth, 1797).

[101] Nachtigal, "Bruckstücke einer Vorlesung," 126.

[102] Nachtigal, "Bruckstücke einer Vorlesung," 125.

[103] Nachtigal, "Bruckstücke einer Vorlesung," 120.

religion. While they may have been necessary in the past, the modern age revealed their obsolete nature. In Nachtigal's day, people were supposedly more rational and no longer needed to be taught these errors by the church or in the universities.[104] Nachtigal's hope was not only to recognize the existence of these accommodations in order to make sense of the biblical text but also to rid the perpetuation of these antiquated concepts in the modern age.

Georg Lorenz Bauer

The final voice in the century's accommodation debate was Georg Lorenz Bauer (1755–1806). Bauer was the son of a pastor in Hiltpoltstein. After completing his studies at the University of Altdorf, he went on to replace his teacher Johann Andreas Michael Nagal (1710–1788) as professor of rhetoric and oriental languages. In 1805, he accepted a position in oriental studies at the University of Heidelberg. However, his tenure ended prematurely with his death less than a year later. Bauer was committed to a rationalistic historical criticism, as was typified in his *Entwurf einer Hermeneutik des Alten und Neuen Testaments* (1799). A common theme repeated throughout his scholarship was the concept of ancient myth; as with Gabler, Bauer advanced the understanding that the Bible, especially the Old Testament, incorporated ancient myths from their surrounding cultures.[105]

Though the work had a larger scope, Bauer acknowledged the accommodation debate and how his understanding aligned him with a certain cohort of like-minded scholars.[106] While differentiating between two definitions of accommodation, Bauer argued that the doctrine included the use of error. As a wise teacher had to address his students according to their abilities, the biblical authors used what was available for their purposes.[107] This inevitably included errors and other preexisting misunderstandings. However, such use of accommodation was justified by

---

[104] Nachtigal, "Bruckstücke einer Vorlesung," 114, 115.

[105] Georg Lorenz Bauer, *Hebräische Mythologie des alten und neuen Testaments, mit Parallelen aus der Mythologie anderer Völker, vornemlich der Griechen und Römer*, 2 vols. (Leipzig: Weygand, 1802).

[106] Georg Lorenz Bauer, *Entwurf einer Hermeneutik des Alten und Neuen Testaments* (Leipzig: Weygand, 1799), 124. Bauer referenced Teller, Hemert, Vogel, Behn, Stäudlin, Eichhorn, Eckermann, Heringa, and Carus.

the fact that they merely used preexisting error without introducing new error. Bauer also argued that because the end purpose of teaching truth overshadowed the temporary allowance of misconceptions, accommodation to error was valid.[108]

Bauer outlined four principles to follow when identifying accommodation in the Bible.[109] First, passages such as Acts 15:21 were to be interpreted as accommodations since it was alluded to in the text. Second, if a contradiction was found within the Bible, it could be assumed that at least one of the passages contained an accommodation to error. For instance, since Paul presented opposing positions on predestination in Romans 2:6 and Romans 9–11, predestination was rightly interpreted as an accommodation to erroneous thinking. The same held true for God's kingdom described sometimes as earthly and sometimes as spiritual. As expressed in John 3; 19:36 and Luke 20:35–36, the notion of an earthly kingdom was an accommodation to mistaken Jewish expectations.

Third, if the Bible affirmed the belief of something that was known to be impossible, then it could be assumed that it was an accommodation. Such erroneous beliefs often referred to supernatural matters, such as demon possession, the healing properties of the pool at Bethesda, or Jesus's resurrection.[110] While ancient Israel may not have known any better, Bauer argued that rational and modern interpreters could easily recognize such supernatural acts as accommodations to antiquated thinking. Fourth, if the text referred to folk custom, then it should not only be interpreted as an accommodation to Jewish notions but also understood to have no instructional value for today. As with Krug, this affected not only ceremonies but also doctrinal matters such as Old Testament sacrifices and Jesus's atonement on the cross.

---

[107] Bauer, *Entwurf einer Hermeneutik*, 125.

[108] Bauer, *Entwurf einer Hermeneutik*, 121.

[109] Bauer, *Entwurf einer Hermeneutik*, 123–124.

[110] As for the resurrection, also see Georg Lorenz Bauer, *Biblische Theologie des Neuen Testaments* (Leipzig: Weygand, 1800–1802), 1:316–380.

Conclusion

While the 1790s marked the end of the century, it was only the middle point of the accommodation debate. During the apex of the debate, Socinian accommodation dominated much of the literature. Behn continued the issue of Jesus's teaching, common to the previous decade. Krug introduced the issue of the fear of God and how that accommodated motif had far-reaching effects on various doctrines. Senff argued that Socinian accommodation was in keeping with God as Father and that propitiatory sacrifice was but part of this accommodation. Carus examined the church fathers' use of the doctrine to justify Socinian accommodation, which became a common practice throughout the debate.

In addition to the rationalistic manifestation of Socinian accommodation witnessed in the preceding decades, the 1790s also saw the development of Kantian accommodation. Kant's division of pure religious faith and ecclesiastical faith resulted in a reconceptualization of traditional doctrines and theological terms. Socinian accommodation provided theological and historical justification for the philosopher. Kant's influence can be seen in theological scholars such as Schmid, who followed a similar line of reasoning.

In Planck we see the struggle to harmonize Scripture as divine and human words. The ambiguity of his position was a result of trying to adhere to not only historical-critical methods but also a supernatural understanding of the Bible. Nevertheless, the century came to a close with several works committed to the Socinian position. Whether it is was through a series of articles or Bauer's monograph, the debate shifted decidedly toward Socinian accommodation.

Bibliography

Anonymous. "Bruchstück einer Vorlesung: Ueber die Accommodationen im Neuen Testament." *Magazin für die Religionsphilosophie, Exegese und Kirchengeschichte* 2, part 2 (1798): 249–53.

———. "Ist die Lehre von den Akkommodationen im N. T. Neologie?" *Magazin für Religionsphilosophie, Exegese und Kirchengeschichte* 2, part 2 (1798): 638–39.

Baumgarten-Crusius, Ludwig Friedrich Otto. *Grundzüge der biblischen Theologie*. Jena: Frommann, 1828.

Bauer, Georg Lorenz. *Biblische Theologie des Neuen Testaments*. 4 vols. Leipzig: Weygand, 1800–1802.

———. *Entwurf einer Hermeneutik des Alten und Neuen Testaments*. Leipzig: Weygand, 1799.

———. *Hebräische Mythologie des alten und neuen Testaments, mit Parallelen aus der Mythologie anderer Völker, vornemlich der Griechen und Römer*. 2 vols. Leipzig: Weygand, 1802.

Behn, Hermann Friedrich. *Ein kleiner Beytrag zu Untersuchung der Frage: Ob und wie weit es einem weisen Manne überhaupt, und besonders einem göttlichen Lehrer anständig und erlabut sey, sich zu den Meynungen und Irrthümern anderer herabzulassen?* Breslau: Meyer, 1791.

———. *Ueber die Lehrart Jesu und seiner Apostel: in wie fern dieselben sich nach den damals herrschenden Volksmeinungen bequemt haben*. Lübeck: Christian Gottfried Donatius, 1791.

Beiser, Frederick C. *Fate of Reason: German Philosophy from Kant to Fichte*. Cambridge, MA: Harvard University Press, 1987.

Carus, Friedrich August. *Historia antiquior sententiarum ecclesiae graecae de accommodatione Christo inprimis et Apostolis tributa*. Leipzig: Schulze, 1793.

Cramer, Petrus Christianus. *Dissertatio de sapientissima Jesu Christi in vero se Messia declarando oikonomia*. Copenhagen: P. M. Höpffneri, 1792.

DiCenso, James. *Kant's Religion within the Boundaries of Mere Reason: A Commentary*. Cambridge: Cambridge University Press, 2012.

Dorrien, Gary J. *Kantian Reason and Hegelian Spirit: The Idealistic Logic of Modern Theology*. Malden, MA: Wiley-Blackwell, 2012.

Dresde, Friedrich Wilhelm. *De falalci Fausti Socini libros Sacros interpretandi ratione*. Wittenberg: Charisius, 1790.

Eckermann, Jakob Christoph Rudolf. *Handbuch für das systematische Studium der christlichen Glaubenslehre*. 4 vols. Altona: Johann Friedrich Hammerich, 1801–1803.

———. *Theologische Beyträge*. 6 vols. Altona: Johann Friedrich Hammerich, 1792–1799.

Eichhorn, Johann Gottfried. *Allgemeine Bibliothek der biblischen Litteratur* 1–14 (1787–1801).

Franke, Georg Samuel. *De ratione qua est critica philosophia ad interpretationem librorum, inprimis sacrorum*. Schleswig: Serringhaus, 1794.

Hamann, Johann Georg. *Briefwechsel*. Edited by Walther Ziesemer and Arthur Henkel. 7 vols. Wiesbaden: Insel, 1955–1975.

Hauff, Karl Viktor. *Bemerkungen über die Lehrart Jesu mit Rücksicht auf jüdische Sprache- und Denkungsart*. Offenbach: C. L. Brede, 1788.

———. "Gedanken über die Frage: ob und inwiefern sich Jesus und die Apostel zu einigen jüdischen Ideen herabgelassen haben?," in *Beyträge zur Beförderung des vernünftigen Denkens in der Religion* 15 (1791): 1–25.

Hofer, Johann Evangelist. *De Kantiana S. Scripturae interpretatione programma.* Salisburg: Salisburg, 1800.

Kant, Immanuel. *Religion within the Boundaries of Mere Reason and Other Writings.* Translated and edited by Allen Wood and George Di Giovanni. Cambridge Texts in the History of Philosophy. Cambridge: Cambridge University Press, 1998.

Krug, Wilhelm Traugott. *Fundamentalphilosophie.* Züllichau, Darnmannsch, 1803.

———. *Principium, cui religionis christianae auctor doctrinam de moribus superstruxit, ad tempora eius atque consilia aptissime et accommodatissime constitutum.* Wittenberg: Dürr, 1792.

Kuehn, Manfred. *Kant: A Biography.* Cambridge: Cambridge University Press, 2001.

Nachtigal, Johann Carl Christoph. "Bruckstücke einer Vorlesung: Ueber die Akkommadationen, besonders im N. T." *Magazin für Religionsphilosophie, Exegese und Kirchengeschichte* 5, part 1 (1801): 109–30.

Nitzsch, Karl Ludwig. *De Iudicandis Morum Praeceptis In Novo Testamento A Communi Omnium Hominum Ac Temporum Usu Alienis.* Wittenberg: Dürr, 1791–1802.

Nösselt, Johann August. *Animadversiones in sensum librorum sacrorum moralem.* Halle: Hendel, 1795.

Planck, Gottlieb Jakob. *Einleitung in die Theologische Wissenschaften.* 2 vols. Leipzig: Siegfried Lebrecht Crusius, 1794–1795.

Pölitz, Karl Heinrich. *Beytrag zur Kritik der Religionsphilosophie und Exegese unseres Zeitalters.* Leipzig: Breitkopf, 1795.

Sauter, Michael J. *Visions of the Enlightenment: The Edict on Religion of 1788 and the Politics of the Public Sphere in Eighteenth-Century Prussia.* Leiden: Brill, 2009.

Schmid, Johann Wilhelm. *Ueber christliche Religion: deren Beschaffenheit und zweckmäßige Behandlung als Volkslehre und Wissenschaft für das gegenwärtige Zeitalter.* Jena: Wolfgang Stahl, 1797.

Schmidt, Johann Ernst Christian. *Ueber den Einfluss der Kantischen unterscheidung der Geschaefte des historishen und moralischen Auslegers auf die Schrifterklarung.* In *Bibliothek für Kritik und Exegese des Neuen Testaments und älteste Christengeschichte.* Hadamar: Gelehrtenbuchhandlung, 1797.

Senff, Carl Friedrich. *Versuch über die Herablassung Gottes in der christlichen Religion zu der Schwachheit der Menschen.* Leipzig: Barth, 1792.

Stauss, August Christian. *Utrum philosophica Scripturae interpretatio, quam commendavit Kantius, admitti possit in explicando N. T.* Wittenberg: Tzschiedrich, 1795.

Storr, Gottlob Christian. **Bemerkungen über Kants philosophische Religionslehre.** Tübingen: Cotta, 1794.

Vogel, Paul Joachim Siegmund. *Aufsätze theologischen Inhalts.* 2 vols. Nürnberg and Altdorf: Monath and Kußler, 1796–1799.

Winkler, Ernst Gottlob. *Versuch über Jesus Lehrfähigkeiten und Lehrart: in sofern sich diese zur Fassungskraft der Zuhörer herabläßt, und für die Religionslehrer Muster ist.* Leipzig: Barth, 1797.

Wurm, Jakob Gottlieb. *Observationes ad philosophicum Kantii de hermeneutica sacra decretum.* Tübingen: Fues, 1799.

CHAPTER 6

The End of the Accommodation Debate, 1800–1835

Recounting the advancements in theology and hermeneutics within the second half of the eighteenth century, Wilhelm David Fuhrmann posited that historical criticism developed over the span of 40 years.[1] Writing just after the turn of the nineteenth century, Fuhrmann already detected an acute awareness of the significant changes that had occurred during this formative period.[2] Fuhrmann contended that one of the core tenets of historical criticism was the unveiling of the historical context of the passage. This not only included the proper translation of the original words but also what the ancient world thought and why ancient Israel thought in these particular ways. By gaining a full understanding of biblical times, the modern interpreter could come to the true meaning of the text. Beyond a simplistic and literalistic reading, historical criticism opened up avenues of further comprehension and ultimately a more accurate interpretation of the Bible.

---

[1] Wilhelm David Fuhrmann, *Die Aufhellungen der neueren Gottesgelehrten in der christlichen Glaubenslehre, von 1760 bis 1805* (Leipzig: Weigandschen, 1807).

[2] For an overview of the developments in historical criticism, see Christian Ludwig Wilhelm Stark, "Ueber das oberste Princip der wahren Interpretation, und über die Frage, welche Erklärungsart des N. Testaments die richtigste sey?," in *Beiträge zur Vervollkommnung der Hermeneutik insbesondere der des Neuen Testamentes* (Jena: Schmid, 1817). Stark briefly mentioned accommodation and how the doctrine impacted our understanding of to what extent Jesus held the beliefs of his countrymen.

It should be noted that for the most part, the rise of historical criticism and the ongoing accommodation debate overlapped during this period. Fuhrmann recognized this timing, leading him to conclude that the accommodation debate played a major role in the development of historical criticism. According to Fuhrmann, the doctrine of accommodation was the key to aligning the characteristics of the historical text with the message of universal religion. Once one understood that the Bible included accommodations to the "prevalent mentality, to the modes of conception and even to the prejudices and mistaken and false or faulty opinions of folk religion," one could begin to see how the historical setting shaped the biblical text.[3] Forced to speak according to the limitations of the times, the Bible contained many elements that under different circumstances the biblical authors would have omitted. The doctrine of accommodation brought together the Bible and the "new philosophical propositions," otherwise known as historical criticism.[4] It allowed the interpreter to maintain the importance of Scripture and at the same time address its supposed inaccuracies.

Though biblical interpretation benefited greatly from Ernesti's philological approach, he proved to be too timid in his exegesis, in Fuhrmann's assessment. Fearing the deterioration of the authority of the Bible, Ernesti refrained from appropriating the recent advances in historical criticism.[5] Specifically, Fuhrmann claimed that Ernesti's hesitation and stunted potential as an exegete was due to his failure to implement a Socinian accommodation. Without the use of the doctrine, Ernesti limited himself to philology and did not take full advantage of the historical-critical method. Fuhrmann's comments coincide with my previous argument that Ernesti's use of the doctrine was somewhat ambiguous.

If the doctrine of accommodation was what separated Ernesti's philological approach from a fully developed historical-critical approach, Semler's use of the doctrine cemented his role in the progression of historical criticism. Though Fuhrmann traced the doctrine to the church fathers, Socinians, Grotius, and Lightfoot, it was not until Semler that accommodation was deployed in its modern use.[6] Semler was the first

---

[3] Fuhrmann, *Aufhellungen der neueren Gottesgelehrten*, 1:150.
[4] Fuhrmann, *Aufhellungen der neueren Gottesgelehrten*, 1:160.
[5] Fuhrmann, *Aufhellungen der neueren Gottesgelehrten*, 1:163.
[6] Fuhrmann, *Aufhellungen der neueren Gottesgelehrten*, 1:152–153, 166.

to combine the Socinian definition with the historical-critical method. Perhaps not for his originality but for his efforts as a promoter, Teller was also deemed an important figure in the modern use of the doctrine.[7] The partnering of Socinian accommodation with the historical-critical method by eighteenth-century rationalists formed a defining characteristic of rationalistic theology.

The use of accommodation in conjunction with historical criticism continued to progress after the Enlightenment. This partnership was sustained into the early nineteenth century as the central position of Socinian accommodationists. However, that relationship would be challenged by two opposing reactions. First, because the two were intertwined, finding fault in one also resulted in faulting the other. Since the inception of the Socinian doctrine, Augustinian accommodationists had disputed the legitimacy of deviating from their definition of accommodation. However, due to the partnership with historical criticism, objections were no longer limited to Socinian accommodation but were extended to historical criticism.

The Socinian accommodationists argued that their use of accommodation was validated by the historical research of ancient Israel. For instance, through the historical study of Israel and its surrounding cultures, it was shown that mental illness was commonly mistaken for demon possession. To facilitate the learning process, Jesus and the apostles incorporated this misunderstanding into their teaching without introducing further error or jeopardizing the communication of truth. Thus, modern interpreters rested assured when interpreting demon possession as cases of mental illness because they based it on the historical study of ancient Israel.

Augustinian accommodationists countered not just on theological grounds that Socinian accommodation was irreconcilable with God and the authority of Scripture but also on rational grounds that Socinian accommodationists were undermined by their own argument. They contended that historical criticism failed to produce the evidence that Socinian accommodationists claimed it did. For example, when they asserted that the mentally ill were misdiagnosed as demon possessed, one would expect historical proof supporting this allegation. However, there was no evidence that the demon possessed were in fact mentally ill. The

---

[7] Fuhrmann, *Aufhellungen der neueren Gottesgelehrten*, 1:169–171.

so-called historical-critical method relied not on carefully researched facts but on theological presuppositions that imposed certain assumptions on the historical setting of the Bible. The possibility of a natural explanation did not disprove the supernatural. Without historical evidence showing that the supposed errors were, in fact, actual errors, Socinian accommodationists were unconvincing in their case for legitimacy and failed to show that historical criticism was supported by historical research.

The second response to the partnership between Socinian accommodation and historical criticism came from proponents of the historical-critical method. This new voice questioned the hierarchical system of Socinian accommodation. At the same time, they also doubted the use of Augustinian accommodation. The relationship between accommodation and historical criticism proved to be unfruitful, not based on what Augustinian accommodationists proposed but because the doctrine itself was outmoded. These historical critics argued that the doctrine falsely assumed that Jesus and the apostles were in a position to accommodate to others. As members of the nation of Israel raised during ancient times, the logical expectation would be that Jesus and the apostles held the prevalent ideas and beliefs of their day to be true. Unless there was strong historical reason to contend otherwise, it could not be argued that they possessed knowledge that others did not. Thus, regardless of Augustinian or Socinian interpretations, new developments in historical criticism made the doctrine of accommodation obsolete. We will see that this understanding of accommodation had much to do with the closing of the debate.

SHIFTS IN THE NINETEENTH-CENTURY ACCOMMODATION DEBATE

A common trait of many works of the late accommodation debate was to provide a summary of the events up to that point. This often took the form of a rehearsal of significant themes, such as New Testament teaching, demonology, and atonement. Accompanying this historiography was the defining of accommodation in its two forms. Lastly, there was usually some sort of breakdown or categorization of scholars according to their position on the doctrine. This is the pattern we find in Georg Friedrich Seiler's (1733–1807) *Biblische Hermeneutik* (1800), the century's first contribution to the accommodation debate.

Georg Friedrich Seiler: A Prototype for the Debate's Last Phase

Seiler spent his entire academic career at Erlangen, where he also received his education. Beginning with a professorship in theology in 1770, he went on to become the university preacher in 1772, then the superintendent of the Lutheran church in 1788, all the while rising within the ranks of the university. Throughout his career, Seiler received offers from various universities such as Göttingen and Leipzig, hoping to lure him to their theology departments. Despite these overtures, he chose to remain in Erlangen, becoming the city's leading theologian.

Seiler's theology fell somewhere between rationalism and orthodox supernaturalism. In his *Ueber die Gottheit Christi, beides für Gläubige und Zweifler* (1775), he defended Christ's deity against the Arian and Socinian position. He upheld the Bible as supernatural revelation, maintaining the veracity of many events that his colleagues denied. His hermeneutics was typified by a grammatical-historical approach, making much use of philology. Equally as important to his hermeneutics was the use of historical criticism. This last point was not lost on Jodocus Heringa. Commenting on the *Biblische Hermeneutik*, Heringa lamented that Seiler had given so much credence to the new exegetical methods of the eighteenth century. Nevertheless, he praised the work as the best of its kind. As the preeminent work on hermeneutics, Heringa found it appropriate for a Dutch translation—granted, with extensive annotations to balance out Seiler's use of historical criticism.[8]

According to Seiler, the doctrine of accommodation was to be understood as both an accommodation to error and a "compliance" with error.[9] While some supernaturalists insisted on only a limited form of accommodation, Seiler held that the doctrine was correctly understood only when both components were included in its definition. The

---

[8] Heringa's translation was published as *Bijbelsche Uitlegkunde, of Grondstellingen en regelen, ter verklaaring der Heilige Schriften des Ouden en Nieuwen Testaments*, trans. and ed. Jodocus Heringa (Leiden: A. and J. Honkoop, 1804). This edition with Heringa's notes was translated into English as *Biblical Hermeneutics: or, the Art of Scripture Interpretation*, trans. William Wright, with notes, strictures, and supplements from the Dutch of Jodocus Heringa (London: Frederick Westley and A. H. Davis, 1835).

[9] Georg Friedrich Seiler, *Biblische Hermeneutik, oder Grundsätze und Regeln zur Erklärung der heil. Schrift des Alten und Neuen Testaments* (Erlangen: Bibelanstalt, 1800), 363.

compliance with error was a "necessary means" for communication, regardless of natural or supernatural revelation.[10] Humanity had certain limitations that God had to overcome in order to provide his truth. But there was also a "conditional condescension." Here Seiler had in mind the historical context of the Bible. Given the preexisting ideology, thought patterns, and pedagogical needs of ancient Israel, God had to tailor his revelation specifically to these limitations. This conditional condescension occurred in words and actions, in form and matter, passively and actively, in part and whole, perpetually and temporarily.[11] Finally, there was a "special" accommodation reserved for the manner in which the New Testament appropriated the Old Testament. This exegetical use of accommodation addressed why the New Testament authors at times used the Old Testament without taking into consideration the meaning of the text within its original context.

Seiler stipulated four principles for using the doctrine properly.[12] First, there was no accommodation in the text if such accommodation would negatively impact the teaching of morality. Second, though the use of errors was an integral component of the doctrine, this did not mean Jesus or the apostles supported these errors. Their method of accommodation only appropriated preexisting error, which they opposed when circumstances allowed. Third, there was no accommodation to error when it compromised the essential tenets of the faith. Fourth, it was a prudent and common practice for Jesus and the apostles to allow error to remain without correction since an abrupt rectification would have done more harm than good. These principles were integral to the Socinian camp, which Seiler identified as consisting of Teller, Stäudlin, Behn, van Hemert, Eichhorn, and Carus, and which was opposed by Storr and Hauff.[13]

It is fitting that with the first work of the nineteenth century, we see an inclination to what contributed to the end of the accommodation debate. Seiler set his discussion of accommodation within a section on Jesus's teaching and introduction of "new instructions." It was his

---

[10] Seiler, *Biblische Hermeneutik*, 366.

[11] Seiler, *Biblische Hermeneutik*, 367–368.

[12] Seiler, *Biblische Hermeneutik*, 379–380.

[13] To Seiler's list of accommodationists, Heringa added Steinbart, Meyer, and the authors in Henke's *Magazin*, who were opposed by Schaefer, Bang, and himself. Heringa, *Bijbelsche Uitlegkunde*, 378–381.

contention that Jesus intended not to reject Mosaic Law outright but to provide a correction to centuries of misunderstanding the Law. The modern interpreter had to turn to "universally recognized principles of true rational religion" in order to best decipher these corrections from the unfortunate inaccuracies associated with a text so situated within its historical setting.[14] These errors or "subjective conceptions"—often but not necessarily attributed to accommodation—were "imperfections" that the modern exegetic needed both to correct and to look beyond in order to come to the true meaning of a text. For example, in agreement with Krug, Seiler identified Paul's admonition of God's wrath as an error or accommodation that needed to be corrected in the modern age.

While this seems like standard fare for the accommodation debate, Seiler's subsequent remarks anticipated the end of the debate. He continued to insist that these "subjective conceptions" or "imperfections" were also found in Jesus, even though he qualified this claim by differentiating the extent to which these imperfections appeared in Jesus and other biblical figures. For Seiler, there were "no nocuous error" within Jesus's beliefs.[15] But with the words "no nocuous error," we begin to see one of the reasons why the debate ended. Up to this point, accommodation to error was necessary due to the limited capacity of ancient Israel. At times, God needed to accommodate even to his chosen spokesmen, such as the Old Testament prophets and New Testament apostles. However, there was always an unerring mediator of this accommodation, whether it was the biblical author or Jesus himself.

In contrast, Seiler's statement assumed that Jesus held to some innocuous errors.[16] Given these innocuous errors, his role as mediator of God's accommodation became compromised. Since Jesus held to some errors, as small as they may be, at some point God would need to accommodate to him. This shift signaled the turning point for the doctrine of accommodation. Eighteenth-century accommodation would eventually become obsolete in later stages of historical criticism. The constant disclaimer that a small number of biblical figures possessed truth but condescended to falsehood for the benefit of their audience grew to become

---

[14] Seiler, *Biblische Hermeneutik*, 357.

[15] Seiler, *Biblische Hermeneutik*, 360.

[16] For Seiler's definition of Israel's innocuous errors see Seiler, *Biblische Hermeneutik*, 377–378.

too cumbersome. Instead, historical critics began to argue that the biblical authors, and even Jesus himself, were no different from their audience. Hence, because they were in no position to accommodate to the needs of others, the doctrine of accommodation became no longer necessary.

This new voice within the accommodation debate, though adhering to a Socinian definition, differed from the Socinian camp. Against the Augustinian position, Socinian accommodation maintained that God's revelation condescended to the limited capacities of ancient Israel through the use of preexisting errors. This adaptation of truth was a temporary measure to ensure the communication of universal and rational religion. Within this system of accommodation was a hierarchy of knowledge. God possessed all truth, but while he shared his truth with his messengers, they did not all receive an equal degree of understanding. Moses possessed greater knowledge than the nation, and thus he condescended to establish a system of laws and punishment based on their simplistic needs for order and piety. In the New Testament, the apostles were given a special dispensation of truth that their fellow countrymen did not possess. Finally, Jesus as God's ambassador surpassed all human comprehension, initiating a wide range of further accommodations in the New Testament.

The new strand of Socinian accommodation agreed that the doctrine used the erroneous ideology of the ancient Near East. Where the new Socinian accommodationists differed was on the hierarchy of accommodation. Rather than maintaining an awkward system of who could accommodate to whom, the new Socinian accommodationists moved toward casting aside these various levels. Instead, they viewed all figures within the Bible, including Jesus, as holding to the opinions that were prevalent during their time. The biblical authors were products of their historical context, working within the same customs, thought patterns, and beliefs as their countrymen. There was no reason to assume that they possessed, or were even capable of possessing, knowledge that was drastically different. Hence, the use of accommodation was limited to God only. As we will see later, the doctrine of accommodation was entirely lost once the Bible was set on equal footing with other ancient religious writings, possessing no actual revelation from God. If the use of accommodation was limited to God, the doctrine was rendered void if God was no longer the author of the Bible and was removed from the writing process.

Anton Theodor Hartmann: A New Layer of Complexity

The accommodation debate was further complicated by Anton Theodor Hartmann (1774–1838).[17] It may very well have been Eichhorn who turned Hartmann on to the doctrine when he came under his tutelage at Göttingen. After his time at Göttingen, Hartmann became known for his development of historical-critical exegesis, especially in Pentateuch studies. He emphasized the importance of understanding the customs and beliefs of the ancient Near East for the interpretation of the Old Testament. Before succeeding Werner Karl Ludwig Ziegler (1763–1809) at Rostock, Hartmann served as a prorector for the city of Herford. During this period he wrote *Hat sich Jesus für den von Gott verheissenen Messias wirklich gehalten, oder hat er sich blos nach den Erwartungen seiner Zeitgenossen accomodirt?*, in which Hartmann painstakingly recounted the narrative of Israel's messianic expectations.

Hartmann argued that the messianic concept was a byproduct of the oppression Israel encountered under centuries of captivity and foreign rule. Whether it was Egyptian, Assyrian, Persian, or Roman rule, the Israelites longed for a savior to release them from their captivity. The prophets spoke of a second David, who would free the nation and bring together the scattered remnant. In New Testament times, the concept of atonement was grafted into the messianic motif. As Jesus's prominence grew, the idea that he would undergo a sacrificial death for the sins of mankind became an integral component of the messiah concept.

In addition to giving a naturalistic explanation of Jesus's rise as the messiah, Hartmann also questioned Socinian accommodationists such as Eckermann. While Eckermann argued for the prolific use of accommodation to error within the New Testament, Hartmann contended that his position was inconsistent. When interpreting the Bible like any other religious text, there was no reason to believe that Jesus and the apostles possessed greater truth than others in their surroundings.[18] It was only

---

[17] Fuhrmann makes brief mention of Hartmann as indicative of the ongoing nature of the accommodation debate and its continuing importance for the interpretation of the Bible. Fuhrmann, *Aufhellungen der neueren Gottesgelehrten*, 1:159.

[18] Anton Theodor Hartmann, *Hat sich Jesus für den von Gott verheissenen Messias wirklich gehalten, oder hat er sich blos nach den Erwartungen seiner Zeitgenossen accomodirt?*, in *Blicke in den Geist des Urchristenthums* (Düsseldorf: Johann Heinrich Christoph Schreiner, 1802), 62–63.

natural to assume that Jesus and the apostles, having been brought up as Jews during the Second Temple period, thought the same way and believed the same things as other Second Temple Jews. In fact, many of the apostles were from the lowest class, as equally uneducated as the majority of Israel.[19] Eckermann, though, failed to see how his position on accommodation was inconsistent with this modern understanding of the Bible.

Opposed to Eckermann, Hartmann preferred Georg Lorenz Bauer's use of the doctrine.[20] Though Bauer was not as consistent as Hartmann desired, he did situate the beliefs of Jesus and the apostles within their historical context more than Eckermann. Hartmann found hints of this position in Bauer's *Biblische Theologie des Neuen Testaments* (1800–1802). As we have seen in the previous chapter, Bauer addressed the doctrine at greater length in his *Entwurf einer Hermeneutik des Alten und Neuen Testaments*. However, the nineteenth-century shift in Socinian accommodation was more evident in his *Biblische Theologie*.

Hartmann was encouraged to see Baur state that Jesus and the apostles believed that Jesus was, in fact, the fulfillment of messianic prophecies. Hence, they did not accommodate when addressing prophecies in the New Testament.[21] This was also true of the existence of demons and cases of demon possession. Jesus and the apostles did not believe that demon possession were cases of mental illness; rather, they thought they were actual oppressions from evil spirits.[22] However, it was Hartmann's contention, along with Bauer, that Jesus and the apostles were ignorant of their erroneous beliefs in these matters. Jesus and the apostles were right not to apply the doctrine of accommodation in these cases, for as with others in their historical time, they believed them to be true. However, they were simply

---

[19] Hartmann, *Hat sich Jesus für den von Gott verheissenen Messias wirklich gehalten*, 73.

[20] Hartmann also admired Gottlob Wilhelm Meyer's (1768–1816) stance that Paul did not accommodate when addressing messianic prophecies but rather believed them to be true. Gottlob Wilhem Meyer, *Entwickelung des Paulinischen Lehrbegriffs: Ein Beitrag zur Kritik des christlichen Religionsystems* (Altona: Johann Friedrich Hammerich, 1801). Also see Gottlob Wilhelm Meyer, *Grundriß einer Hermeneutik des Alten und Neuen Testaments und einer Anleitung zur populären und praktischen Schrifterklärung* (Göttingen, Johann Friedrich Römer, 1801). This work is a short hermeneutic with brief comments on the use of accommodation.

[21] Georg Lorenz Bauer, *Biblische Theologie des Neuen Testaments* (Leipzig: Weygand, 1800–1802), 2:159; 3:171, 189.

[22] Bauer, *Biblische Theologie*, 2:233, 252, 365.

wrong in not understanding that these supposed supernatural phenomena were only natural occurrences.

Karl Christian Tittmann: A New Approach to Defending Augustinian Accommodation

I have argued that when combined with historical criticism, the Socinian form of accommodation gained much ground in the last decade of the eighteenth century. In the early nineteenth century, we witness a renewed effort to affirm the Augustinian position. However, Augustinian proponents also changed their strategy by focusing on combatting the bond between historical criticism and Socinian accommodation. They did not limit their accusations to a misunderstanding of the doctrine but instead included how the errors of Socinian accommodation and historical criticism fed off each other. Augustinian accommodationists contended that neither Socinian accommodation nor historical criticism honored a true understanding of the historical setting, resulting in a skewed interpretation of the Bible.

Charles Hodge (1797–1878) aimed to display the dangerous relationship between Socinian accommodation and historical criticism when he published a translation of Karl Christian Tittmann's (1744–1820) preface to his commentary on the Gospel of John.[23] Speaking of Socinian accommodation, Hodge wrote, "Perhaps few causes have operated more extensively and effectually, in promoting erroneous opinions than the prevalence of this doctrine."[24] He identified Semler as the one who renewed this doctrine through his development of historical criticism. The danger of this approach was in its ability to use supposed scientific methods and deem any doctrine an accommodation to error. Though

---

[23] Karl Christian Tittmann, *Meletemata Sacra, sive Commentarius Exegetico-Critico-Dogmaticus in Evangelium Ioannis* (Leipzig: Weidmannia, 1816), 3–34. The preface was added in the 1816 edition of the work and did not appear in the original 1786 publication. Hodge also translated Christian Daniel Beck's *Monogrammata Hermeneutices* (Leipzig: Schwickertum, 1803). Beck's assessment of the doctrine followed the common nineteenth-century format. After relating past themes of the debate, he defined the doctrine as either an accommodation of manner or matter, and he traced accommodation to matter to the Socinians and Grotius. Christian Daniel Beck, "Monogrammata Hermeneutices," *Biblical Repertory and Theological Review* 1 (1825): 25–27.

[24] Charles Hodge, "Introduction," *Biblical Repertory and Theological Review* 1 (1825): 125.

a preface to a commentary, Tittmann's short piece addressed this very concern and, through Hodges's translation, reached a significantly larger audience than a preface normally would.

For Tittmann, accommodation had traditionally been understood as an adaptation of manner. For instance, Paul used Old Testament ideas, such as the priesthood and the Melchizedek figure, to instruct Jews that Jesus was the messiah.[25] This pedagogical tool never compromised the principles of faith lest one could argue that the accommodation only served those of ancient times and had no relevance or authority for the modern age. The Socinian use of the doctrine was exacerbated by a supposedly historical method of interpretation that did not give due diligence to a grammatical and textual approach.

According to Tittmann, historical criticism did not uncover the *usus loquendi* of the text.[26] Rather, the presuppositions of the method made speculations beyond the text. For instance, since in the Socinian view, God or the biblical authors used an accommodation to error, the true meaning of the text had to exist beyond the mistaken doctrines of demonology, Jesus's atoning death, and the resurrection. For Tittmann, historical criticism had more to do with eighteenth-century rationalism than a truly scientific and historical approach. On the other hand, a grammatical method did not carry with it philosophical or theological presuppositions that distorted the text, but instead, it limited the interpreter to uncovering the historical meaning. Also, alluding to the shift in Socinian accommodation, Tittmann argued that historical criticism eroded the distinction between Jesus and the thinking of his day. As a result, he anticipated that the doctrine of accommodation would become obsolete and that Christianity would be reduced to eighteenth-century "natural religion" or nineteenth-century "mystical theology."[27]

---

[25] Karl Christian Tittmann, "Historical Interpretation," *Biblical Repertory and Theological Review* 1 (1825): 131.

[26] Tittmann, "Historical Interpretation," 133–134.

[27] Tittmann, "Historical Interpretation," 138.

Discussion of Accommodation in Journals

The discussion of accommodation in journals served as part of the Augustinian accommodation resurgence. Beginning in 1801, a series of articles articulated the historical position. In the *Magazin für christliche Dogmatik und Moral*, edited by Johann Friedrich Flatt, Wilhelm Todias Lang argued that Socinian accommodation committed two inconsistencies. First, the doctrine did not align with God's character. The divine qualities of perfection and holiness made the use of error for the communication of truth nonsensical. This also applied to the character of God's revelation. Using Kant's terminology, Lang questioned the validity of accommodation to error as a method of teaching truth. Admittedly, the "Ding an sich" ("thing-in-itself") of divine truth may have required an accommodation, but the type of accommodation remained in question. Lang was not arguing against idealists by supporting a belief in the thing-in-itself; rather, his application of the principle was to highlight the inconsistency of the Socinian position. The use of error to explicate the thing-in-itself or religious truth would be at odds with God and the truth to which it referred.[28] The use of error would oppose divine truth.[29]

The second inconsistency concerned historical data. Though Socinian accommodationists claimed that the mistaken beliefs of ancient Israel necessitated an accommodation of error, they failed to convince that this was indeed the case. What defined the modern use of heterodox accommodation was the partnership between Socinian accommodation and historical criticism. This relationship was crafted by Semler but fostered by many others in the eighteenth century. One of the claimed strengths of the Socinian position was that it did justice to the historical context of the Bible.[30] By deciphering between the erroneous beliefs of ancient

---

[28] Wilhelm Todias Lang, "Ueber die a priori und a posteriori aufgestellten Principiend der Beurtheilung, was in der christlichen Religionsurkunde locale und temporelle oder allgemeingültige Lehre sei? aus dem Standpuncte des Offenbarungsgläubigen," *Magazin für christliche Dogmatik und Moral* 7 (1801): 14–19.

[29] Lang, "Ueber die a priori und a posteriori aufgestellten Principiend," 29.

[30] See Karl Friedrich Stäudlin's three-part series "Über die blos historische Auslegung der Bücher des N. T.," *Kritisches Journal der neuesten theologischen Literatur* 1, no. 4, 2, no. 1, 2, no. 2 (1814).

Israel and the truth, Socinian accommodation held the key to discovering God's message of universal religion.

As we have seen with Tittmann, Lang challenged the extent to which Socinian accommodation actually relied on a historical approach. The common charge against Socinian accommodation and historical criticism was that they lacked historical evidence that an accommodation to error actually occurred.[31] Without historical evidence to this effect, the allegations of Socinian accommodationists were merely speculations of the historical situation based on theological presuppositions. The historical data did not support Socinian claims. In fact, historical evidence failed to prove that demon possession did not actually occur. While it was reasonable to assume that mental illness was at least sometimes mistaken for demon possession, this did not disprove the possibility of demon possession. The same held true for other matters, such as the concept of a messiah. Explaining the development of a prophesied messiah by a study of the oppressive history of Israel did not negate the supernatural factor in its development.[32] Lang recounted much of the same thinking in a follow-up article a year later.[33]

During Friedrich Gottlieb Süskind's (1767–1829) editorship of the *Magazin für christliche Dogmatik und Moral*, he examined the Socinian claim that the inheritance of Adam's sin was an accommodation to error.[34] Paul taught in Romans 5 that sin entered the world through the actions of Adam. This sin was passed to all mankind. Paul also contended that as sin entered the world through one man, so also was salvation delivered through the actions of a single person. Jesus's death and resurrection provided justification for all. Socinian accommodationists argued that the concept of inherited sin was a ploy to instruct a life of morality.

---

[31] Lang, "Ueber die a priori und a posteriori aufgestellten Principiend," 27.

[32] Lang, "Ueber die a priori und a posteriori aufgestellten Principiend," 30.

[33] Wilhelm Todias Lang, "Etwas über die Principien a priori und a posteriori, durch welche man das Locale und Temporelle von der allgemeingültigen Lehre in der christlichen Offenbarungsurkunde scheiden will, aus dem Standpuncte des Offenbarungsgläubigen," *Magazin für christliche Dogmatik und Moral* 8 (1802): 99–140.

[34] Friedrich Gottlieb Süskind, "Bemerkungen über die Hypothese, daß Paulus Röm 5:12 ff. sich zu jüdischen Meinungen akkommodirt habe," *Magazin für christliche Dogmatik und Moral* 13 (1806): 68–97. Also see Friedrich Gottlieb Süskind, "Ueber die Gränzen der Pflicht, keine Unwahrhelt zu sagen," *Magazin für christliche Dogmatik und Moral* 13 (1806): 1–67.

Adam did not pass his sin on to others, but the concept proved to be profitable for the instruction of holy living.

If this were true, Süskind posited that we should find historical precedence for the belief that humankind inherited the sins of a single person. Perhaps we would see this belief shared by the surrounding cultures of ancient Israel. At the very least, it should be shown that the concept of inherited sin was a prevalent belief in Hebrew theology. Such a historical presentation, however, did not exist. Ancient Israel did not adhere to a doctrine that humankind inherited the sins of Adam. Instead, Paul appeared to have introduced the concept. Historical research did not support the claim that inherited sin was an accommodation to erroneous Jewish thinking.

Johann Gottlieb Crell continued the dialogue in the *Magazin für biblische Interpretation*.[35] Crell's article treated the messianic prophecies fulfilled in the book of Matthew and the issue of whether accommodation played a role within these prophecies. While he recognized the different uses of the doctrine, for his purposes in this article Crell wished to concentrate on two methods. First, verbal accommodation occurred when the New Testament author employed an Old Testament passage without due diligence to its original meaning or context. Second, real or actual accommodation was condescension to Jewish error in "abilities, opinions, and attitudes."[36] After examining several fulfilled prophecies, he concluded that neither verbal nor real accommodation was used in prophecy.[37]

Prophecy and Accommodation

The issue of prophecy had played a role throughout the accommodation debate, albeit a minor one.[38] While cosmology, demonology, and New Testament teaching garnered most of the attention, the topic of prophecy did appear from time to time. It was not until this late stage of the

---

[35] Also see a pair of articles in the 1802 and 1803 editions of the *Journal für Prediger* to see how the doctrine was expounded in the context of homiletics.

[36] Johann Gottlieb Crell, "Ueber Accommodationem in Neuen Testamente und vorzüglich im Matthäus," *Magazin für biblische Interpretation* 1, no. 2 (1806): 231.

[37] The prophecies are found in Matt. 4:14; 12:17–21; 21:4–5; 27:9, 35.

[38] For example, see Johann Christoph Doederlein, *Institutio theologi christiani in capitibus religionis theoreticis* (Nürnberg and Altdorf: Monath and Kussler, 1797), 2:215–228.

debate that the issue of prophecy featured more prominently, as visible in how Hartmann and Crell addressed the issue of messianic prophecies.[39]

Varied Voices

Carl Christian Flatt (1772–1843), brother of Johann Friedrich Flatt, added to his teacher's understanding of prophecy in his German translation of Storr's *Doctrinae christianae pars theoretica*. In addressing the issue of the authority of the Old Testament, Storr came to the issue of whether Jesus's and the apostles' statements of fulfilled Old Testament prophecy were to be considered accommodation or not. Storr understood that those who contended for an accommodation proposed that Jesus's and the apostles' claims of prophecy were accommodations to the errors and opinions of the people in their time. Thus, the Old Testament passages were not in fact prophecies but merely passages cited as prophecy to accommodate to Jesus's and the apostles' audience. Jesus and the apostles knowingly misrepresented the Old Testament to adhere to the erroneous expectations and opinions of their hearers.

Storr charged his opponents with creating an "arbitrary supposition," "violating the commonly accepted rules of interpretation," and denying the "esteem and credibility" of Jesus and the apostles.[40] He cited Matthew 26:24, 31; Luke 22:37; and 24:44–47 to show that Jesus claimed Old Testament prophecies for himself when addressing his own disciples. John 17:12 further showed how Jesus claimed that a prophecy applied to him even in his prayer. Paul also included prophecy in his dealings with Timothy and the opponents of Judaism, who would have had no expectations of prophecy.

Flatt proceeded to give five "principal arguments" against the understanding that prophecies held by Jesus and his apostles were accommodations. First, Jesus's and the apostles' "moral character" made it impossible to hold such an understanding. Second, the fact that their miracles confirmed their authority as teachers was incongruous with the notion that Jesus and the apostles would promote any sort

---

[39] For an example outside of Germany, see Wessel Scholten, *Specimen hermeneutico-theologicum: De appellatione tou Giou tou Anthrōpou, qua Iesus se Messiam professus est* (Utrecht: Paddenburg and Schoonhoven, 1809).

[40] Gottlob Christian Storr, *Lehrbuch der Christlichen Dogmatik*, trans. Carl Christian Flatt (Stuttgart: Johann Benedict Metzler, 1803), 191.

of misrepresentation or error. Third, this theory of accommodation rendered the whole of Scripture uncertain. Neither those who held to this understanding nor Scripture itself provided a rule or category to decipher between passages that should be understood as accommodation to erroneous notions and those that should not. As Storr and Flatt rephrased the concern, there was no standard to differentiate between which passages were to be understood universally and which temporally. Fourth, the historical evidence that showed Jesus's teachings as accommodation dependent on Jewish expectations was lacking, and anyway, a connection between Jewish opinion and Jesus's teaching did not mandate an accommodation when the Jewish understanding contained no falsehood. Fifth, it had not been proven that this way of accommodation was necessary.

Flatt returned to the issue of accommodation when answering the claim that Jesus's atonement on the cross was an accommodation merely to reconcile the Jewish understanding of ritual sacrifices.[41] The authors offered three arguments against this thinking. First, Jesus never promised the end of ritual sacrifices, which thus necessitated his atonement on the cross. Therefore, Jesus's atonement did not need to be understood as an accommodation by any means. Second, in Romans, Paul had the optimal opportunity to correct all misunderstanding concerning atonement. However, Paul did not teach that Christ's death on the cross was an accommodation to the absolution of Jewish sacrifices. Third, the authors called attention to the "circumstantial" nature of the comparison between the cross and Old Testament sacrifices. Fourth, the crux of the apostles' teaching was founded on Jesus's death on the cross and not on man's "repentance and good works."

Speaking to the breadth of views on the topic, Seiler in the *Biblische Hermeneutik* discussed four ways to interpret fulfilled prophecies in the New Testament.[42] First, one could interpret these prophecies as actual predictions of the future that were fulfilled through the historical actions of Jesus. Second, one might say that the Old Testament prophets believed their claims for the future would come true, even though Jesus and the apostles knew that they had spoken in error. By claiming

---

[41] Storr, *Lehrbuch der Christlichen Dogmatik*, 614. Also see Gottlob Christian Storr, *Ueber den eigentlichen Zweck des Todes Jesu* (Nuremberg: Rawschen, 1800), 101–114.

[42] Seiler, *Biblische Hermeneutik*, 389–391.

that these prophecies were fulfilled by Jesus, the apostles were providing a mystical or allegorical interpretation that accommodated to these "exegetical errors." Third, one could make the case that God saw that the prophets truly believed in their false prophecies and chose to accommodate to these errors by fulfilling them through Jesus. Fourth, one might argue that the prophets, along with Jesus and the apostles, believed that they were true prophecies, which were fulfilled by Jesus; however, the truth was that they were mistaken—there were no actual prophecies.

Though providing these options, Seiler refrained from articulating his position and instead called for all to respect the position of others regardless of what it was. Heringa appreciated Seiler's tone and ecumenical spirit but stated that the first option was the only valid choice worthy of Jesus's character. To think otherwise would be heterodoxy.[43] William Wright also balked at Seiler's omission, questioning how one could uphold the Bible as God's revelation without adhering to the first option.[44]

Georg Christian Knapp: A Clearly Orthodox View

Though Seiler's ambiguity makes it difficult to pinpoint his exact beliefs, Georg Christian Knapp (1753–1825) made his opinions explicitly known. Born near Halle, he conducted his studies at the university, where he attended the lectures of Semler and Nösset. After further studies at Göttingen, he returned to Halle in 1777, earning full professorship 5 years later. In addition to familiarity with Semler and Nösset, at Göttingen he became acquainted with fellow accommodationist Zachariae. As a Pietist, Knapp was committed to the supernaturalism of the Bible and the refutation of rationalistic theology. According to Knapp, the misinterpretation of messianic prophecies as accommodations to error could be traced to Semler's use of the doctrine.[45]

Though published posthumously in 1827 by Knapp's son-in-law Johann Karl Thilo (1794–1853), the *Vorlesungen über die christliche Glaubenslehre* lectures were given in 1789 during the height of the

---

[43] Heringa, *Bijbelsche Uitlegkunde*, 386.
[44] Wright, trans., *Biblical Hermeneutics*, 443.
[45] Georg Christian Knapp, *Vorlesungen über die christliche Glaubenslehre, nach dem Lehrbegriff der evangelischen Kirche* (Halle: Waisenhauses, 1827), 2:129.

accommodation debate. Knapp's discussion of accommodation was firmly situated within the ongoing accommodation debate of the eighteenth century. His time at Halle and Göttingen would have ensured his encounter with the debate through fellow accommodationists Semler, Nösset, and Zachariae. Even if Knapp had not been introduced to the doctrine through Semler, Nösset, or Zachariae, it would not have been possible to study biblical interpretation during this time without some exposure to the debate. Of the various topics addressed in the *Lectures*, Knapp included several sections dedicated to the doctrine of accommodation. Rather than treating the doctrine comprehensively, Knapp limited his study to the issues of demonology and messianic prophecy.

Donald W. Dayton identifies Knapp's *Vorlesungen* as a prime example of Pietism's unity with the Enlightenment and discontinuity with orthodox Lutheran exegesis.[46] However, Knapp's discussion of accommodation reveals two problems with Dayton's argument. First, it problematizes Dayton's understanding of the Enlightenment. Dayton's failure to clearly define what he means by the Enlightenment or by Enlightenment biblical criticism not only misinterprets Knapp but also the Enlightenment. Second, Knapp's doctrine of accommodation shows direct opposition to biblical critics such as Johann Salomo Semler and an alignment with the orthodox doctrine of Scripture.

Knapp held that the literal interpretation of demons was the long-standing position of the church. It was not until more recent days that "new" theologians began doubting the existence of demons.[47] Particularly, it was eighteenth-century developments in historical criticism that questioned the reality of evil spirits. Knapp identified Semler as the main promoter of this understanding, though it had originated with Bekker and Farmer. Against this use of Socinian accommodation, Knapp argued that a careful reading of the Gospels revealed inconsistencies with such reasoning.

First, Jesus's desire was to free his audience from the errors that were prevalent in their day.[48] Given this objective, for Jesus to

---

[46] Donald W. Dayton, "The Pietist Theological Critique of Biblical Inerrancy," in *Evangelicals and Scripture: Tradition, Authority and Hermeneutics*, ed. Vincent Bacote, Laura C. Miguélez, and Dennis L. Okholm (Downers Grove, IL: InterVarsity Press, 2004), 84.

[47] Knapp, *Vorlesungen*, 1:370.

[48] Knapp, *Vorlesungen*, 1:370–371.

propagate the error of the existence of demons and demon possession would be counterproductive to his entire ministry. Second, if Jesus understood the existence of demons to be false opinion, then he would have avoided the topic as much as possible, resorting to such language only when absolutely necessary to complete his mission. However, passages such as John 8:38, 44 show that Jesus willingly raised the issue without provocation.[49] This is inconsistent with what we would expect from one who understood demons as accommodations to error. Finally, John 16:23–24 showed that Jesus reserved some teaching for only the disciples who were given greater revelation. Surely, if the existence of demons were false, he would have told his disciples as much. No such teaching was given.[50] Knapp concluded that such a use of accommodation resulted in Jesus being either a fallible teacher or one with a compromised moral character.

Knapp's *Vorlesungen* demonstrates an alignment with the orthodox understanding of Scripture on a well-defined issue. The doctrine of demonology was a crucial doctrine for the accommodation debate, becoming a favored topic of discussion for no less than Semler, the father of biblical criticism. Knapp's rejection of Semler's use of accommodation and interpretation of demon possession goes against Dayton's argument. Instead, Knapp's use of accommodation confirms the continuity between Pietism and Orthodoxy on the issue of biblical criticism.

Though Semler is most often associated with the use of accommodation in interpreting demon possession, Knapp argued that the misinterpretation of messianic prophecies should also be attributed to Semler.[51] In the *Vorlesungen* Knapp addressed the most prevalent arguments in Semler's use of the doctrine.[52] For instance, according to Semler, since the Jews were given to allegorical interpretation, Jesus and the apostles allegorized passages of the Old Testament as prophecies fulfilled by Jesus. Also, the messianic concept was a psychological coping mechanism for the oppression suffered during the exile. Finally, due to the limited capacities of the common person, an accommodation of a prophesied messiah was needed to bring him gradually to truth. Hence, the

---

[49] Knapp, *Vorlesungen*, 1:371.
[50] Knapp, *Vorlesungen*, 1:371.
[51] Knapp, *Vorlesungen*, 2:129.
[52] Knapp, *Vorlesungen*, 2:129–130.

messianic prophecies were not fulfilled predictions, a truth that Jesus and the apostles understood.

Knapp responded to these claims with four counterarguments denying any accommodation to error in the Bible.[53] First, the prevalence of allegorical interpretation during New Testament times was greatly exaggerated. While this method of interpretation was used, it was a secondary method. Josephus (AD 37–100) did not make any significant mention of the interpretive tool. Philo (20 BC–AD 40), who did make much use of the approach, introduced allegory as a new interpretive method, dating allegory after the time of the New Testament. Hence, the marginalized use of allegorical interpretation did not merit a whole system of accommodations.

Second, the occasions when allegorical interpretation was used, such as Galatians 4:24 and Hebrews 7, the biblical author made clear that he was using this method. Third, when New Testament figures refrained from alluding to Old Testament prophecies, it was due to the Gentiles' lack of familiarity with the prophecies and not because the prophecies were false. The Epistles and passages such as Acts 8:26–35; 10:43 showed how the apostles attempted to rectify the situation but how it remained an ongoing process.

Finally, there were no definitive cases of accommodation to error in the Bible. Knapp stated that neither Jesus nor the disciples ever taught a concept or doctrine that they thought was false. Knapp did acknowledge that the Old Testament contained teachings that were temporary and would be further clarified at a later point. For instance, the limitations of the Mosaic Law were corrected by the coming of Jesus.[54] But to use an allegorical interpretation to argue that the Law was an accommodation to error would have violated the original purpose of the Law. To avoid such erroneous interpretations, one had to limit an allegorical interpretation of prophecy to only passages stating that an allegorical method had been used.

Knapp's doctrine of accommodation decidedly positioned him against historical critics such as Semler and aligned him with orthodox hermeneutics. Knapp continued the Augustinian understanding of accommodation, arguing against the Socinian approach that eighteenth-century

---

[53] Knapp, *Vorlesungen*, 2:130–131.
[54] Knapp, *Vorlesungen*, 2:134–135.

historical critics championed. Contrary to Dayton, Knapp does not show accommodation to be an issue of Pietist versus Orthodox hermeneutics and one in favor of Enlightenment exegesis. Semler would be a better candidate for Dayton's argument. At the same time, though Semler does show a pietistic influence in his hermeneutics, it would be inaccurate to identify him as a Pietist given his rejection of the tradition.[55] And thus, Dayton's argument remains unconvincing.

Ernst Wilhelm Hengstenberg: Another Defense of the Historic View

While Knapp credited Semler with interpreting messianic prophecies as accommodations, Ernst Wilhelm Hengstenberg (1802–1869) contended that Eckermann was responsible for this idea. Originally from Bonn, where Hengstenberg began his education, he moved to Berlin to study under August Neander (1789–1850) and August Tholuck (1799–1877). Financially unable to complete his degree, Hengstenberg took a position as a tutor in Basel, where he eventually earned a position in the university. In 1824, he returned to Berlin initially as a privatdozent and eventually as a professor.

According to Hengstenberg, the premise of Eckermann's position was that Jesus and the apostles used the existing beliefs of the messianic motif and Jesus's role as the fulfillment of these prophecies to promote God's truth. However, Hengstenberg showed Eckermann's argument to be historically inaccurate. For instance, the prevalent understanding of the messiah called for one who would be an authoritative ruler and would free them from their oppressors.[56] Jesus's ministry on earth could hardly have been characterized in such terms. As the messiah, Jesus did not free the Israelites from their foreign rulers or gain any political power. In fact, it was under Roman authority that he was put to death. If the messianic prophecies were an accommodation to the prevalent ideas of ancient

---

[55] Eric Carlsson, "Pietism and Enlightenment Theology's Historical Turn: The Case of Johann Salomo Semler," in *The Pietist Impulse in Christianity*, ed. Christian T. Collins Winn, Gehrz Collins, Carlson Christopher, and Eric Holst (Cambridge: James Clarke, 2012), 97–106.

[56] Ernst Wilhelm Hengstenberg, *Christologie des Alten Testaments und Commentar über die Messianischen Weissagungen der Propheten* (Berlin: Ludwig Oehmigke, 1829–1835), 1:170–171.

Israel, why did Jesus come in such a humble form rather than as a conquering hero? If these were accommodations to erroneous expectations, when these expectations went so grossly unfilled, they would have created the opposite reaction and undermined Jesus's mission.

Hengstenberg also objected to the idea that the messiah motif was of purely human origins. On the one hand, the modern interpreter would not have been wrong to assume that centuries of foreign rule contributed to the development of the messiah concept. On the other hand, a psychological explanation for the need of a messiah did not mean that messianic prophecies could be explained on purely naturalistic grounds. It was understandable that the nation of Israel would develop a concept of a savior who would free them from their foreign rulers. And it was also entirely plausible that since God knew the nation longed for such a figure, he would use the concept to instruct his people. However, just because the messiah concept existed in the minds of the Israelites did not necessitate an accommodation to error. Proponents of historical criticism failed to provide historical evidence for their interpretation of messianic prophecies and instead simply forced their interpretation, which was based on the presupposition that prophecies were impossible.

THE END OF THE ACCOMMODATION DEBATE

It would be too convenient to expect a clear-cut end to the accommodation debate. If one side had conceded defeat, or if the historical evidence provided some quantitative way to determine the victor, our present task would be much easier. Instead, we see the continued struggle between rationalists and supernaturalists over the proper use of the doctrine. Teacher against student, the debate ended without resolution. The familiar theme of demonology continued to be debated, spreading beyond the boundaries of Germany. To complicate matters even more, the Socinian camp was fragmented by a group of historical critics who argued for the expulsion of the doctrine altogether. The debate ended without a decisive settlement.

Karl Gottlieb Bretschneider: The Tension of a Rational Supernaturalist

With his training in theology at Leipzig, Karl Gottlieb Bretschneider (1776–1848) chose the path of a clergyman after serving as a privatdozent in Wittenburg. During his early years, Bretschneider came under the tutelage of Reinhard. Through this relationship, Bretschneider gained his first position as a pastor in Schneeberg. After returning to Wittenburg for a degree, he was appointed the superintendent of Gotha, a position he held until his death.

As a rational supernaturalist, Bretschneider clearly felt the pain of attempting to adhere to two supposedly contradictory positions. Misunderstood by supernaturalists and rationalists alike, Bretschneider could only maintain his own theological integrity without being swayed one way or the other. As a case in point, his *Probabilia de evangelii et epistolarum Ioannis Apostoli indole et origine cruditorum* (1820) was not favorably received. Though he maintained that he never questioned the authenticity of the Gospel of John, critics perceived the work to be a direct attack on its authorship and authority. Bretschneider argued that the study was for the greater good of Johannine scholarship and the confirmation of its authenticity. It was his opinion that the negative reception of this work resulted in him being passed up for Tittmann's chair in Dresden.

The doctrine of accommodation was another area in which he differed from his rationalist colleagues. For Bretschneider, accommodation to error should be understood as a historical-philosophical criticism of Christian dogma.[57] Along with the moral interpretation of Reinhard and the critical philosophy of Kant, the doctrine of accommodation in its modern form attempted to discover the essentials of Christianity beyond a plain reading of the text.

Differentiating between various methods of accommodation, Bretschneider used two rubrics to define the extent to which God condescended through revelation.[58] First, the doctrine was to be understood as either negative/*dissimulatio* or positive/*simulatio*. The former classification referred to a passive omission in which God chose not to correct error. The latter gave the appearance that the error was, in fact, true by

---

[57] Karl Gottlieb Bretschneider, *Systematische Entwickelung aller in der Dogmatik vorkommenden Begriffe nach den symbolischen Schriften der evangelisch-lutherischen Kirche und den wichtigsten dogmatischen Lehrbüchern ihrer Theologen* (Leipzig: Johann Ambrosius Barth, 1819). 130. Due to the unavailability of the original publication, I am using the second edition.

[58] Bretschneider, *Systematische Entwickelung*, 137. Karl Gottlieb Bretschneider, *Handbuch der Dogmatik der evangelisch-lutherischen Kirche* (Leipzig: Johann Ambrosius Barth, 1822), 1:271–273. Due to the unavailability of the original publication, I am using the second edition.

affirming its legitimacy. The second rubric divided the doctrine between an accommodation of either form or matter. An accommodation of form was a didactic method, which a prudent teacher used to adapt a subject to the capacity of his student, whereas an accommodation of matter altered the actual content of the teaching, using what was not necessarily true to advise what was true. Common doctrines challenged by negative accommodation included the inspiration of the Old Testament, the existence of the spirit world, Jesus as the messiah, Jesus's role as humankind's atonement, and the resurrection.[59]

Bretschneider rejected accommodation of matter based on eight arguments.[60] First, there were no definitive examples of such an accommodation in the Bible. While it was true that the biblical accounts, especially in the Old Testament, shared similarities with the surrounding cultures, it should not have been surprising that other cultures and religions shared a certain amount of truth with Christianity. Second, an accommodation to error was not morally permissible of God and his messengers—that would jeopardize all revelation. Third, such accommodation would have made God the "greatest promoter" of error. Jewish error would have eventually faded away or have been corrected in modern times, but with God's sanction of these errors, they would have remained in perpetuity. Fourth, accommodation of matter would have compromised the essentials of Christianity, which were inextricably tied to doctrines such as the atonement, the resurrection, and the promise of eternal life. Fifth, there would have been no need for it. If doctrines such as the spirit world or the resurrection were accommodations to error, why did Jesus teach these doctrines to those, such as the Sadducees, who did not believe them to be true? Sixth, these supposed accommodations were of such importance, expressed through their frequency and detail, that if they were errors, they would have been proven false. Seventh, regardless of the audience—learned or uneducated, Jew or Gentile—the message was always the same. If these were accommodations to the audience, one would have expected to see different messages tailored to each audience. Finally, Jesus and the apostles emphasized and validated the authority of their teaching, claiming that no additions were needed.

---

[59] For Bretschneider's assessment of positive accommodation demonology, see Bretschneider, *Handbuch der Dogmatik*, 1:652–662.

[60] Bretschneider, *Handbuch*, 1:273–280.

Johann Friedrich Ernst Kirsten: Hope in Universal, Moral Religion

Bretschneider's assessment of the doctrine was not passed on to his student Johann Friedrich Ernst Kirsten. In a short dissertation, Kirsten reiterated much of Bretschneider's discussion. More a summary than an original work, *De Accommodatione Jesu et Apostolorum ad Errores* (1816) briefly overviewed several objections to the accommodation to error, but in the end, Kirsten opposed Bretschneider and sided with the Socinian camp.[61]

According to Kirsten, Semler held center court in the accommodation debate. While Semler and the "religious orthodox" could both agree that the doctrine was a necessary pedagogical tool, Semler made his departure when he promoted an accommodation to error.[62] Against the orthodox, Semler and company argued that the doctrine understood biblical authors to use preexisting errors when condescending to their audience. The orthodox countered with three objections.[63] First, using a pedagogical argument, they contended that if Jesus taught a propitiatory atonement while at the same time knowingly accommodating to the misunderstanding of sacrifice that would be an absolute *reductio ad absurdum*. Second, proponents of an accommodation to error worked from an a priori conviction rather than from a study of the biblical text. The third objective, which Kirsten found more convincing, raised the dangerous possibility of interpreters claiming any doctrine as an accommodation to error.

In Kirsten's response to these objections, he first turned to Paul's ministerial approach in 1 Corinthians 9:19–23. The success of Paul's mission was based on his ability to adapt according to his audience. To Jews he spoke as a Jew, to a Gentile he taught as one outside the law, and to the weak he became weak. The principle of accommodation was a practical and astute method of instruction, not a contradiction reduced to absurdity. To the charge that Socinian accommodation

---

[61] Bretschneider identified Kirsten within the Socinian camp in *Systematische Entwickelung*. Kirsten's understanding was more in tune with Julius August Ludwig Wegscheider (1771–1849). See Julius August Ludwig Wegscheider, *Institutiones theologicae christianae dogmaticae* (Halle: Gebauer, 1817), 53–55.

[62] Johann Friedrich Ernst Kirsten, *De Accommodatione Jesu et Apostolorum ad Errores Judaeorum* (Arnstadt: Trommsdorff, 1816), 2.

[63] Kirsten, *De Accommodatione Jesu et Apostolorum*, 2–4.

was based on an a priori conviction, Kirsten turned to the prophecies claiming that Elijah would precede the messiah's coming. Jesus knowingly accommodated to these erroneous expectations when he identified John the Baptist as the fulfillment of this prophecy. This interpretation was based not on an a priori understanding of the possibility of prophecy but on John 1:19–23, where John stated that he was not the fulfillment of Elijah's first coming. Lastly, Kirsten did believe that there was some truth behind the fear that the doctrine could be abused so as to reject any doctrine. Similar to Behn, he argued that the guiding principle for accommodation depended on the specific doctrines in question. Readers were to safeguard against this abuse on a case-by-case basis. Universal and moral religion would reveal when accommodation was being used beyond its appropriate parameters.

Johann Jahn: A Continued Appeal to the Church Fathers

In a return to the doctrine of demonology, the Catholic scholar Johann Jahn (1750–1816) carried on the discussion of accommodation outside the debate's usual geographical boundaries. Born in Moravia, Jahn conducted his studies at Olomouc and Bruck. After returning to Bruck and then Olomouc to teach Old Testament studies and languages, he was called to Vienna as professor of oriental languages and biblical archeology. His research on the latter subject was the distinguishing mark of his scholarship.

Jahn was reprimanded for arguing against a literal reading of demon possession in the New Testament. Proposing that accounts of demon possession were, in fact, undiagnosed cases of mental illness was hardly novel by the late eighteenth century. Nevertheless, his position on demonology and the publication of his *Einleitung ins Alte Testament* (1792) landed him in opposition to the archbishop of Vienna. Though never accused of heresy, Jahn was faulted for compromising the faith of the uneducated. To censure Jahn, his 1804 revised Latin introduction to the Old Testament and his *Archaeologia Biblica* (1805) were banned. The latter work contained a treatment on demon possession.[64]

---

[64] Johann Jahn, *Archaeologia Biblica in compendium redacta* (Vienna: Christoph Friedrich Wappler and Beck, 1804), 311–329. In addition to the accommodation debate theme of demonology, Jahn also wrote on the messianic prophecies in *Vaticinia prophetarum de Jesu Messia* (1815).

Opposition was unrelenting until Jahn was removed from his position at the university a year later.

Due to Jahn's censorship, it is unclear when he wrote his treatment on the church fathers' use of accommodation. "Was hielten die Kirchenväter von der Accommodation?" appeared posthumously in a collection of six treatises under the title *Nachträge zu seinen theologischen Werken* (1821). But with its publication in Tübingen, it may have received a broader readership than had it been published elsewhere at an earlier date.

Jahn's familiarity with the debate was evident from the very beginning. After recounting the different definitions of the doctrine, specifically Reinhard's understanding, Jahn continued with his study of the church fathers. The majority of the treatise consists of lengthy quotations from Clement of Alexandria, Tertullian, Origen, Athanasius, John Chrysostom, Jerome, and Augustine. Jahn concluded that with his study one could see that the church fathers commonly used the doctrine to interpret the errors contained in the Bible without accusing God of being deceptive. The fathers argued that these errors were the existing thoughts of ancient Israel, which God used without affirming or denying them.[65] Jahn also argued that with this understanding of accommodation, modern interpreters could make sense of the supposed demon possession described in the biblical account. Though not a treatment of accommodation, the third treatise of the *Nachträge* argued that his interpretation of demonology was based on his study of the church fathers and the scholarship of both Farmer and Semler.[66]

Peter Fourerius Ackermann reworked Jahn's *Archaeologia Biblica* in his *Archaeologia Biblica breviter exposita* (1826), maintaining the importance of demon possession to the debate.[67] In the same fashion as his

---

[65] Johann Jahn, "Was hielten die Kirchenväter von der Accommodation?" in *Nachträge zu seinen theologischen Werken* (Tübingen: Heinrich Laupp, 1821), 60.

[66] Johann Jahn, "Was lehret die Bibel vom Teufel, von den gefallenen Engeln, von den Dämonen, und bösen unreinen Geistern?," in *Nachträge zu seinen theologischen Werken* (Tübingen, Heinrich Laupp, 1821), 60.

[67] The issue of demon possession continued to be discussed until the end of the debate. As late as 1835, Ludwig August Kähler (1775–1855) kept the issue alive. Through a series of three short works, Kähler addressed the historical nature of the belief in demon possession and whether it was an accommodation to error or not. Ludwig August Kähler, *Dissertationis de accommodatione legitima, a Jesu, cum diaboli mentionem faciebat, usurpata, conclusio, ubi Scriptura concedente et ratione dictante demonstratur, doctrinam communem de diabolo abhorrere a Theologia Christiana* (Königsberg: Hartung, 1834–1835).

republication of Jahn's *Einleitung*, Ackermann's revised work was a thinly veiled effort to skirt the censorship of Jahn. As Jahn's successor at Vienna, Ackermann notably developed these works so they did not deviate from his predecessor. While he recognized that the discussion of accommodation had been addressed by Irenaeus against the Gnostics, by Bekker, and also by Farmer, Ackermann dated the accommodation debate as occurring during the previous 50 years. Being careful not to reap the same consequences as Jahn, Ackermann was more diplomatic in his discussion of demon possession. However, it is easy to see that Ackermann supported Jahn's view.[68]

The Signs of Finality

The end of the accommodation debate was signaled by the appearance of summaries, often in encyclopedic fashion. As short synopses, they stuck to the following configuration: defining accommodation in its two forms, recounting the topics of the debate and listing works associated with each position. This was the same arrangement found in early nineteenth-century studies but in an abridged format.

For example, August Hahn (1792–1863) included a brief summary of the debate in his *Lehrbuch der christlichen Glaubens* (1828).[69] Though a discussion of the doctrine could be traced back to the church fathers, Hahn claimed that it was not until the seventeenth century that the doctrine became a matter of debate. The reformers remained faithful in upholding the historical definition, which Hahn defined as a negative or formal accommodation. Opposed to negative accommodation, the seventeenth century witnessed the development of positive accommodation, or an accommodation of material and matter. Especially visible with the Cartesians, this latter form of accommodation interpreted cosmological and doctrinal matters as errors of ancient Israel. In the eighteenth century, positive accommodation was used to discredit the supernatural world, as seen in the scholarship of Semler. To the naturalists and rationalists of these centuries, positive accommodation became an "integral

---

[68] Peter Fourerius Ackermann, *Archaeologia Biblica breviter exposita* (Vienna: Fridrich Volke, 1826), 223–234.

[69] August Hahn, *Lehrbuch der christlichen Glaubens* (Leipzig: Friedrich Christian Wilhelm Vogel, 1828), 62–69. Also see August Hahn, *An die Evangelische Kirche zunächst in Sachsen und Preußen: Eine offene Erklärung* (Leipzig: Vogel, 1827), 87–97.

part" of their ideology.[70] Hahn ended his entry with a list of positive and negative accommodationists.

As a supernaturalist, Hahn deemed Semler problematic for the proper understanding of accommodation. On the other hand, Johann Traugott Leberecht Danz (1769–1851) held Semler and company as the key to the doctrine.[71] His précis of the debate followed the same format but claimed that the Bible contained numerous errors at the time of its writing. These errors were not introduced by God nor promoted by the biblical authors. Instead, through an accommodation of preexisting ideas, God's message was communicated through historical means. Again following the same format, Danz repeated the themes now very familiar to readers of this book, along with a list of many of the works we have discussed.[72]

Conclusion

The rationalistic understanding of accommodation established in the eighteenth century endured into the nineteenth century. Rationalists such as Kirsten maintained Semler's use of Socinian accommodation alongside historical-critical methods. The two formed a partnership, giving Socinian accommodation validity through historical evidence and giving historical criticism a theological explanation for many traditionally unacceptable conclusions about the biblical text. Through accommodation, the biblical figures were viewed as using the erroneous thoughts of their audience to gradually teach God's truth. Since God used preexisting errors, the modern interpreter was tasked with deciphering the true message behind these historical anomalies.

At the same time, the Socinian definition of accommodation evolved during the nineteenth century. The hierarchy of accommodations was deemed too cumbersome by certain historical critics. Earlier adherents of Socinian accommodation had constructed a system of accommodations in which biblical figures possessed more knowledge than other figures, thus

---

[70] Hahn, *Lehrbuch*, 68.

[71] Johann Traugott Leberecht Danz, *Encyklopädie und Methodologie der theologischen Wissenschaften* (Weimar: Wilhelm Hoffmann, 1832), 282–287.

[72] Danz's list of works is not as balanced as Hahn, providing many more Socinian sources. For an even more concise summary, see Johann Traugott Leberecht Danz, *Universal-Wörterbuch der theologischen, kirchen—und religionsgeschichtlichen Literatur* (Leipzig: Fest, 1843), 17–18.

creating a rift between the biblical figures and their historical context. For the new historical critics, though, it became more natural to align them with their historical context. Jesus, the apostles, the prophets, and the biblical authors were not in a special position to accommodate to others. They were all limited by their historical context, adhering to the same customs, beliefs, and ideologies of their times. Only God was in a position to accommodate. By including the preexisting misunderstandings of the biblical figures, God was able to communicate a universal religion within a historically situated means.

During the final stage of the debate, we also witnessed a resurgence of Augustinian accommodation. While efforts to combat Socinian accommodation in the early 1800s were not as numerous as the Socinian works of the 1790s, they did amount to a significant pushback. A key component of their argument was the claim that Socinian accommodationists lacked historical evidence. Socinian accommodation not only violated the sanctity of God and his revelation but also failed to live up to its own assertions of historical accuracy. While historical research did provide a plausible cause for certain occurrences, such as the development of the messiah concept, it proved to be inconclusive in many areas. It was simply too far of a stretch to claim accommodation to error when it could not be definitively shown that there was any error.

While one would wish that the debate had come to a more decisive end with clear delineations and quantitative results, we are faced with a more complex scenario. Though the use of both historical and Socinian accommodation continued, the debate did come to an end. Accommodationists ceased to dialogue with one another, allowing the debate to dissipate without recourse. Part of the reason for this less-than-climactic end was the shift within the Socinian camp. Through research of the biblical-writing process, nineteenth-century accommodationists developed the idea that applying the doctrine to the biblical figures constituted an antiquated concept. Rather, the biblical figures were fully situated within their historical context, without any knowledge that would be atypical for the time period. Since God was the only one in a position to accommodate, debating the extent to which Jesus and the apostles applied the doctrine had become a nonissue.

Bibliography

Ackermann, Peter Fourerius. *Archaeologia Biblica breviter exposita.* Vienna: Fridrich Volke, 1826.

Beck, Christian Daniel. *Monogrammata Hermeneutices: Librorum Novi Fœderis.* Leipzig: Schwickertum, 1803.

Bretschneider, Karl Gottlieb. *Handbuch der Dogmatik der evangelisch-lutherischen Kirche.* Leipzig: Johann Ambrosius Barth, 1822.

———. *Systematische Entwickelung aller in der Dogmatik vorkommenden Begriffe nach den symbolischen Schriften der evangelisch-lutherischen Kirche und den wichtigsten dogmatischen Lehrbüchern ihrer Theologen. Nebst der Literatur, vorzüglich der neuern, über alle Theile der Dogmatik.* Leipzig: Johann Ambrosius Barth, 1825.

Carlsson, Eric. "Pietism and the Enlightenment Theology's Historical Turn: The Case of Johann Salomo Semler." In *The Pietist Impulse in Christianity*, edited by Christian T. Collins Winn, Gehrz Collins, Carlson Christopher, and Eric Holst, 97–106. Cambridge: James Clarke, 2012.

Crell, Johann Gottlieb. "Ueber Accommodationem in Neuen Testamente und vorzüglich im Matthäus." *Magazin für biblische Interpretation* 1, no. 2 (1806): 193–252.

Danz, Johann Traugott Leberecht. *Encyklopädie und Methodologie der theologischen Wissenschaften.* Weimar: Wilhelm Hoffmann, 1832.

———. *Universal-Wörterbuch der theologischen, kirchen—und religionsgeschichtlichen Literatur.* Leipzig: Fest, 1843.

Dayton, Donald W. "The Pietist Theological Critique of Biblical Inerrancy." In *Evangelicals and Scripture: Tradition, Authority and Hermeneutics*, edited by Vincent Bacote, Laura C. Miguélez, and Dennis L. Okholm, 76–89. Downers Grove, IL: InterVarsity Press, 2004.

Doederlein, Johann Christoph. *Institutio theologi christiani in capitibus religionis theoreticis.* 2 vols. Nürnberg and Altdorf: Monath and Kussler 1797.

Fuhrmann, Wilhelm David. *Die Aufhellungen der neueren Gottesgelehrten in der christlichen Glaubenslehre, von 1760 bis 1805.* Leipzig: Weigandschen, 1807.

Hahn, August. *An die Evangelische Kirche zunächst in Sachsen und Preußen: Eine offene Erklärung.* Leipzig: Friedrich Christian Wilhelm Vogel, 1827.

———. *Lehrbuch der christlichen Glaubens.* Leipzig: Friedrich Christian Wilhelm Vogel, 1828.

Hartmann, Anton Theodor. *Hat sich Jesut für den von Sott verheissenen Messias wirklich gehalten, oder blos nach den Hoffnungen und Erwartungen feiner Zeitgenossen accomodirt?* In *Blicke in den Geist des Urchristenthums.* Düsseldorf: Schreiner, 1802.

Hengstenberg, Ernst Wilhelm. *Christologie des Alten Testaments und Commentar über die Messianischen Weissagungen der Propheten.* 3 vols. Berlin: Ludwig Oehmigke, 1829–1835.

Hodge, Charles. "Introduction to Charles Christian Tittmann on Historical Interpretation," *Biblical Repertory* 1 (1825): 125–127.

Jahn, Johann. *Archaeologia Biblica in compendium redacta.* Vienna: Christoph Friedrich Wappler and Beck, 1804.

———. "Was hielten die Kirchenväter von der Accommodation?" In *Nachträge zu seinen theologischen Werken.* Tübingen: Heinrich Laupp, 1821.

———. "Was lehrt die Bibel vom Teufel, von den gefallenen Engeln, von den Dämonen, und bösen unreinen Geistern?," in *Nachträge zu seinen theologischen Werken.* Tübingen, Heinrich Laupp, 1821.

Kähler, Ludwig August. *Dissertationis de accommodatione legitima, a Jesu, cum diaboli mentionem faciebat, usurpata, conclusio, ubi Scriptura concedente et ratione dictante demonstratur, doctrinam communem de diabolo abhorrere a Theologia Christiana.* Königsberg: Hartung 1834–1835.

Kirsten, Johannes Fridericus Ernestus. *De accommodatione Jesu et apostolorum ad errores Judaeorum.* Arstadiae: Trommsdorff, 1816.

Knapp, Georg Christian. *Vorlesungen über die christliche Glaubenslehre, nach dem Lehrbegriff der evangelischen Kirche.* 2 vols. Halle: Waisenhauses, 1827.

Lang, Wilhelm Todias. "Etwas über die Principien a priori und a posteriori, durch welche man das Locale und Temporelle von der allgemeingültigen Lehre in der christlichen Offenbarungsurkunde scheiden will, aus dem Standpuncte des Offenbarungsgläubigen." *Magazin für christliche Dogmatik und Moral,* 8 (1802): 99–140.

———. "Ueber die a priori und a posteriori aufgestellten Principiend der Beurtheilung, was in der christlichen Religionsurkunde locale und temporelle oder allgemeingültige Lehre sei? aus dem Standpuncte des Offenbarungsgläubigen." *Magazin für christliche Dogmatik und Moral,* 7 (1801): 1–67.

Meyer, Gottlob Wilhem. *Entwickelung des Paulinischen Lehrbegriffs: Ein Beitrag zur Kritik des christlichen Religionsystems.* Altona: Johann Friedrich Hammerich, 1801.

———. *Grundriß einer Hermeneutik des Alten und Neuen Testaments und einer Anleitung zur populären und praktischen Schrifterklärung.* Göttingen, Johann Friedrich Römer, 1801.

Scholten, Wessel. *Specimen hermeneutico-theologicum: De appellatione tou Giou tou Anthrōpou, qua Iesus se Messiam professus est.* Utrecht: Paddenburg and Schoonhoven, 1809.

Seiler, Georg Friedrich. *Biblische Hermeneutik oder Grundsätze und Regeln zur Erklärung der Heil. Schrift des Alten und Neuen Testaments.* Erlangen: Bibelanstalt, 1800.

Stark, Christian Ludwig Wilhelm. *Ueber das oberste Princip der wahren Interpretation, und über die Frage, welche Erklärungsart des N. Testaments die richtigste sey? Beiträge zur Vervollkommnung der Hermeneutik insbesondere der des Neuen Testaments.* Jena: Schmid, 1817–1818.

Stäudlin, Karl Friedrich. "Über die blos historische Auslegung der Bücher des N. T." *Kritisches Journal der neuesten theologischen Literatur* 1:4 (1814): 321–348.

———. "Über die blos historische Auslegung der Bücher des N. T." *Kritisches Journal der neuesten theologischen Literatur* 2:1 (1814): 1–39.

———. "Über die blos historische Auslegung der Bücher des N. T." *Kritisches Journal der neuesten theologischen Literatur* 2:2 (1814): 113–148.

Storr, Gottlob Christian. *Lehrbuch der christlichen Dogmatik.* Translated by Carl Christian Flatt. Stuttgart: Johann Benedict Metzler, 1803.

Süskind, Friedrich Gottlieb. "Bemerkungen über die Hypothese, daß Paulus Röm 5:12 ff. sich zu jüdischen Meinungen akkommodirt habe." *Magazin für christliche Dogmatik und Moral* 13 (1806): 68–97.

———. "Ueber die Gränzen der Pflicht, keine Unwahrheit zu sagen." *Magazin für christliche Dogmatik und Moral* 13 (1806), 1–67.

Tittmann, Karl Christian. *Meletemata Sacra, sive Commentarius Exegetico-Critico-Dogmaticus in Evangelium Ioannis.* Leipzig: Weidmannia, 1816.

Wegscheider, Julius August Ludwig. *Institutiones theologicae christianae dogmaticae.* Halle: Gebauer, 1817.

CHAPTER 7

Conclusion

The doctrine of accommodation contends that a chasm exists between God and his creation. Despite being created in God's image, man is bound by a limited mental capacity. Thus, we're faced with this dilemma: how does God communicate his religion of truth to humankind, which lacks comprehension? It has been argued since the patristic age that God condescended his revelation by accommodating to the needs of humankind. God uses the same strategy in the Bible as a wise teacher who adapts his lesson according to the learning ability of his student. The doctrine facilitates humanity's encounter with revelation by providing a means of divine communication catered to the profane. Like the hypostatic union, in which Jesus upheld his full deity while living as a human, God's revelation encases divine truth in human words.

THE DOCTRINE OF ACCOMMODATION: A STORY OF CONTROVERSY

The Augustinian understanding of accommodation contends that the harmonization of God's condescension with his perfection results in an inerrant Bible. God's condescension never compromised the authority or integrity of Scripture. This meant that accommodation was an act in form and manner, not material and matter. The former stipulated an accommodation in the way God communicates, while the latter included alterations to the content of God's communication. An accommodation of manner was the standard understanding since the patristic age, throughout the medieval period, and in the time of the reformers.

In the sixteenth century, we witnessed the beginnings of a challenge to the Augustinian definition. The Socinians incorporated within the doctrine the understanding that accommodations were made not merely in the manner of revelation but also in its content. For the Socinians, the inclusion of ancient Israelite customs and beliefs inevitably involved the use of errors and misunderstanding as a part of God's instruction. Socinian accommodation argued that only by employing misconceptions was God able to communicate superior knowledge to a less-than-superior audience.

Though the sixteenth-century Socinians mounted the first challenge to the Augustinian definition, the Socinian definition was not popularized until the seventeenth century. Also, while German Lutherans most extensively discussed and used accommodation in the eighteenth century, the Dutch Reformed made the most use of the doctrine in the seventeenth century. Specifically, it was the Cartesio-Cocceians who appropriated the Socinian definition, using the doctrine to harmonize biblical passages with scientific discoveries that they seemingly opposed. For example, the book of Joshua recounted an instance when God prevented the movement of the sun to ensure Israel won on the battlefield. Modern science showed that the biblical passage could not be taken at face value since the earth actually orbits around a stationary sun. The doctrine of accommodation was used to explain how God was not instructing Israelites about the earth's orbit or advancing the misunderstanding of the sun's orbit but merely using preexisting errors to communicate a greater truth. God adapted revelation according to the thoughts of ancient Israel by using scientifically inaccurate language. Cartesio-Cocceians employed the doctrine to explain many cosmological passages, such as the earth's alleged four corners, the rising and setting of the sun, and the light of the moon.

Against this innovation, the Voetians attempted to maintain the accommodation doctrine of Augustine and Calvin. They agreed with the Cartesio-Cocceian belief that the central objective of the Bible was to communicate the message of salvation. However, in opposition to the Cartesio-Cocceians, the Voetians contended that this objective did not negate the accuracy of nonsalvific matters. To say otherwise would mean God was a liar and deceiver. Augustinian accommodation accounted for such cosmological issues without including errors. God adapted his revelation to include phenomenological language, which addressed appearances and not scientific descriptions. This accommodation of manner used everyday language without violating scientific accuracy. As one would put it today, saying that the sun rises and sets is a colloquial way of describing what appears to happen when the earth rotates. To describe the sun as such is not an error but only a common way to describe the phenomenon.

As the Cartesio-Cocceians and Voetians debated the proper understanding of the doctrine, the writing of Meyer's *Philosophia S. Scripturae Interpres* exacerbated the issue. Though the work only briefly addressed the doctrine, the Cartesian principles it laid out for the interpretation of the Bible forced Cartesio-Cocceians to defend the logical conclusions of their position. This included the use of Socinian accommodation, which Cartesio-Cocceian accommodationists Wittichius and van Velthuysen publicly endorsed, leading other Cartesio-Cocceians to join in the defense of Socinian accommodation. The polarization of the controversy also had an effect on the historical position as well. Previously uncommitted scholars such as Maresius, no friend of Voetius, sided with the Voetians in safeguarding the Augustinian definition.

The publication of Spinoza's *Tractatus Theologico-Politicus* further propagated Socinian accommodation. Spinoza's use of the doctrine radicalized accommodation. Freed from Cartesian dualism, Spinoza extended the doctrine beyond mere cosmological issues and applied an accommodation to error in various doctrinal matters. While Bekker's use of the doctrine was the culmination of Cartesio-Cocceian accommodation, Spinoza's doctrine would become the foundation of eighteenth-century Socinian accommodation.

During the early years of the Aufklärung, Cartesio-Cocceian accommodation was passed on to the Lutheran rationalists of the eighteenth century. The trajectory from the Socinians to the Cartesio-Cocceians and finally to Lutheran rationalists was facilitated by Leibnizian and Wolffian philosophy. This new German philosophy ordered the world within a set of laws that excluded supernatural occurrences, and Socinian accommodation provided the theological and exegetical credence for descriptions of events that were scientifically improbable. It was Baumgarten who combined Wolffian philosophy with Socinian accommodation in a new hermeneutic. Drawing on the Wolffian distinction between the text of the Bible and God's revelation, Socinian accommodation explained how God's revelation of truth was enclosed within flawed human words.

While the Socinian trajectory jumped confessions, eighteenth-century Augustinian Lutherans drew more from seventeenth-century Lutherans than from the Voetians. The expression of accommodation found in Luther was continued by Quenstedt, Calov, and Deyling. They argued that God's condescension upheld the accuracy of all matter within the Bible and not merely matters of faith. This Augustinian definition continued into the eighteenth century with both orthodox and Pietist Lutherans affirming it. While the two parties clashed in other matters, on the matter of accommodation they put their differences aside to deal with the greater threat of Socinian accommodation. Löscher and Lange were no strangers to polemics, often dueling partners in one of the fiercest confrontations between orthodox and Pietists, but their agreement on accommodation aligned them against a common enemy.

To this point, the discussion of the doctrine was significant but still only in the preliminary stages leading up to the accommodation debate. The actual debate occurred approximately from the last third of the eighteenth century through the first third of the nineteenth century and was marked by a high volume of works within this relatively short period. The concentration of works often took the form of full monographs dedicated to the doctrine that were in direct dialogue with each other. The first monograph in the debate was Zachariae's 1762 biblical theology, in which he argued for an accommodation to error, articulated within a rationalistic system.

Along with the change in philosophical partnership, Socinian accommodation reached its peak during the Enlightenment. The single most important progression of Socinian accommodation occurred through the scholarship of Semler. Progressing beyond his teacher Baumgarten, Semler combined rationalism, historical criticism, and Socinian accommodation together to move in a profoundly different direction. The prevalence of rationalism greatly increased the awareness and use of Socinian accommodation. However, as significant as rationalism was to the cause of Socinian accommodation, even more crucial was the development of historical criticism. The two formed a partnership that outlived rationalism and the eighteenth century and morphed into the modern use of Socinian accommodation. Previous to this partnership, the doctrine could be isolated or marginalized as only one aspect of biblical interpretation. With the rise of historical criticism and the significant role Socinian accommodation played in this rise, the doctrine reached its apex. Accommodation provided historical criticism the theological and exegetical justification for a historical approach to biblical interpretation, while historical criticism provided the doctrine with historical validity of an accommodation to error. Thus Semler was the most important figure in establishing the modern use of Socinian accommodation.

Another characteristic of the accommodation debate was the wide range of theological issues attached to the doctrine. This shift began to take place with Spinoza's *Tractatus Theologico-Politicus* and Bekker's *De Betooverde Weereld*, as well as Schmidt's Wertheim Bible. However, it was not until the accommodation debate that the wide range of possibilities for the doctrine emerged.

For Semler, it was the specific issue of New Testament demon possession. The literal reading of the New Testament took the historical accounts of demon possession at face value: since Jesus and the apostles conducted their healings as if an evil spirit or spirits dwelled within the human subject, readers traditionally believed they were on safe grounds to assume that the possession was genuine. However, Semler contended that this assumption was naïve. Relying on the scholarship of Bekker and Farmer, he proposed that the cases of demon possession were in fact misdiagnosed episodes of mental illness. Through the historical and critical research of the ancient Near East, Semler argued that Israel lacked knowledge of mental health issues, and as a result, what should have been diagnosed as schizophrenia could only be explained with supposed spiritual powers outside the order of the world. This did not mean spirits such as demons actually existed. Rather, the use of evil spirits was an accommodation to error. By using this preexisting but misguided understanding of the existence of demons, Jesus and the apostles were able to continue their teaching of divine truth without hindering their message by unnecessarily confronting their audience over the point.

The last issue, the teaching ministry of Jesus and the disciples, became the central question of the accommodation debate. To what extent did Jesus and the apostles use the doctrine of accommodation? Proponents of the Augustinian position stipulated that accommodation in New Testament teaching was expressed by manner and form. Jesus and the apostles did not propagate error, affirm any existing error, or introduce new error into their teaching. However, they did adapt their teaching in a form best suited for their audience.

Opposed to the Augustinian position, eighteenth-century Socinian accommodationists argued that Jesus and the apostles included the errors of ancient Israel within their teaching. Their main objective was to correct only those errors that directly impeded understanding God's universal religion. The use of other errors aided in this goal. Not only were Jesus and the apostles thus freed from the obligation of correcting all errors, especially important given the short time allotted to them, they were also given a tool that facilitated their mission.

However, Semler and company were not the only ones applying a historical approach to the interpretation of the Bible. Augustinian accommodationist Storr advanced a historical interpretation free of Semler's historical criticism. For instance, Storr acknowledged that it was very probable that ancient Israel often misdiagnosed mental illness—historical research confirmed their lack of knowledge concerning modern medical advancements. However, historical research also indicated that Jesus and the apostles fully believed they were exorcizing actual demons. A historical reading of the Bible did not necessitate an accommodation of error. A possible natural explanation of biblical events did not negate a supernatural source. Semler's use of accommodation assumed conclusions that Augustinian accommodation and interpretation in a historical sense did not find defensible.

Socinian accommodationists were most prevalent in the last decade of the eighteenth century. The number of Socinian works in the 1790s greatly outnumbered the works of Augustinian accommodationists. What these Socinian accommodationists shared was the continued impulse to couple the doctrine with rationalistic historical criticism. They also exhibited a greater awareness of the supposed advantages of interpreting the Bible in a modern age. Thus, since the modern age was privileged with an improved use of reason, they felt a sense of responsibility to decipher the accommodations of error from the truth of God's revelation.

During this middle period of the debate, Socinian accommodation continued to evolve. The doctrine was continually applied to different theological concepts previously unexplored. One such area was Jesus's role as propitiatory sacrifice on the cross. Socinian accommodationists called into question the salvific value of Jesus's atonement, arguing that Jesus's death was an accommodation to the Jewish system of sacrifice. The belief that God required a blood sacrifice should be attributed to ancient paganism, not to God's need for a sacrifice. While the sacrificial system and Jesus's atonement made sense to people accustomed to such a belief, the modern age did not need such accommodations since it had done away with antiquated notions of God's wrath and Jesus's propitiatory atonement.

Socinian accommodation also acquired yet another new philosophical backing. By the end of the eighteenth century, the Leibnizian-Wolffian system, which replaced Cartesianism, was displaced by Kantian critical philosophy. In efforts to develop a comprehensive system of critical and autonomous reason, Kant attempted to situate faith within practical reason. In the realm of practical reason, rational faith could give meaning to morality. It also freed religion from ecclesiastical and political authorities. Socinian accommodation offered theological justification for Kant's reconceptualization of traditional doctrines. While the church may have attempted to control the masses through oppressive dogmas, universal religion set aside dogmatic rule for rational faith. However, Kant did not want to jettison the biblical text in its entirety. With the understanding of accommodation to error, the rational Christian could maintain the importance of the biblical text since universal truth existed behind the error.

By the end of the eighteenth century, rationalism began to wane, losing some of its prevalence with the rise of the Sturm und Drang, romanticism, and idealism. This is not to say that rationalism ceased to exist after the Enlightenment. Rather, its lost stature helps explain why Socinian accommodation did not continue to rely on rationalism. Instead, it leaned more heavily on historical criticism, and this partnership forged during the eighteenth century lived on into the next.

As the debate came to a close within the first third of the nineteenth century, the Augustinian position mounted a resurgence, making a concerted effort to combat the Socinian definition not only in Germany but also in America, where Hodge defended the Augustinian definition. The refocused Augustinian party concentrated their criticism on the lack of historical evidence supporting Socinian accommodationists' claims. The latter defended an accommodation to error through the use of a historical-critical approach to interpreting the Bible. They claimed both that historical criticism supplied the scientific evidence to support the existence of error within the biblical text and that Socinian accommodation provided the theological justification for such a historical approach to hermeneutics. However, historical accommodationists challenged the historical accuracy of their findings, charging historical critics of clouding their interpretation with presuppositions they brought to the text. A historical study of ancient Israel presented an entirely different picture, one that acknowledged the errors of the Israelites but also did not necessitate the existence of these errors in the biblical text. Providing natural reasons for beliefs such as demon possession and the expectation of a messiah was not the same as disproving supernatural causes that coincided with natural causes. The partnership between historical criticism and Socinian accommodation was shown to be cyclical and lacking historical support for their allegations.

The accommodation debate came to an end around the first third of the nineteenth century. The last monograph dedicated to the doctrine was published in 1835. However, even before that point, most had come to realize that the debate had ended. Late treatments of the doctrine often took the form of summaries of the debate. They carried a tone of completion for the debate and not for the continued use of the doctrine. Without a proclamation of a winner or a statement of concession, the debate came to a close.

The debate dissolved in part because the Socinian party itself fragmented into two groups. Socinian accommodationists had typically maintained a hierarchy of accommodations. God stood in a position where he had to accommodate his revelation to others, including his chosen messengers. Since accommodation to error was strongly connected to the thinking of the day, with the improvement of knowledge came different accommodations. Thus, Moses's accommodation differed from the prophets, whose accommodation differed even more from New Testament teaching. With each progression of knowledge came a different stage in accommodation, forming a system or hierarchy of accommodation. At the top was Jesus, who accommodated to his apostles. Nineteenth-century Socinian accommodationists deemed this hierarchy of accommodation too cumbersome. Instead, they reasoned that if they situated the biblical figures, including Jesus, within their historical context, they could avoid this complex structure. God's accommodation to mankind included the use of error; however, only God was in a position to accommodate to others. Thus, Jesus and the apostles were constrained by the same beliefs of other New Testament Jews, including their erroneous beliefs. This new understanding of Socinian accommodation greatly diminished the importance of the doctrine, or at the very least, the need to continue debating its significance.

Beyond the Debate

Even after the debate, the doctrine continued to be used in significant ways, as seen in the philosophy of Schleiermacher and in Neander's *Das Leben Jesu Christi* (1837).[1] Neander's work and the work of others in the first quest show that the doctrine was appropriated in the quest for the historical Jesus. However, the doctrine faced an even greater challenge than maintaining its Augustinian definition or expanding it to include the use of error. As the interpretation of the Bible moved more toward approaching Scripture as a book of ancient culture, the doctrine lost its importance altogether. The Bible began to be treated as a work of literature. It contained the history, customs, beliefs, and religious practices of ancient Israel. But as a human work, it did not contain divine revelation, nor was it directed by a divine source. As a purely human work, there was no need for the doctrine of accommodation. The biblical figures, including Jesus, held the same beliefs as the others within their time. Since God did not play any role in the Bible's composition, there was entirely no accommodation from a divine source.

Frei credited David Friedrich Strauss (1808–1874) with the abrogation of the doctrine. As a "mythophile," Strauss argued that the meaning of the text could only be found in the consciousness of the biblical author.[2] This consciousness was conditioned by the religious and cultural context of the author. By insisting on a purely historical explanation for the author's intentions, Strauss jettisoned the doctrine of accommodation completely. Albert Schweitzer (1875–1965) also deemed Strauss's work a critical turning point for the doctrine. However, in the quest for the historical Jesus, Schweitzer claimed that this understanding first occurred in Karl August Hase's *Das Leben Jesu zunächst für akademische Studien* (1829).[3] According to Schweitzer, Hase was the first to oppose the "rationalistic" interpretation of Jesus when he refrained from

---

[1] August Neander, *Das Leben Jesu Christi* (Hamburg: Friedrich Perthes, 1837), 212–214. Lutz Danneberg, "Schleiermacher und das Ende des Akkommodationsgedankens in der *hermeneutica sacra* des 17. und 18. Jahrhunderts," in *200 Jahre "Reden über die Religion,"* ed. Ulrich Barth and Claus-Dieter Osthövener (Berlin: de Gruyter, 2000), 194–246.

[2] Hans W. Frei, *The Eclipse of Biblical Narrative: A Study in Eighteenth and Nineteenth Century Hermeneutics* (New Haven, CT: Yale University Press, 1974), 234.

[3] Albert Schweitzer, *The Quest for the Historical Jesus: A Critical Study of Its Progress from Reimarus to Wrede*, trans. W. Montgomery (London: Adam and Charles Black, 1910), 61.

applying the doctrine to Jesus's teaching. Instead, Hase interpreted the errors of Jesus's teaching as originating from Jesus himself, who was fully contextualized within his historical setting. Regardless of who was first to disregard accommodation, the doctrine was lost in the development of nineteenth-century biblical interpretation and specifically during the quest for the historical Jesus.

Significance of the Study

Since the disappearance of the doctrine, we have only recently seen a rejuvenation of interest in it. Jack Rogers and Donald McKim revived the doctrine of accommodation so that it once again plays a considerable role in biblical interpretation. Despite John Woodbridge's critique of Rogers's and McKim's understanding of accommodation, the doctrine continues to be misunderstood in contemporary scholarship. Scholars such as Peter Enns and Kenton Sparks show little awareness of the doctrine's history. As with Rogers and McKim, these recent scholars confuse the Augustinian definition with the modern use of Socinian accommodation. They call on the likes of John Chrysostom, Augustine, Calvin, and Luther to redefine the Augustinian position as the Socinian definition found in the eighteenth century. These authors make little mention, if at all, of the various ways the doctrine has been understood. The accommodation debate is never discussed. And they fail to relay the differences between Augustinian and Socinian accommodation. Instead, the Socinian definition is assumed as the Augustinian definition, forced upon historical figures such as the church fathers and the reformers.

As with eighteenth-century rationalists, the promotion of Socinian accommodation today has much to do with historical criticism. The works in which these authors discuss the doctrine are often written with the express purpose of validating historical criticism. These scholars also make the case that the need for historical criticism is based not on liberal theology or on efforts antagonistic to the authority of the Bible but on the historical context of the Bible. To best understand oddities and other elements that do not align with a modern understanding, we must examine the original context of the passage. The historical-critical approach uncovers the erroneous thinking of ancient Israel. However, we are told not to fear the conclusions of historical criticism because God often accommodated to misunderstandings in biblical times in order to communicate divine truth. As historical criticism is said to reveal the layers of meaning behind the falsities contained in the biblical text, the modern exegete is exhorted not to fret, for it is only bringing to light God's original intent through the accommodation to error.

The intention of this present study was first to define the Augustinian position. While it has not recounted a history of the doctrine from its inception to the present age, the study has shown that the definition affirmed throughout the majority of the doctrine's existence was one of manner and form, which never compromised the accuracy or authority of the Bible. From there it was argued that the challenge to the standard definition arose from the sixteenth-century Socinians' reconceptualization of accommodation, resulting in two mutually exclusive definitions of the doctrine. It was the objective of the study to discuss the intricacies of debating the doctrine from the seventeenth century to the nineteenth century and especially during the Enlightenment.

In doing so, I have argued that the doctrine played a pivotal role in the history of biblical interpretation. For both Augustinian and Socinian accommodationists, the doctrine served a critical purpose for comprehending the way divine revelation was expressed through human thoughts and words. Further, by scrutinizing the accommodation debate and how the doctrine became an integral component of the historical-critical method, we have come to better understand the nature and foundations of historical criticism. Given the way the debate and the rise of historical criticism overlapped, it is no surprise that they worked in conjunction. Socinian accommodation provided the theological justification for historical criticism, while the findings of historical criticism supported the claims of Socinian accommodation.

Finally, such a study can help prevent contemporary misunderstandings of the doctrine—particularly the conflating of Socinian and Augustinian accommodation so common today. A discussion of the accommodation debate offers readers the lessons of those who debated the doctrine over centuries. The hope is that after examining the accommodation debate, one realizes more fully that how one defines and uses the doctrine of accommodation has significant implications for how one views and interprets the Bible, ancient history, and a whole spectrum of Christian doctrines.

Bibiliography

Danneberg, Lutz. "Schleiermacher und das Ende des Akkommodationsgedankens in der *hermeneutica sacra* des 17. und 18. Jahrhunderts." In *200 Jahre "Reden über die Religion,"* edited by Ulrich Barth and Claus-Dieter Osthövener, 194–246. Berlin: de Gruyter, 2000.

Frei, Hans W. *The Eclipse of Biblical Narrative: A Study in Eighteenth and Nineteenth Century Hermeneutics.* New Haven, CT: Yale University Press, 1974.

Neander, August. *Das Leben Jesu Christi.* Hamburg: Friedrich Perthes: 1837.

Schweitzer, Albert. *The Quest of the Historical Jesus: A Critical Study of Its Progress from Reimarus to Wrede.* Translated by W. Montgomery. London: Adam and Charles Black, 1910.

BIBLIOGRAPHY

Primary Sources

Ackermann, Peter Fourerius. *Archaeologia Biblica breviter exposita.* Vienna: Fridrich Volke, 1826.

Anonymous. "Bruchstück einer Vorlesung: Ueber die Accommodationen im Neuen Testament." *Magazin für die Religionsphilosophie, Exegese und Kirchengeschichte* 2, part 2 (1798): 249–53.

———. "Ist die Lehre von den Akkommodationen im N. T. Neologie?" *Magazin für Religionsphilosophie, Exegese und Kirchengeschichte* 2, part 2 (1798): 638–39.

Bahrdt, Karl Friedrich. *Briefe über die Bibel im Volkston.* Halle: Johann Friedrich Dost, 1782.

Bang, Johann Christian. *Verhandeling, waarin ondersogt wordt, in hoe verre Jesus en zyne Apostelen zich geschikt hebben naar de vatbaarheid der Jooden in het vorstellen der Christelijke leere.* Amsterdam: Allart, 1789.

Basedow, Johann Bernhard. *Methodischer Unterricht in der überzeugenden Erkenntniss der biblischen Religion.* Altona: Iverson, 1764.

———. *Philalethie: Neue Aussichten in die Wahrheiten und Religion der Vernunft bis in die Gränzen der glaubwürdigen Offenbarung.* Altona: Iverson, 1764.

Bauer, Georg Lorenz. *Biblische Theologie des Neuen Testaments.* 4 vols. Leipzig: Weygand, 1800–1802.

———. *Entwurf einer Hermeneutik des Alten und Neuen Testaments.* Leipzig: Weygand, 1799.

———. *Hebräische Mythologie des alten und neuen Testaments, mit Parallelen aus der Mythologie anderer Völker, vornemlich der Griechen und Römer.* 2 vols. Leipzig: Weygand, 1802.

Bauer, Karl Ludwig. *Logica Paullina, vel notatio rationis, qua utatur Paullus Apostolus in verbis adhibendis, interpretando, definiendo, enuntiando, argumentando, et methodo univers.* Halae Magdeburg: Orphanotrophei, 1774.

Baumgarten, Siegmund Jacob. *Ausführlicher Vortrag der Biblischen Hermeneutik.* Halle: Johann Justinus Gebauer, 1769.

———. *Auslegung des Buches Hiob.* Halle: Johann Andreas Bauer, 1740.

———. *Evangelische Glaubenslehre.* Halle: Gebauer, 1759–1760.

———. *Untersuchung Theologischer Streitigkeiten.* Halle: Gebauer, 1762–1764.

Baumgarten-Crusius, Gottlob August. *Schrift und Vernunft für denkende Christen.* Berlin: Joachim Pauli, 1796.

Baumgarten-Crusius, Ludwig Friedrich Otto. *Grundzüge der biblischen Theologie.* Jena: Frommann, 1828.

Beck, Christian Daniel. *Monogrammata Hermeneutices: Librorum Novi Fœderis.* Leipzig: Schwickertum, 1803.

Behn, Hermann Friedrich. *Ein kleiner Beytrag zu Untersuchung der Frage: Ob und wie weit es einem weisen Manne überhaupt, und besonders einem göttlichen Lehrer anständig und erlabut sey, sich zu den Meynungen und Irrthümern anderer herabzulassen?* Breslau: Meyer, 1791.

———. *Ueber die Lehrart Jesu und seiner Apostel: in wie fern dieselben sich nach den damals herrschenden Volksmeinungen bequemt haben.* Lübeck: Christian Gottfried Donatius, 1791.

Bekker, Balthasar. *De Betoverde Weereld.* 2 vols. Amsterdam: Daniel van den Dalen, 1691–1693.

———. *De Philosophia Cartesiana Admonitio Candida & Sincera.* Wesel: Hoogenhuysen, 1668.

———. *Naakte Uitbeeldinge van alle de vier boeken der Betoverde weereld.* Amsterdam: Daniel van den Dalen, 1693.

———. *Uitlegginge van den Propheet Daniel.* Amsterdam: Daniel van den Dalen, 1688.

Beyer, Carl August. *De difficultate judicii super disputatione veterum ecclesiae doctorum kat' oikonomian.* Leipzig: Langenheimius, 1766.

Bock, Friedrich Samuel. *Lehrbuch für die neueste Polemik.* Halle: Johann Jacob Gebauer, 1782.

Bois, Jacobus du. *Dialogus theologico-astronomicus.* Leiden: Petrus Leffen, 1653.

———. *Naecktheyt van de Cartesiaensche Philosophie: Ontbloot in een antwoort Op een Cartesiaensch Libel Genaemt Bewys, dat het gevoelen van die gene die leeren der Sonne-Stilstandt.* Utrecht: Johannes van Waesberge, 1655.

Bretschneider, Karl Gottlieb. *Handbuch der Dogmatik der evangelisch-lutherischen Kirche.* Leipzig: Johann Ambrosius Barth, 1822.

———. *Systematische Entwickelung aller in der Dogmatik vorkommenden Begriffe nach den symbolischen Schriften der evangelisch-lutherischen Kirche und den wichtigsten dogmatischen Lehrbüchern ihrer Theologen. Nebst der Literatur,*

vorzüglich der neuern, über alle Theile der Dogmatik. Leipzig: Johann Ambrosius Barth, 1825.
Calov, Abraham. *Systema Locorum Theologicorum.* Wittenberg: Sumptibus A. Hartmann, 1655.
Calsov, Christoph Friedrich. *Antiscripturariis, speciatim Werthemiensi.* Jena: Ritter, 1737.
Calvin, John, *Commentaries on the First Book of Moses, Called Genesis.* Translated by John King. 2 vols. Edinburgh: Calvin Translation Society, 1847.
Carpzov, Johann Benedict. *Historia Critica Veteris Testamenti autore Richardo Simone oratione inaugurali discussa.* Leipzig: Grossius, 1684.
Carus, Friedrich August. *Historia antiquior sententiarum ecclesiae graecae de accommodatione Christo inprimis et Apostolis tributa.* Leipzig: Schulze, 1793.
Cramer, Petrus Christianus. *Dissertatio de sapientissima Jesu Christi in vero se Messia declarando oikonomia.* Copenhagen: P. M. Höpffneri, 1792.
Crell, Johann Gottlieb. "Ueber Accommodationem in Neuen Testamente und vorzüglich im Matthäus." *Magazin für biblische Interpretation* 1, no. 2 (1806): 193–252.
Danz, Johann Traugott Leberecht. *Encyklopädie und Methodologie der theologischen Wissenschaften.* Weimar: Wilhelm Hoffmann, 1832.
———. *Universal-Wörterbuch der theologischen, kirchen—und religionsgeschichtlichen Literatur.* Leipzig: Fest, 1843.
Descartes, René. *Philosophical Writings.* Translated by John Cottingham, Robert Stoothoff, and Dugald Murdoch. 3 vols. Cambridge: Cambridge University Press, 1984–1991.
Detharding, Georg. *Commentatio theologica de accommodatione verbi divini ministri ad captum vulgi.* Göttingen: Dieterich, 1782.
Deyling, Salomon. *Observationum Sacrarum in qua Multa Scripturae Veteris ac Novi Testamenti Dubia Vexata Sovunutur.* Leipzig: S. H. F. Lanckisii, 1735.
Diestel, Ludwig. *Die socinianische Anschauung vom Alten Testamente: in ihrer geschichtlichen und theologischen Bedeutung.* Gotha: R. Besser, 1862.
———. *Geschichte des Alten Testamentes in der christlichen Kirche.* Jena: Mauke, 1869.
Doederlein, Johann Christoph. *Institutio theologi christiani in capitibus religionis theoreticis.* 2 vols. Nürnberg and Altdorf: Monath and Kussler 1797.
Dresde, Friedrich Wilhelm. *De falalci Fausti Socini libros Sacros interpretandi ratione.* Wittenberg: Charisius, 1790.
Eckermann, Jakob Christoph Rudolf. *Handbuch für das systematische Studium der christlichen Glaubenslehre.* 4 vols. Altona: Johann Friedrich Hammerich, 1801–1803.
———. *Theologische Beyträge,* 6 vols. Altona: Johann Friedrich Hammerich, 1792–1799.

Eichhorn, Johann Gottfried. *Allgemeine Bibliothek der biblischen Litteratur* 1–14 (1787–1801).
———. *Einleitung in das Alte Testament*. 3 vols. Leipzig: Weidmannischen Buchhandlung, 1780–1783.
———. *Einleitung in das Neue Testament*. 5 vols. Leipzig: Weidmannischen Buchhandlung, 1804–1827.
Eifert, Carl Traugott. *Untersuchung der Frage: Könnte nicht die mosaische Erzählung vom Sündenfalle buchstäblich wahr, und durch den Fall ein erbliches Verderben auf die Menschen gekommen seyn?* Halle: Hemmerde, 1781.
Ernesti, Johann August. *Institvtio Interpretis Novi Testamenti*. Leipzig: Weidmanni, 1761.
———. *Neue theologische Bibliothek: darinnen von den neuesten theologischen Büchern und Schriften Nachricht gegeben wird*. Leipzig: Bernard Christoph Breitkopf, 1760–1771.
Fairbairn, Patrick. *Hermeneutical Manual: Or, Introduction to the Exegetical Study of the Scriptures of the New Testament*. Edinburgh: T&T Clark, 1858.
Farmer, Hugh. *Letters to the Rev. Dr. Worthington: In Answer to his Late Publication, Intitled, An Impartial Enquiry into the Case of the Gospel Demoniacks*. London: J. Buckland and G. Robinson, 1778.
Franke, Georg Samuel. *De ratione qua est critica philosophia ad interpretationem librorum, inprimis sacrorum*. Schleswig: Serringhaus, 1794.
Fuhrmann, Wilhelm David. *Die Aufhellungen der neueren Gottesgelehrten in der christlichen Glaubenslehre, von 1760 bis 1805*. Leipzig: Weigandschen, 1807.
Gess, Wolfgang Friedrich. *Briefe über einige theologische Zeit-Materien: besonders über den Accommodations-Grundsaz in Hinsicht auf einige positive Lehren der christlichen Religion*. Stuttgart: Erhard, 1797.
Grapius, Zacharias. *Systema novissimarum controversiarum, seu theologia, recens controversa*. 4 vols. Rostock: Georg. Ludov. Fritschuum, 1719.
Hahn, August. *An die Evangelische Kirche zunächst in Sachsen und Preußen: Eine offene Erklärung*. Leipzig: Friedrich Christian Wilhelm Vogel, 1827.
———. *Lehrbuch der christlichen Glaubens*. Leipzig: Friedrich Christian Wilhelm Vogel, 1828.
Hakvoord, Barend. *De schole van Christus waar in de gansche belydenis der gereformeerde godsdienst beknoptelyk voorgesteld*. Amsterdam: Goeree, 1689.
Hamann, Johann Georg. *Briefwechsel*. Edited by Walther Ziesemer and Arthur Henkel. 7 vols. Wiesbaden: Insel, 1955–1975.
———. *Sämtliche Werke*. Edited by Josef Nadler. 6 vols. Vienna; Herder, 1949–57.
Hamer, Petrus. *Voorlooper tot de volstrekte wederlegginge van het gene de heeren, Orchard, Daillom en Bekker*. Dordrecht: Cornelis Wilgaarts, 1692.
Hartmann, Anton Theodor. *Hat sich Jesut für den von Sott verheissenen Messias wirklich gehalten, oder blos nach den Hoffnungen und Erwartungen*

feiner Zeitgenossen accomodirt? In *Blicke in den Geist des Urchristenthums.* Düsseldorf: Schreiner, 1802.

Hauff, Karl Viktor. *Bemerkungen über die Lehrart Jesu mit Rücksicht auf jüdische Sprache- und Denkungsart.* Offenbach: C. L. Brede, 1788.

———. "Gedanken über die Frage: ob und inwiefern sich Jesus und die Apostel zu einigen jüdischen Ideen herabgelassen haben?," in *Beyträge zur Beförderung des vernünftigen Denkens in der Religion* 15 (1791): 1–25.

Hemert, Paulus van. *Oratio de prudenti christi, apostolorum, atque evangelistarum consilio, sermones suos et scripta, ad captum atque intellectum vulgi, quantum illud fieri potuit, accommodantium.* Amsterdam: M. Schalekamp, 1791.

———. *Über Accommodationen im Neuen Testament oder Beantwortung der Frage: haben Christus und die Apostel in ihren Schriften sich zuweilen nach den herrschenden Volksbegriffen bequemt.* Leipzig: Blothe, 1797.

Hengstenberg, Ernst Wilhelm. *Christologie des Alten Testaments und Commentar über die Messianischen Weissagungen der Propheten.* 3 vols. Berlin: Ludwig Oehmigke, 1829–1835.

Heringa, Jodocus Ezn. *Über die Lehrart Jesu und seiner Apostel mit Hinsicht auf die Religionsbegriffe ihrer Zeitgenossen.* Offenbach: Weiss & Brede, 1792.

Hess, Johann Jakob, *Geschichte der drey letzten Lebensjahre Jesu.* Zurich: Orell, Geßner, Füeßlin, 1768.

Hodge, A. A. and B. B. Warfield, "Inspiration," *Presbyterian Review* 2 (1881), 225–60.

Hodge, Charles. "Introduction to Charles Christian Tittmann on Historical Interpretation," *Biblical Repertory* 1 (1825): 125–27.

Hofer, Johann Evangelist. *De Kantiana S. Scripturae interpretatione programma.* Salisburg: Salisburg, 1800.

Jaeger, Johann Wolfgang. *Historia Ecclesiastica cum Parallelismo Profanae.* 2 vols. Hamburg: Samuelis Heylii, 1709, 1717.

Jahn, Johann. *Archaeologia Biblica in compendium redacta.* Vienna: Christoph Friedrich Wappler and Beck, 1804.

———. "Was hielten die Kirchenväter von der Accommodation?" In *Nachträge zu seinen theologischen Werken.* Tübingen: Heinrich Laupp, 1821.

———. "Was lehret die Bibel vom Teufel, von den gefallenen Engeln, von den Dämonen, und bösen unreinen Geistern?," in *Nachträge zu seinen theologischen Werken.* Tübingen, Heinrich Laupp, 1821.

Kähler, Ludwig August. *Dissertationis de accommodatione legitima, a Jesu, cum diaboli mentionem faciebat, usurpata, conclusio, ubi Scriptura concedente et ratione dictante demonstratur, doctrinam communem de diabolo abhorrere a Theologia Christiana.* Königsberg: Hartung, 1834–1835.

Kant, Immanuel. *Religion within the Boundaries of Mere Reason and Other Writings.* Translated and edited by Allen Wood and George Di Giovanni.

Cambridge Texts in the History of Philosophy. Cambridge: Cambridge University Press, 1998.

Keil, Karl August Gottlieb. *Analekten für das Studium der exegetischen und systematischen Theologie.* 4 vols. Leipzig: Barth, 1812–1822.

———. *De historica librorum sacrorum interpretatione ejusque necessitate.* Leipzig: Sommeria, 1788.

Kirsten, Johannes Fridericus Ernestus. *De accommodatione Jesu et apostolorum ad errores Judaeorum.* Arstadiae: Trommsdorff, 1816.

Knapp, Georg Christian. *Vorlesungen über die christliche Glaubenslehere, nach dem Lehrbegriff der evangelischen Kirche.* 2 vols. Halle: Waisenhauses, 1827.

Koelman, Jacobus. *Wederlegging van B. Bekkers Betoverde Wereldt.* Amsterdam: Johannes Boekholt, 1692.

Krug, Wilhelm Traugott. *Fundamentalphilosophie.* Züllichau, Darnmannsch, 1803.

———. *Principium, cui religionis christianae auctor doctrinam de moribus superstruxit, ad tempora eius atque consilia aptissime et accommodatissime constitutum.* Wittenberg: Dürr, 1792.

Lang, Georg Heinrich. *Zur Beförderung des nützlichen Gebrauches des Wilhelm Abraham Tellerischen Wörterbuchs des neuen Testaments.* 4 vols. Anspach: Benedict Friederich Haueisen, 1778–1785.

Lang, Wilhelm Todias. "Etwas über die Principien a priori und a posteriori, durch welche man das Locale und Temporelle von der allgemeingültigen Lehre in der christlichen Offenbarungsurkunde scheiden will, aus dem Standpuncte des Offenbarungsgläubigen." *Magazin für christliche Dogmatik und Moral,* 8 (1802): 99–140.

———. "Ueber die a priori und a posteriori aufgestellten Principiend der Beurtheilung, was in der christlichen Religionsurkunde locale und temporelle oder allgemeingültige Lehre sei? aus dem Standpuncte des Offenbarungsgläubigen." *Magazin für christliche Dogmatik und Moral,* 7 (1801): 1–67.

Lange, Joachim. *Bescheidene und ausführliche Entdeckung der falschen und schädlichen Philosophie in dem Wolffianischen Systemate metaphysico.* Halle: Wäysenhauses, 1724.

———. *Modesta disquisitio novi philosophiae systematis de Deo, Mundo et homine.* Halle: Orphanotropheum, 1723.

Leibniz, Gottfried Wilhelm. *Phoranomus seu de potentia et legibus Naturae.* In *Opuscules et fragments inedits de Leibniz.* Edited by Louis Courturat. Paris: Alcan, 1903.

Lessing, Gotthold Ephraim. *Die Erziehung des Menschengeschlechts.* Berlin: Christian Friedrich Voss and Son, 1780.

Leydekker, Melchior. *Der Goddelykheid en Waarheid der H. Schriften.* 2 vols. Utrecht: Ottho de Vries, 1692.

———. *Dissertatio historico-theologica, de vulgato nuper cl. Bekkeri volumine, et Scripturarum authoritate ac veritate, pro Christiana religione apologetica.* Utrecht: Clerck, 1692.

———. *Fax Veritatis, seu exercitationes ad nonnullas controversias quae hodie in Belgio potissimum moventur.* Leiden: Lugduni Batavorum, 1766.

Löscher, Valentin Ernst. *Praenotiones theologicae contra naturalistarum et fanaticorum omne genus atheos, deistas, indifferentistas, antiscripturarios.* Wittenberg: Gerdesius, 1708.

Lüderwald, Johann Balthasar. *Die allegorische Erklärung der drey ersten Capitel Mosis.* Helmstädt: Johann Heinrich Kühnlin, 1781.

———. *Die Wahrheit Gewißheit der Auferstehung Jesu Christi.* Helmstädt: Kühnlin, 1778.

———. *Gedanken von dem Unterscheid der Lehre und des Lehrvortrags im Christenthum in Absicht auf seine nationellen Vorzüge.* Helmstädt: Kühnlin, 1781.

Maas, A. J. "Exegesis," The Catholic Encyclopedia, ed. Charles G. Herbermann, Edward A. Pace, Condé B. Pallen, Thomas J. Shahan, and John J. Wynne. New York: Encyclopedia Press, 1907–1912, 5:695.

Maresius, Samuel. *De Abusu Philosophiae Cartesianae.* Groningae: Tierck Everts, 1670.

———. *Disputationes Theologicae prior refutatoria libelli de philosophia Interprete Scripturae.* Groningen: Johannis Collenus, 1667.

Mastricht, Petrus van. *Novitatum Cartesianarum Gangraena, Nobiliores plerasque Corporis Theologici Partes arrodens et exedens.* Amsterdam: Jansson, 1676.

———. *Theologia Theoretico-Practica: Qua, per singula capita theologica, pars exegetica, dogmatica, elenchtica & practica, perpetua successione conjugantur.* 2 vols. Utrecht: Thomas Appels, 1699.

———. *Vindiciae veritatis et authoritatis Sacrae Scripturae in rebus philosophicis.* Utrecht: Johannis Waesberge, 1655.

Mencke, Otto. *Acta Eruditorum.* Leipzig: Grosse and Gleditsch, 1692.

Meyer, Gottlob Wilhem. *Entwickelung des Paulinischen Lehrbegriffs: Ein Beitrag zur Kritik des christlichen Religionsystems.* Altona: Johann Friedrich Hammerich, 1801.

———. *Grundriß einer Hermeneutik des Alten und Neuen Testaments und einer Anleitung zur populären und praktischen Schrifterklärung.* Göttingen, Johann Friedrich Römer, 1801.

Meyer, Johann Andreas. *Beitrag zur endlichen Entscheidung der Frage: "In wiefern haben die Lehren und Vorschriften des Neuen Testaments blos eine locale und temporelle Bestimmung, und in wiefern sind dieselben von einem allgemeinen und stets gültigen Ansehen?"* Hannover: Helwingschen Hof-Buchhandlung, 1806.

Meyer, Lodewijk. *Philosophia Sive Scripturae Interpres.* Amsterdam: Eleutheropoli, 1666.

———. *Philosophy as the Interpreter of Holy Scripture.* Translated by Samuel Shirley. Milwaukee, Marquette University Press, 2005.

Michaelis, Johann David. *Einleitung in die göttlichen Schriften des Neuen Bundes.* 2 vols. Göttingen: Vandenhoeck, 1765–66.

———. *Mosaiches Recht.* 6 vols. Frankfurt: J. G. Garbe, 1770–75.

Molinaeus, Johannes. *De Betoverde Werelt van D. Balthazar Bekker . . . Onderzogt en Wederlegst.* Rotterdam, Barent Bos, 1692.

Mosheim, Johann Lorenz. *Sittenlehre der Heiligen Schrift.* Helmstädt: Christian Friedrich Weygand, 1735.

Nachtigal, Johann Carl Christoph. "Bruckstücke einer Vorlesung: Ueber die Akkommadationen, besonders im N. T." *Magazin für Religionsphilosophie, Exegese und Kirchengeschichte* 5, part 1 (1801): 109–30.

Neander, August. *Das Leben Jesu Christi.* Hamburg: Friedrich Perthes: 1837.

Nitzsch, Karl Ludwig. *De Iudicandis Morum Praeceptis In Novo Testamento A Communi Omnium Hominum Ac Temporum Usu Alienis.* Wittenberg: Dürr, 1791–1802.

Nösselt, Johann August. *Animadversiones in sensum librorum sacrorum moralem.* Halle: Hendel, 1795.

Oetinger, Friedrich Christoph. *Biblisches und emblematisches Wörterbuch, dem Tellerischen Wörterbuch und Anderer falschen Schrifterklärungen entgegen gesezt.* Hildesheim: Georg Olms, 1776.

Opitz, Ernst. *De accommodationis Christi et apostolorum didacticae natura.* Wittenberg: Tzschiedrichius, 1789.

Pappelbaum, Georg Theophil. *De Christo sapienter ac licite simulante et dissimulante.* Stargard: Joannis Ludouici Kunstii, 1763.

Pisanski, Georg Christoph. *Adversaria de Accommodationibus Veteris Testamenti in Novo Obviis.* Göttingen: Wedeliane, 1781.

Planck, Gottlieb Jakob. *Einleitung in die Theologische Wissenschaften.* 2 vols. Leipzig: Siegfried Lebrecht Crusius, 1794–1795.

Pölitz, Karl Heinrich. *Beytrag zur Kritik der Religionsphilosophie und Exegese unseres Zeitalters.* Leipzig: Breitkopf, 1795.

Poppo, Volkmar Conrad. *Spinozismus detectus, oder vernünfftige Gedanken von dem wahren Unterscheid der philosophischen und mathematischen Methode oder Lehr-Art.* Weimar: Mumbachen, 1721.

Quenstedt, Johannes Andreas. *Theologia Didactico-Polemica sive Systema Theologiae.* Leipzig: Thomam Fritsch, 1702.

Rambach, Johann Jakob. *Hypothesis de Scriptura sacra ad erroneos vulgi conceptus adcommodata.* Halle: Henckel, 1729.

———. *Institutiones Hermeneuticae Sacrae, variis observationibus copiosissimisque exemplis biblicis illustratae.* Jena: Hartungius, 1723.

Reinhard, Franz Volkmar. *System der christlichen Moral.* 5 vols. Wittenberg: Zimmermann, 1791–1792.

———. *Utrum et quando possint oratores divini in administrando munere suo demittere se ad vanas hominum opiniones.* Wittenberg: Adamus Christianus Charisius, 1782.

———. *Versuch über den Plan, welchen der Stifter der christlichen Religion zum Besten der Menschheit entwarf.* Wittemberg: Samuel Gottfried Zimmermann, 1784.

Reuss, Jeremias Friedrich. *Disquisitio theologico-hermeneutica de Oeconomia, qua in docendo ipse etiam Dominus usus esse dicitur.* Tübingen: Fues, 1773.

Revius, Jacobus. *Analectorum theologicorum disputatio XXI.* Leiden: Johannis Nicolai van Dorp, 1647.

———. *Kartesiomanias pars altera, qua ad secundam partem rabiosae Assertionis Tobiae Andreae respondetur.* Leiden: Hieronymum de Vogel, 1655.

———. *Methodi Cartesianae consideratio theologica.* Leiden: Hieronymum de Vogel, 1648.

Rosenmüller, Johann Georg. *Einige Bemerkungen, das Studium der Theologie betreffend.* Erlangen: Palm, 1794.

———. *Historia interpretationis librorum sacrorum in Ecclesia Christiana.* Leipzig: Hildburghusae, 1795–1814.

Sartorius, Ernst. *Drei Abhandlungen über wichtige Gegenstände der exegetischen und systematischen Theologie.* Göttingen: Dieterichschen, 1820.

Schaefer, Franz Peter. *De Christo et Apostolis in tradenda religione ad hominum captum sese demittentibus.* Mainz: Alef, 1787.

Schleiermacher, Friedrich Daniel Ernst. *Einleitung ins neue Testament.* Berlin: Reimer, 1834–1864.

———. *Hermeneutics: The Handwritten Manuscripts.* Edited by H. Kimmerle. Missoula, MT: Scholars Press, 1977.

Schmid, Johann Wilhelm. *Ueber christliche Religion: deren Beschaffenheit und zweckmäßige Behandlung als Volkslehre und Wissenschaft für das gegenwärtige Zeitalter.* Jena: Wolfgang Stahl, 1797.

Schmidt, Christian Friedrich. *Iudaeorum qui Christi tempore vixerunt de eodem varias opiniones accommodata ad Loca N. T. enarrar et ad Solemnem Doctoris Theologi Inaugurationem.* Wittenberg: Litteris Caroli Christiani Dürrii, 1775.

Schmidt, Johann Ernst Christian. *Ueber den Einfluss der Kantischen unterscheidung der Geschaefte des historishen und moralischen Auslegers auf die Schrifterklarung.* In *Bibliothek für Kritik und Exegese des Neuen Testaments und älteste Christengeschichte.* Hadamar: Gelehrtenbuchhandlung, 1797.

Schmidt, Johann Lorenz. *Die göttlichen Schriften vor den Zeiten des Messie Jesus.* Wertheim: Johann Georg Nehr, 1735.

Scholten, Wessel. *Specimen hermeneutico-theologicum: De appellatione tou Giou tou Anthrōpou, qua Iesus se Messiam professus est.* Utrecht: Paddenburg and Schoonhoven, 1809.

Schoock, Martin. *De Scepticismo*. Groningen: Henrici Lussinck, 1652.
Schott, Heinrich August. *Epitome Theologiae Chritianae Dogmaticae in usum scholarum academicarum adornata*. Leipzig: Barth, 1811.
Schweitzer, Albert. *The Quest for the Historical Jesus: A Critical Study of Its Progress from Reimarus to Wrede*. Translated by W. Montgomery. London: Adam and Charles Black, 1910.
Seiler, Georg Friedrich. *Biblische Hermeneutik oder Grundsätze und Regeln zur Erklärung der Heil. Schrift des Alten und Neuen Testaments*. Erlangen: Bibelanstalt, 1800.
———. *Die Weissagung und ihre Erfüllung, ist von mir mehr über diese Materie gesagt worden*. Erlangen: Bibelanstalt, 1794.
———. *Jesus Christus der Wahrheitslehrer kein Volkstäuscher*. Erlangen: Palm, 1787.
———. *Über die göttlichen Offenbarungen, vornehmlich die welche Jesus und seine Gesandten empfangen haben*. 2 vols. Erlangen: Bibelanstalt, 1796.
———. *Ueber die Gottheit Christi, beides für Gläubige und Zweifler*. Leipzig: Schwickertchen, 1775.
Semler, Johann Salomo. *Abfertigung der neuen Geister und alten Irtümer in der Lohmannischen Begeisterung zu Kemberg, nebst theologischem Unterricht von dem Ungrunde der gemeinen Meinung von leiblichen Besitzungen des Teufels und Bezauberungen der Christen*. Halle: Gebauer, 1760.
———. *Abhandlung von freier Untersuchung des Canon*. 4 vols. Halle: Hemmerde, 1771–1775.
———. *Apparatus ad liberalem Novi Testamenti interpretationem*. Halle: Rengeriana, 1764.
———. *Beantwortung der Fragmente eines Ungenannten: insbesondere vom Zweck Jesu und seiner Jünger*. Halle: Erziehungsinst. 1779.
———. *Dissertatio theologico-hermeneutica de Daemoniacis, quorum in Evangeliis fit mentio*. Halle: Hendel, 1760.
———. *Dissertatio theologico-hermeneutica de discrimine notionum vulgarium et christianarum in libris N. T. observando*. Halle: Hendel, 1770.
———. *Programmata Academica Selecta*. Halle: Hemmerde, 1779.
———. *Über historische, gesellschaftliche und moralische Religion der Christen*. Leipzig: Beer, 1786.
———. *Umständliche Untersuchung der dämonischen Leute oder sogenannten Besessenen*. Halle: Gebauer, 1762.
———. Neue Theologische Bibliothek 3 (1762) 778–808.
———. *Unterhaltungen mit Herrn Lavater über die freie practische Religion*. Leipzig: Weidmann and Reich, 1787.
———. *Untersuchung und Beleuchtung der sogenannten biblischen Dämonologie*. Danzig: Flörke, 1778.

———. *Versuch einer biblischen Dämonologie oder Untersuchung der Lehre der heiligen Schrift vom Teufel und seiner Macht*. Halle: Hemmerde, 1776.

———. *Vorbereitung zur Theologie Hermeneutik*. 8 vols. Halle: Hemerde, 1761–1769.

Senff, Carl Friedrich. *Versuch über die Herablassung Gottes in der christlichen Religion zu der Schwachheit der Menschen*. Leipzig: Barth, 1792.

Socinus, Faustus. *De auctoritate Sacrae Scripturae*. Amsterdam: n.p., 1588.

———. *Defensio Animadversionum Fausti Socini Senensis in Assertiones Theologicas Collegii Posnaniensis de Trino et uno Deo: Adversus Gabrielem Eutropium*. Raków: Sternacki, 1618.

Socinus, Faustus, et al. "Epitome of a Colloquium Held in Rakow in the Year 1601." In *The Polish Brethren: Documentation of the History and Thought of Unitarianism in the Polish-Lithuanian Commonwealth and in the Diaspora, 1601–1685*, edited by George Huntston Williams. Harvard Theological Studies 30. Missoula, MT: Scholars Press, 1980.

Spinoza, Benedict de. "Letter 75." In *The Letters*. Translated by Samuel Shirley, with an introduction and notes by Steven Barbone, Lee Rice, and Jacob Adler. Indianapolis, IN: Hacket, 1995.

———. *Theological-Political Treatise*. Translated by Michael Silverthorne and Jonathan Israel. Cambridge: Cambridge University Press, 2007.

Stark, Christian Ludwig Wilhelm. *Ueber das oberste Princip der wahren Interpretation, und über die Frage, welche Erklärungsart des N. Testaments die richtigste sey? Beiträge zur Vervollkommnung der Hermeneutik insbesondere der des Neuen Testaments*. Jena: Schmid, 1817–1818.

Stäudlin, Karl Friedrich. *Ideen zur Kritik des Systems der christlichen Religion*. Göttingen: Vandenhoek and Ruprecht, 1791.

———. "Über die blos historische Auslegung der Bücher des N. T." *Kritisches Journal der neuesten theologischen Literatur* 1:4 (1814): 321–348.

———. "Über die blos historische Auslegung der Bücher des N. T." *Kritisches Journal der neuesten theologischen Literatur* 2:1 (1814): 1–39.

———. "Über die blos historische Auslegung der Bücher des N. T." *Kritisches Journal der neuesten theologischen Literatur* 2:2 (1814): 113–148.

Stauss, August Christian. *Utrum philosophica Scripturae interpretatio, quam commendavit Kantius, admitti possit in explicando N. T.* Wittenberg: Tzschiedrich, 1795.

Steinbart, Gotthelf Samuel. *System der reinen Philosophie; oder, Glückseligkeitslehre des Christenthums*. Züllichau: Waysenhaus and Frommann, 1778.

Storr, Gottlob Christian. *Bemerkungen über Kants philosophische Religionslehre*. Tübingen: Cotta, 1794.

———. *De sensu historico*. In *Opuscula Academica ad Interpretationem Librorum Sacrorum Pertinentia*, 1:1–88. Tubingen: Joannis Georgii Cottae, 1796. Originally published in Tübingen: Fuesianis, 1778.

———. *Doctrinae christianae pars theoretica e sacris literis repetita.* Stuttgart: Johann Benedict Metzler, 1793.

———. *Lehrbuch der christlichen Dogmatik.* Translated by Carl Christian Flatt. Stuttgart: Johann Benedict Metzler, 1803.

———. *Ueber den eigentlichen Zweck des Todes Jesu.* Nuremberg: Rawschen, 1800.

Suicer, Johann Caspar. *Thesaurus Ecclesiasticus.* Amsterdam: J. Henricum Wetstenium, 1682.

Süskind, Friedrich Gottlieb. "Bemerkungen über die Hypothese, daß Paulus Röm 5:12 ff. sich zu jüdischen Meinungen akkommodirt habe." *Magazin für christliche Dogmatik und Moral* 13 (1806): 68–97.

———. "Ueber die Gränzen der Pflicht, keine Unwahrheit zu sagen." *Magazin für christliche Dogmatik und Moral* 13 (1806), 1–67.

Teller, Wilhelm Abraham. *Die Religion der Vollkommnern.* Berlin: Mylius, 1792.

———. *Wörterbuch des Neuen Testaments zur Erklärung der christlichen Lehre.* Berlin: Mylius, 1772.

Terry, Milton S. *Biblical Hermeneutics: A Treatise on the Interpretation of the Old and New Testaments.* New York: Phillips & Hunt, 1883.

Tholuck, August. *A Commentary on the Epistle to the Hebrews.* 2 vols. Translated by James Hamilton. Edinburgh: Thomas Clark, 1842.

Tittmann, Karl Christian. *Meletemata Sacra, sive Commentarius Exegetico-Critico-Dogmaticus in Evangelium Ioannis.* Leipzig: Weidmannia, 1816.

Töllner, Johann Gottlieb. *Grundriß einer erwiesenen Hermeneutik der heiligen Schrift.* Züllichau: Waisenhaus, 1765.

Unselt, Samuel Fridericus. *Dissertatio philologica de locorum Veteris Testamenti in Novo accommodatione orthodoxa.* Leipzig: Breitkopf, 1766.

Velthuysen, Lambertus van. *Bewys, Dat het gevoelen van die genen, die leeren der Sonne Stilstandt, En des Aertycks Beweging niet strydich is met Godts-Woort.* Utrecht: Jaer onses Herren, 1655.

———. *Bewys, Dat noch de Leere van der Sonne Stilstant, En des Aertryx Bewegingh, Noch de gronden vande Philosophie van Renatus Des Cartes strijdig sijn met Godts Woort. Gestelt tegen een Tractaet van J. du Bois.* Utrecht: Jaer onses Herren, 1656.

———. *Dissertatio de usu rationis in rebus theologicis, et praesertim in interpretatione S. Scripturae.* Rotterdam: Reinier Leers, 1667.

———. "Epistola XLII." In *Spinoza Opera*, 4. Heidelberg: Carl Winters, 1925.

Voetius, Gijsbertus. *Thersites heautontimorumenos. Hoc est, Remonstrantium hyperaspistes, catechesis, et liturgiae Germanicae, Gallicae, et Belgicae denuo insultans.* Utrecht: Abrahami ab Herwiick et Hermanni Ribbius, 1635.

Vogel, Paul Joachim Siegmund. *Aufsätze theologischen Inhalts.* 2 vols. Nürnberg and Altdorf: Monath and Kußler, 1796–1799.

Waeyen, Johannes van der. *De betooverde weereld van D. Balthasar Bekker ondersogt en weederlegt.* Franeker: Strik and Horreus, 1693.

Walten, Eric. *Aardige Duyvelary.* Rotterdam: Pieter van Veen, 1691.

———. *Brief Aan sijn Excellentie, de Heer Graaf van Portland.* Hague: Meyndert Uytwerf, 1692.

Warfield, B. B. *The Inspiration and the Authority of the Bible.* Philadelphia: Presbyterian and Reformed, 1948.

Wegscheider, Julius August Ludwig. *Institutiones theologicae christianae dogmaticae.* Halle: Gebauer, 1817.

Wette, Wilhelm Martin Leberecht de. *Biblische Dogmatik Alten und Neuen Testaments.* Berlin: Realschulbuchhandlung, 1813.

Windheim, Christian Ernst. *De erroribus vulgi in libris sacris non probatis.* Göttingen: Vandenhoeck, 1748.

Winkler, Ernst Gottlob. *Versuch über Jesus Lehrfähigkeiten und Lehrart: in sofern sich diese zur Fassungskraft der Zuhörer herabläßt, und für die Religionslehrer Muster ist.* Leipzig: Barth, 1797.

Wittichius, Christophorus. *Consensus veritatis in Scriptura divina et infallibili revelatae cum veritate philosophica a Renato Des Cartes detecta.* 2nd ed. Leiden: Cornelii Boutesteyn & Cornelii Lever, 1682. Originally published in Neomagi: Wyngaerden, 1659.

———. *Dissertationes Duae, Quarum prior De S. Scripturae in rebus Philosophicis abusu examinat.* Amsterdam: Ludovicum Elzevirium, 1653.

Wolff, Christian. *Der Anfangs-Gründe Aller Mathematischen Wiessenschaften.* Halle: Renger, 1717.

———. *Philosophia rationalis.* Leipzig: Rengeriana, 1728.

Wolzogen, Lodewijk. *De Scripturarum Interprete adversus Exercitatorem Paradoxum.* Utrecht: Linde, 1668.

Wurm, Jakob Gottlieb. *Observationes ad philosophicum Kantii de hermeneutica sacra decretum.* Tübingen: Fues, 1799.

Zachariae, Gotthilf Traugott. *Theologische Erklärung der Herablassung Gottes zu den Menschen.* In Gotthilf Traugott Zachariae, *Philosophisch-Theologische Abhandlungen als Beilagen zur Biblischen Theologie,* ed. Christian Gottlieb Perschke, 541–800. Lemgo: Meyer, 1776. Originally published in Bützow: Wismar, 1762.

Secondary Sources

Ashley, Clinton M. "John Calvin's Utilization of the Principle of Accommodation and Its Continuing Significance for an Understanding of Biblical Language." PhD diss., Southwestern Baptist Theological Seminary, 1972.

Asselt, Willem J. van. *The Federal Theology of Johannes Cocceius (1603–1669)*. Studies in the History of Christian Thought 100. Leiden: Brill, 2001.

———. "Scholasticism in the Time of High Orthodoxy (ca. 1620–1700)," in *Introduction to Reformed Scholasticism*, ed. Willem J. van Asselt, trans. Albert Gootjies, Reformed Historical-Theological Studies. Grand Rapids, MI: Reformation Heritage, 2011.

Balserak, Jon. *Divinity Compromised: A Study of Divine Accommodation in the Thought of John Calvin*. Studies in Early Modern Religious Reforms 5. Dordrecht: Springer, 2006.

———. "The God of Love and Weakness: Calvin's Understanding of God's Accommodating Relationship with His People." *Westminster Theological Journal* 62, no. 2 (2000): 177–95.

Battles, Ford Lewis. "God Was Accommodating Himself to Human Capacity." *Interpretation* 31, no. 1 (1977): 19–38.

Bayer, Oswald. *A Contemporary in Dissent: Johann Georg Hamann as a Radical Enlightener*. Translated by Roy A. Harrisville and Mark C. Mattes. Grand Rapids, MI: Eerdmans, 2012.

———. *Zeitgenosse im Widerspruch: Johann Georg Hamann als radikaler Aufklärer*. Munich: Piper, 1988.

Benin, Stephen D. "The 'Cunning of God' and Divine Accommodation." *Journal of the History of Ideas* 45, no. 2 (1984): 179–91.

———. *The Footprints of God: Divine Accommodation in Jewish and Christian Thought*. SUNY Series in Judaica. Albany: State University of New York Press, 1993.

———. "Sacrifice as Education in Augustine and Chrysostom." *Church History* 52, no. 1 (1983): 7–20.

Beiser, Frederick C. *Fate of Reason: German Philosophy from Kant to Fichte*. Cambridge, MA: Harvard University Press, 1987.

Betz, John R. *After Enlightenment: The Post-Secular Vision of J. G. Hamann*. Malden, MA: Wiley-Blackwell, 2009.

———. "Enlightenment Revisited: Hamann as the First and Best Critic of Kant's Philosophy." *Modern Theology* 20, no. 2 (2004): 291–301.

———. "Glory(ing) in the Humility of the Word: The Kenotic Form of Revelation in J. G. Hamann." *Letter & Spirit* 6 (2010): 141–179.

Bizer, Ernst. "Die reformierte Orthodoxie und der Cartesianismus." *Zeitschrift für Theologie und Kirche* 55, no. 3 (1958): 306–72.

Bollacher, Martin. "Wilhelm Abraham Teller: Ein Aufklärer der Theologie." In *Über den Prozess der Aufklärung in Deutschland im 18. Jahrhundert*, edited by Hans Erich Bödeker and Ulrich Hermann, 39–52. Göttingen: Vandenhoeck & Ruprecht, 1987.

Brecht, Martin, ed. *Geschichte des Pietismus*. 4 vols. Göttingen: Vandenhoeck & Ruprecht, 1993–2004.

Bunge, Wiep van. "Balthasar Bekker's Cartesian Hermeneutics and the Challenge of Spinozism." *British Journal for the History of Philosophy* 1, no. 1 (1993): 55–79.

———. "Eric Walten (1663–1697): An Early Enlightenment Radical in the Dutch Republic." In *Disguised and Overt Spinozism around 1700*, edited by Wiep van Bunge and Wim Klever, 41–54. Leiden: Brill, 1996.

———. *From Stevin to Spinoza: An Essay on Philosophy in the Seventeenth-Century Dutch Republic*. Brill's Studies in Intellectual History 103. Leiden, Brill, 2001.

———. "Van Velthuysen, Batelier and Bredenburg on Spinoza's interpretation of the Scriptures." In *L'hérésie spinoziste: La discussion sur le Tractatus theologico-politicus, 1670–1677, et la réception immédiate du spinozisme*, edited by Paolo Cristofolini, 49–65. Amsterdam: APA-Holland University Press, 1995.

Carlsson, Eric. "Pietism and the Enlightenment Theology's Historical Turn: The Case of Johann Salomo Semler." In *The Pietist Impulse in Christianity*, edited by Christian T. Collins Winn, Gehrz Collins, Carlson Christopher, and Eric Holst, 97–106. Cambridge: James Clarke, 2012.

Carson, D. A. *The Gagging of God: Christianity Confronts Pluralism*. Grand Rapids, MI: Zondervan, 1996.

Cole, Graham A. "The Peril of a 'Historyless' Systematic Theology." In *Do Historical Matters Matter to Faith?: A Critical Appraisal of Modern and Postmodern Approaches to Scripture*, edited by James K. Hoffmeier and Dennis R. Magary, 55–69. Wheaton, IL: Crossway, 2012.

Conrad, Sebastian. "Enlightenment in Global History: A Historiographical Critique." *American Historical Review*, 117, no. 4 (2012): 999–1027.

Curran, Mark. *Atheism, Religion and Enlightenment in Pre-revolutionary Europe*. Royal Historical Society Studies in History, New Series. Suffolk, UK: Boydell, 2012.

Danneberg, Lutz. "Schleiermacher und das Ende des Akkommodationsgedankens in der *hermeneutica sacra* des 17. und 18. Jahrhunderts." In *200 Jahre "Reden über die Religion,"* edited by Ulrich Barth and Claus-Dieter Osthövener, 194–246. Berlin: de Gruyter, 2000.

———. "Siegmund Jacob Baumgartens Biblische Hermeneutik." In *Unzeitgemäße Hermeneutik: Verstehen und Interpretation im Denken der Aufklärung*, edited by Axel Bühler, 88–157. Frankfurt: Klostermann, 1994.

Dawes, Gregory W. *The Historical Jesus Question: The Challenge of History to Religious Authority*. Louisville: Westminster John Knox, 2001.

Dayton, Donald W. "The Limits of Evangelicalism: The Pentecostal Tradition." In *The Variety of American Evangelicalism*, edited by Donald W. Dayton and Robert K. Johnston, 36–56. Knoxville: University of Tennessee Press, 1991.

———. "The Pietist Theological Critique of Biblical Inerrancy." In *Evangelicals and Scripture: Tradition, Authority and Hermeneutics*, edited by Vincent

Bacote, Laura C. Miguélez, and Dennis L. Okholm, 76–89. Downers Grove, IL: InterVarsity Press, 2004.

———. "The Use of Scripture in the Wesleyan Tradition." In *The Use of the Bible in Theology: Evangelical Options*, edited by Robert K. Johnston, 121–136. Atlanta: John Knox, 1985.

Dibon, Paul. "Der Cartesianismus in den Niederlanden." In *Die Philosophie des 17. Jahrhunderts*. Vol. 2, *Frankreich und Nierderlande*, edited by Jean-Pierre Schobinger, 349–74. Grundriss der Geschichte der Philosophie. Basel: Schwabe, 1993.

———. "Die Republik der Vereinigten Niederlande." In *Die Philosophie des 17. Jahrhunderts*. Vol. 2, *Frankreich und Nierderlande*, edited by Jean-Pierre Schobinger, 42–86. Grundriss der Geschichte der Philosophie. Basel: Schwabe, 1993.

———. "Scepticisme et orthodoxie reformée dans la Hollande du Siècle d'Or." In *Scepticism from the Renaissance to the Enlightenment*, edited by Richard H. Popkin and Charles B. Schmitt, 55–81. Wolfenbüttler Forschungen 35. Wiesbaden: In Kommission bei O. Harrassowitz, 1987.

DiCenso, James. *Kant's Religion within the Boundaries of Mere Reason: A Commentary*. Cambridge: Cambridge University Press, 2012.

Dickson, Gwen Griffith. *Johann Georg Hamann's Relational Metacriticism*. Theologische Bibliothek Töpelmann 67. Berlin: de Gruyter, 1995.

Dorrien, Gary J. *Kantian Reason and Hegelian Spirit: The Idealistic Logic of Modern Theology*. Malden, MA: Wiley-Blackwell, 2012.

Dowey, Edward A., Jr. *The Knowledge of God in Calvin's Theology*. New York: Columbia University Press, 1952.

Duchatelez, K. "La 'Condescendance' divine et l'histoire du salut." *Nouvelle revue theologique* 95 (1973): 593–661.

Enns, Peter. *Inspiration and Incarnation: Evangelicals and the Problems of the Old Testament*. Grand Rapids, MI: Baker, 2005.

Fix, Andrew. *Fallen Angels: Balthasar Bekker, Spirit Belief, and Confessionalism in the Seventeenth-Century Dutch Republic*. Dordrecht: Kluwer Academic, 1999.

Frei, Hans W. *The Eclipse of Biblical Narrative: A Study in Eighteenth and Nineteenth Century Hermeneutics*. New Haven, CT: Yale University Press, 1974.

Friese, Hans. *Valentin Ernst Löscher*. Berlin: Evangelische Velagsanstalt, 1964.

Funkenstein, Amos. *Theology and the Scientific Imagination: From the Middle Ages to the Seventeenth Century*. Princeton: Princeton University Press, 1986.

Furnish, V. P. "The Historical Criticism of the New Testament: A Survey of Origins." *Bulletin of the John Rylands Library Manchester* 56 no. 2 (1974): 336–70.

Gay, Peter. *The Enlightenment: An Interpretation*. New York: Knopf, 1966, 1969.

Grenz, Stanley J. "Nurturing the Soul, Informing the Mind: The Genesis of the Evangelical Scripture Principle." In *Evangelicals and Scripture: Tradition, Authority, and Hermeneutics*, edited by Vincent Bacote, Laura C. Miguélez, and Dennis L. Okholm, 21–41. Downers Grove, IL: InterVarsity Press, 2004.

Greschat, Martin. *Zwischen Tradition und neuem Anfang: Valentin Ernst Löscher und der Ausgang der lutherischen Orthodoxie.* Witten: Luther, 1971.

Hanson, R. P. C. *Allegory and Event: A Study of the Sources and Significance of Origen's Interpretation of Scripture.* Richmond, VA: John Knox, 1959.

Harris, Jay Michael. *How Do We Know This?: Midrash and the Fragmentation of Modern Judaism.* Albany: State University of New York Press, 1995.

Hayden-Roy, Priscilla. "Sensate Language and the Hermetic Tradition in Friedrich Christoph Oetinger's *Biblisches und Emblematisches Wörterbuch.*" In *Subversive Sublimities: Undercurrents of the German Enlightenment*, edited by Eitel Timm, 58–69. Columbia, SC: Camden House, 1992.

Helseth, Paul Kjoss. *"Right Reason" and the Princeton Mind: An Unorthodox Proposal.* Phillipsburg, NJ: P&R, 2010.

Hirsch, Emanuel. *Geschichte der neuern evangelischen Theologie: im Zusammenhang mit den allgemeinen Bewegungen des europäischen Denkens.* Gütersloh: Mohn, 1952.

Holmgren, Fredrick. "The Pietistic Tradition and Biblical Criticism." *The Covenant Quarterly* 28 (1970): 49–59.

Hope, Nicholas. *German and Scandinavian Protestantism, 1700–1918.* Oxford: Oxford University Press, 1995.

Hornig, Gottfried. *Die Anfänge der historisch-kritischen Theologie.* Göttingen: Vandenhoeck & Ruprecht, 1961.

———. "Wilhelm Abraham Tellers *Wörterbuch* des Neuen Testaments und Friedrich Christoph Oetingers Emblematik." *Das achtzehnte Jahrhundert* (1998): 76–88.

Huijgen, Arnold. *Divine Accommodation in John Calvin's Theology: Analysis and Assessment.* Göttingen: Vandenhoeck & Ruprecht, 2011.

Israel, Jonathan. *The Dutch Republic: Its Rise, Greatness, and Fall, 1477–1806.* Oxford: Clarendon, 1995.

———. *Radical Enlightenment: Philosophy and the Making of Modernity 1650–1750.* New York: Oxford University Press, 2001.

Jellema, Dirk W. "God's 'Baby-Talk': Calvin and the Errors in the Bible." *Reformed Journal* 30, no. 4 (1970): 25–27.

Klauber, Martin, and Glenn Sunshine. "Jean-Alphonse Turrettini on Biblical Accommodation: Calvinist or Socinian?" *Calvin Theological Journal* 25, no. 1 (1990): 7–27.

Kleinig, Vernon P. "Confessional Lutheranism in Eighteenth-Century Germany." *Concordia Theological Quarterly* 60, no. 1–2 (1996): 97–125.

Kuehn, Manfred. *Kant: A Biography.* Cambridge: Cambridge University Press, 2001.
Legaspi, Michael C. *The Death of Scripture and the Rise of Biblical Studies.* Oxford: Oxford University Press, 2010.
Lee, Hoon J. "Accommodation: Orthodox, Socinian, and Contemporary." *Westminster Theological Journal* 75, no. 2 (2013): 335–48.
———. "'Men of Galilee, Why Stand Gazing Up into Heaven?': Revisiting Galileo, Astronomy, and the Authority of the Bible." *Journal of the Evangelical Theological Society* 53, no. 1 (2010): 103–16.
Lindberg, Carter, ed. *The Pietist Theologians: An Introduction to Theology in the Seventeenth and Eighteenth Centuries.* Malden, MA: Blackwell, 2005.
Marshall, I. Howard. *Beyond the Bible: Moving from Scripture to Theology.* Grand Rapids, MI: Baker Academic, 2004.
Mayes, Benjamin T. G. "The Mystical Sense of Scripture according to Johann Jacob Rambach." *Concordia Theological Quarterly* 72, no. 1 (2008): 45–70.
McGowan, A. T. B. *The Divine Spiration of Scripture: Challenging Evangelical Perspectives.* Nottingham: Apollos, 2007.
Muller, Richard A. *Dictionary of Latin and Greek Theological Terms: Drawn Principally from Protestant Scholastic Theology.* Grand Rapids, MI: Baker, 1985.
———. *Post-Reformation Reformed Dogmatics: The Rise and Development of Reformed Orthodoxy, ca. 1520 to ca. 1725.* 4 vols. 2nd ed. Grand Rapids, MI: Baker, 2003.
———. "Reformation, Orthodoxy, 'Christian Aristotelianism,' and the Eclecticism of Early Modern Philosophy." *Nederlands Archief voor Kergeschiedenis* n.s., 81, no. 3 (2001): 306–25.
Mulsow, Martin, and Jan Rohls, eds. *Socinianism and Arminianism: Antitrinitarians, Calvinists and Cultural Exchange in Seventeeth-Century Europe.* Leiden: Brill, 2005.
Olson, Roger E. "Pietism: Myths and Realities." In *The Pietist Impulse in Christianity*, edited by Christian T. Collins Winn, Gehrz Collins, Carlson Christopher, and Eric Holst, 3–16. Cambridge: James Clarke, 2012.
Popkin, Richard. "Cartesianism and Biblical Criticism." In *Problems of Cartesianism*, edited by Thomas M. Lennon and John M. Nicholas, and John W. Davis, 61–81. McGill-Queen's Studies in the History of Ideas 1. Kingston and Montreal: McGill-Queen's University Press, 1982.
Preus, J. Samuel. "Prophecy, Knowledge and Study of Religion." *Religion* 28 (1998): 124–38.
———. *Spinoza and the Irrelevance of Biblical Authority.* Cambridge: Cambridge University Press, 2001.

Preus, Robert D. *The Inspiration of Scripture: A Study of the Theology of the Seventeenth-Century Lutheran Dogmaticians*. Edinburgh: Oliver and Boyd, 1955.
———. *Theology of Post-Reformation Lutheranism*. 2 vols. St. Louis, MO: Concordia, 1970–1972.
Reventlow, Henning Graf. *The Authority of the Bible and the Rise of the Modern World*. Translated by John Bowden. Philadelphia: Fortress, 1984.
Rogers, Jack B., and Donald K. McKim. *The Authority and Interpretation of the Bible: An Historical Approach*. San Francisco: Harper & Row, 1979.
Rotermund, Hans Martin. *Orthodoxie und Pietismus: Valentin Ernst Löschers "Timotheus Verinus" in der Auseinandersetzung mit der Schule August Hermann Franckes*. Theologische Arbeiten 13. Berlin: Evangelische Verlagsanstalt, 1959.
Sailhamer, John H. "Johann August Ernesti: The Role of History in Biblical Interpretation." *Journal of the Evangelical Theological Society* 44, no. 2 (June 2001): 193–206.
———. *The Meaning of the Pentateuch: Revelation, Composition, and Interpretation*. Downers Grove, IL: IVP Academic, 2009.
Sandys-Wunsch, John. "Early Old Testament Critics on the Continent." In *Hebrew Bible / Old Testament: The History of its Interpretation*. Vol. 2, *From the Renaissance to the Enlightenment*, edited by Magne Saebø, 971–984. Göttingen: Vandenhoeck & Ruprecht, 2008.
Sauter, Michael J. *Visions of the Enlightenment: The Edict on Religion of 1788 and the Politics of the Public Sphere in Eighteenth-Century Prussia*. Leiden: Brill, 2009.
Schloemann, Martin. *Siegmund Jacob Baumgarten: System und Geschichte in der Theologie des Überganges zum Neuprotestantismus*. Göttingen: Vandenhoeck & Ruprecht, 1974.
Scholder, Klaus. *The Birth of Modern Critical Theology: Origins and Problems of Biblical Criticism in the Seventeenth Century*. Translated by John Bowden. Philadelphia: Trinity Press International, 1990.
Schweitzer, Albert. *The Quest of the Historical Jesus: A Critical Study of Its Progress from Reimarus to Wrede*. Translated by W. Montgomery. London: Adam and Charles Black, 1910.
Seils, Martin. *Theologische Aspekte zur gegenwärtigen Hamann-Deutung*. Göttingen: Vandenhoeck & Ruprecht, 1957.
Sheehan, Jonathan. *The Enlightenment Bible: Translation, Scholarship, Culture*. Princeton, NJ: Princeton University Press, 2005.
Sorkin, David. *The Religious Enlightenment: Protestants, Jews and Catholics from London to Vienna*. Princeton, NJ: Princeton University Press, 2008.
Sparks, Kenton L. *God's Word in Human Words: An Evangelical Appropriation of Critical Biblical Scholarship*. Grand Rapids, MI: Baker, 2008.

Spaulding, Paul. *Seize the Book, Jail the Author: Johann Lorenz Schmidt and Censorship in Eighteenth-Century Germany*. West Lafayette, IN: Purdue University Press, 1998.

Spindler, Guntram, ed. *Glauben und Erkennen: Die Heilige Philosophie von Friedrich Christoph Oetinger*. Metzingen: Franz, 2002.

Stein, K. James. *Phillip Jacob Spener: Pietist Patriarch*. Chicago: Covenant, 1986.

Stoeffler, F. Ernest. *German Pietism during the Eighteenth Century*. Studies in the History of Religions 24. Leiden: Brill, 1973.

———. *The Rise of Evangelical Pietism*. Studies in the History of Religions 9. Leiden: Brill, 1965.

Sunshine, Glenn. "Accommodation in Calvin and Socinus: A Study in Contrasts." MA thesis, Trinity International University, 1985.

Troeltsch, Ernst. "Historical and Dogmatic Method in Theology." In *Religion in History*. Translated by James Luther Adams and Walter F. Bense, with an introduction by James Luther Adams. Minneapolis: Fortress, 1991.

Vermij, Rienk. *The Calvinist Copernicans: The Reception of the New Astronomy in the Dutch Republic, 1575–1750*. History of Science and Scholarship in the Netherlands 1. Amsterdam: Royal Netherlands Academy of Arts and Sciences, 2002.

Webster, John. *Holy Scripture: A Dogmatic Sketch*. Current Issues in Theology 1. Cambridge: Cambridge University Press, 2003.

Wetzel, Klaus. *Johann Jakob Rambach in Halle und Gießen: Impulse für eine geistliche Ausrichtung von theologischer Arbeit und Theologiestudium*. Fundierte theologische Abhandlungen 5. Wuppertal: Verlag und Schriftenmission der Evangelischen Gesellschaft, 1987.

Willis, E. David. "Rhetoric and Responsibility in Calvin's Theology." In *The Context of Contemporary Theology: Essays in Honor of Paul Lehmann*, edited by Alexander J. McKelway and E. David Willis, 43–64. Atlanta: John Knox, 1974.

Woodbridge, John D. *Biblical Authority: A Critique of the Rogers/McKim Proposal*. Grand Rapids, MI: Zondervan, 1982.

———. "Foreword." In *Do Historical Matters Matter to Faith?: A Critical Appraisal of Modern and Postmodern Approaches to Scripture*, edited by James K. Hoffmeier and Dennis R. Magary, 13–18. Wheaton, IL: Crossway, 2012.

———. "German Responses to the Biblical Critic Richard Simon: From Leibnitz to J. S. Semler." In *Historische Kritik und biblischer Kanon in der deutschen Aufklärung*, edited by Henning Reventlow, Walter Sparn, and John D. Woodbridge, 65–87. Wolfenbütteler Forschungen 41. Göttingen: Hubert & Co., 1988.

Wright, David F. "Accommodation and Barbarity in John Calvin's Old Testament." In *Understanding Poets and Prophets: Essays in Honour of George Wishart Anderson*, edited by A. Graeme Auld, 413–27. Journal for the Study of the Old Testament Supplement Series 152. Sheffield: Sheffield Academic Press, 1993.

———. "Calvin's Accommodating God." In *Calvinus Sincerioris Religionis Vindex*, edited by Wilhelm H. Neuser and Brain G. Armstrong, 3–19. Sixteenth Century Essays and Studies 36. Kirksville, MO: Sixteenth Century Journal Publishers, 1997.

———. "Calvin's 'Accommodation' Revisited." In *Calvin as Exegete*, edited by Peter De Klerk, 171–90. Grand Rapids, MI: Calvin Studies Society, 1995.

———. "Calvin's Pentateuchal Criticism: Equity, Hardness of Heart, and Divine Accommodation in the Mosaic Harmony Commentary." *Calvin Theological Journal* 21, no. 1 (1986): 33–50.

Yeager, Jonathan. *Enlightened Evangelicalism: The Life and Thought of John Erskine*. Oxford: Oxford University Press, 2011.

Index

A

Abraham, 90, 107
Accommodation
  Augustinian, 3, 5, 7, 15, 18, 19, 23, 24, 30, 31, 34, 41, 48, 54, 55, 63, 67, 80, 89, 92, 93, 126, 166, 179, 180, 184, 187, 189, 211, 212, 215, 216, 220, 221
  condescension, 3, 16, 34, 64, 85, 87, 106, 121, 129, 153, 155, 191
  form, 4–6, 19, 48, 50, 69, 77, 107, 131, 145, 147, 181, 187, 201, 205, 211, 214, 215, 221
  manner, 3–5, 119, 120, 132, 135, 182, 211–213, 215, 221
  matter, 3–5, 7, 30, 31, 34, 54, 79, 103, 109, 119, 126, 132, 134, 136, 146, 159, 166, 201, 205, 211, 214
  mode, 3
  Socinian, 5–8, 12–16, 18, 19, 23, 24, 31, 34, 36, 39, 50, 54, 55, 69, 70, 81, 82, 92, 93, 100, 101, 105, 107, 109, 112 114, 117, 122, 123, 132, 133, 135, 136, 142, 145, 155, 164, 167, 172, 178–180, 184, 185, 187–190, 202, 206, 207, 212–214, 216–218, 220, 221
Ackermann, Peter Fourerius, 204, 205
Ancient Near East/Ancient Near Eastern, 2, 16, 37, 38, 40, 52, 54, 159, 164, 184, 185, 215
Atonement, 5, 6, 109, 127, 130, 151, 153–155, 160, 171, 180, 185, 193, 201, 202, 216
  propitiatory sacrifice, 152, 154, 172, 216
Augustine, 3, 4, 13, 23, 204, 212, 220
  Augustinian accommodation, 93, 187, 207, 216

B

Barth, Karl, 12, 71, 156
Basedow, Johann Bernhard, 132–134
Bauer, Georg Lorenz, 170, 186
Baumgarten, Siegmund Jakob, 19, 78, 81, 83–85, 102, 104, 105, 108, 111, 113, 134, 213, 214

Behn, Hermann Friedrich, 143–148, 172, 203
Bekker, Balthasar, 19, 26, 28, 50–55, 79, 133
Berkouwer, G. C., 12, 13
Bible
  authority, 4, 5, 7, 8, 11, 12, 17, 18, 28, 31, 34, 44, 63, 68, 69, 77, 79, 82, 101, 105, 107, 111–117, 119, 132, 133, 178, 220, 221
  authorship, 3, 89, 200
  inerrancy, 4, 5, 7, 8, 17, 18, 31, 63, 76, 89, 111, 113, 114, 119
  inspiration, 3–5, 33, 65, 73, 85, 89, 114, 115
  interpretation, 1, 2, 9–11, 13, 15, 26, 36, 46, 49, 51, 76, 78, 80, 82, 84, 85, 89, 102, 111, 115, 117, 136, 177, 187, 195, 213, 216, 219–221
  New Testament, 10, 13–15, 46, 114–116, 118, 123–125, 127, 128, 144–146, 151, 154, 183, 185, 191, 197, 215, 218
  Old Testament, 7, 13, 64, 82, 107, 115, 116, 121, 123–125, 127, 128, 149, 150, 153, 170, 171, 182, 185, 191–193, 197, 201, 203
Bretschneider, Karl Gottlieb, 199–202

C
Calov, Abraham, 66
Calsov, Christoph Friedrich, 81
Calvin, John
  Calvinist accommodation, 3, 5
Cartesio-Cocceian, 19, 23, 24, 27–31, 33, 34, 36–38, 48–52, 54, 55, 63, 67, 68, 70, 92, 114, 212, 213
Carus, Friedrich August, 155

Chrysostom, John, 204, 220
Church fathers/Patristic age/Patristic fathers, 4, 8, 11, 23, 64, 113, 115, 131, 144, 155, 172, 178, 204, 205, 211, 220
Cocceius, Johannes, 26
Common Sense Realism, 11
Copernicus/Copernican theory, 32, 54, 79
Cosmology, 18, 32, 79, 93, 121, 191
Crell, Johann Gottlieb, 191

D
Danz, Johann Traugott Leberecht, 206
Demonology
  Demon possession, 146, 147, 166, 203, 204
Descartes, René
  Cartesian, 24
Deyling, Salomon, 66
Du Bois, Jacobus, 32

E
Eckermann, Jakob Christoph Rudolf, 185, 186, 198
Eifert, Carl Traugott, 120
Enlightenment, 9, 18, 61, 62, 72, 73, 92, 99–101, 128, 129, 141, 142, 147, 179, 195, 198, 214, 217, 221
Ernesti, Johann August, 101

F
Fairbairn, Patrick, 6
Farmer, Hugh, 114
Flatt, Carl Christian, 192
Flatt, Johann Friedrich, 116, 189, 192
Fuhrmann, David, 177

G

Galileo Galilei, 76
God
  communication, 1, 3, 7, 11, 15, 17, 168, 169, 179, 182, 184, 189, 211
  creator, 30
  Father, 4, 8, 9, 11, 30, 64, 65, 83, 87, 113, 152–155, 167, 168, 172, 204
  fear of God, 149, 151, 172
    Jesus Christ, 5, 10, 18, 40, 44, 64, 78, 91, 100, 106, 109, 116, 118, 119–123, 125–131, 135, 136, 142–148, 151, 152, 154, 155, 160, 161, 168, 169, 171, 172, 177, 179, 180, 182–186, 192–199, 201–203, 207, 215, 216, 218–220; atonement, 5, 109, 127, 130, 151, 152, 154, 171, 185, 193, 201, 202, 216; sonship, 6; reaching ministry, 121, 135, 144, 215
  revelation, 1–4, 8, 12, 14, 16, 17, 25, 29, 39, 41, 43, 44, 88, 90, 91, 112, 127, 132, 164, 165, 182, 184, 194, 201, 211–213, 216, 219
    Trinity, 6, 78, 87, 126, 134; Trinitarian accommodation, 87, 126
Grapius, Zacharias, 68

H

Hahn, August, 205
Hamann, Johann Georg, 9, 19, 62, 85
Hartmann, Anton Theodor, 185
Hase, Karl August, 219
Hauff, Karl Viktor, 118
Heliocentric, 32, 33, 75
Hengstenberg, Ernst Wilhelm, 198
Henke, Philipp Konrad, 167
Herder, Johann, 9
Heringa, Jodocus, 5, 181
Historical criticism/Historical critical method, 1, 2, 5, 6, 10, 12–14, 17, 18, 81, 100, 111–113, 115, 136, 142, 170, 172, 177–181, 187–190, 195, 199, 206, 214, 216–218, 220, 221
History, 1, 2, 7, 8, 15, 16, 23, 29, 40, 46, 67, 74, 84, 85, 90, 111, 121, 144, 155, 160, 167, 190, 219–221
Hodge, Charles, 5, 187
Human capacity
  limitation/weakness, 9

I

Israel, 7, 9, 26, 30, 35, 40, 43, 52, 54, 61, 62, 78, 79, 84, 103, 106–109, 111, 113, 114, 124, 127, 129, 130, 132–134, 136, 145, 149–155, 163, 165, 168, 169, 171, 177, 179, 180, 182–186, 189–191, 199, 204, 205, 212, 215, 219, 220

J

Jaeger, Johann Wolfgang, 69
Jahn, Johann, 203
Judaism
  Jewish expectation/practice/understanding, 8, 64, 129, 130, 135, 154, 166, 171, 193

K

Kant, Immanuel, 18, 86, 141, 156
Kingdom of God
  earthly kingdom, 133

Kirsten, Johann Friedrich Ernst, 202
Knapp, Georg Christian, 194
Krug, Wilhelm Traugott, 148

L
Lange, Joachim, 19, 67, 74
Lang, Wilhelm Todias, 189
Language
   anthropomorphic, 42, 79, 107, 128, 152
   colloquial, 118, 120, 213
   pedagogical, 119
   phenomenological, 4, 30, 39, 41, 78, 80, 118, 120, 152, 166, 213
   vernacular, 148
Leibniz, Gottfried Wilhelm, 75
Lessing, Gotthold, 9
Leydekker, Melchior, 67
Löscher, Valentin Ernst, 19, 67
Lüderwald, Johann Balthasar, 126

M
Maas, A.J, 7
Maresius, Samuel, 38
Mental illness, 53, 54, 114, 118, 120, 146, 147, 166, 179, 186, 190, 203, 215, 216
Meyer, Lodewijk, 35–38, 48, 49, 54, 55, 114
Michaelis, Johann David, 115
Miracle, 35, 44, 45, 103, 114, 153, 160, 192
Moon, 4, 5, 30, 35, 76, 118, 212
Moses
   Mosaic law, 150, 155

N
Nachtigal, Johann Carl Christoph, 168, 169

Naturalism, 62, 70, 82, 85, 134
Neander, August, 198, 219

O
Oetinger, Friedrich Christoph, 110, 111
Opitz, Ernst Wilhelm, 135

P
Pappelbaum, Georg Theophil, 131
Pietism, 67, 70–74, 89, 111, 162, 195, 196
Pisanski, Georg Christoph, 124
Planck, Gottlieb Jakob, 164, 166
Prayer, 154, 192
Prophecy, 41, 44, 87, 115, 116, 125, 127, 156, 191, 192, 195, 197, 203

Q
Quenstedt, Johannes Andreas, 65, 214
Quest for the historical Jesus, 129, 142, 219

R
Rambach, Johann Jacob, 19, 78, 79, 81
Rationalism, 7, 61–63, 70, 82, 85, 90, 100, 110, 129, 141, 162, 165, 181, 188, 214, 217
Reimarus, Hermann Samuel
   Wolfenbüttel Fragments, 9
Reinhard, Franz Volkmar, 128–130, 132, 135, 136, 149, 153, 166, 200, 204
Resurrection, 4–6, 45, 126, 171, 188, 190, 201

S

Sacrifice, 8, 64, 109, 126, 127, 130, 151, 154, 160, 171, 193, 202
Schaefer, Peter, 132, 133, 136
Schmid, Johann Wilhelm, 162
Schmidt, Johann Lorenz, 77
Schoock, Martin, 31, 79
Schweitzer, Albert, 219
Seiler, Georg Friedrich, 5, 180–183
Semler, Johann Salomo, 6, 53, 111, 113, 216
Senff, Carl Friedrich, 151
Socinus, Faustus
  Socinian accommodation, 4
Spinoza, Baruch, 19
Steinbart, Gotthelf Samuel, 132, 134
Storr, Gottlob Christian, 116
Strauss, David Friedrich, 156, 219
Suicer, Johann Caspar, 64
Sun, 4, 30, 32, 41, 76, 79, 82, 106, 120, 152, 212
Süskind, Friedrich Gottlieb, 190

T

Teller, Wilhelm Abraham, 102, 108
Terry, Milton, 7
Tholuck, August, 103, 198
Tittmann, Karl Christian, 187
Turretin, Francis, 10

U

Unselt, Samuel Friedrich, 123

V

van Dale, Anthonie, 69
van Leenhof, Frederik, 77
van Mastricht, Petrus, 48
van Velthuysen, Lambert, 31
Voetian, 19, 24, 25, 27, 32, 35, 36, 38, 48, 54, 55, 212–214
Voetius, Gijsbert, 25

W

Wettstein, Johann Jakob, 6
Windheim, Christian Ernst, 82
Wittichius, Christopher, 19, 29
Wolff, Christian
  Wolffian, 75
Wolzogen, Lodewijk, 37

Z

Zachariae, Gotthilf Traugott, 104

The manufacturer's authorised representative in the EU is Springer Nature Customer Service Centre GmbH, Europaplatz 3, 69115 Heidelberg, Germany. If you have any concerns regarding our products, please contact ProductSafety@springernature.com

Printed and bound by CPI Group (UK) Ltd, Croydon, CR0 4YY

23/03/2026

02076736-0006